THE COMPLETE PATENT BOOK

EVERYTHING YOU NEED TO KNOW TO OBTAIN YOUR PATENT

James L. Rogers
Attorney at Law

SPHINX® PUBLISHING
AN IMPRINT OF SOURCEBOOKS, INC.®
NAPERVILLE, ILLINOIS
www.SphinxLegal.com

First Edition, 2003

Published by: **Sphinx® Publishing, An Imprint of Sourcebooks, Inc.®**

Naperville Office
P.O. Box 4410
Naperville, Illinois 60567-4410
630-961-3900
Fax: 630-961-2168
www.sourcebooks.com
www.SphinxLegal.com

Library of Congress Cataloging-in-Publication Data

Rogers, James L., 1965–
The complete patent book : everything you need to know to obtain your patent / by James L. Rogers.
p. cm.
Includes bibliographical references and index.
ISBN 1-57248-201-X (Paperback)
1. Patent laws and legislation--United States--Popular works. 2. Inventors--United States--Handbooks, manuals, etc. I. Title.
KF3114.6 .R64 2003
346.7304'86--dc21

2002015773

Printed and bound in the United States of America.

VHG Paperback — 10 9 8 7 6 5 4 3 2 1

CONTENTS

SECTION 3: AFTER YOU FILE YOUR APPLICATION

Using Self-Help Law Books

Before using a self-help law book, you should realize the advantages and disadvantages of doing your own legal work and understand the challenges and diligence that this requires.

The Growing Trend

Rest assured that you won't be the first or only person handling your own legal matter. For example, in some states, more than seventy-five percent of divorces and other cases have at least one party representing him or herself. Because of the high cost of legal services, this is a major trend and many courts are struggling to make it easier for people to represent themselves. However, some courts are not happy with people who do not use attorneys and refuse to help them in any way. For some, the attitude is, "Go to the law library and figure it out for yourself."

We at Sphinx write and publish self-help law books to give people an alternative to the often complicated and confusing legal books found in most law libraries. We have made the explanations of the law as simple and easy to understand as possible. Of course, unlike an attorney advising an individual client, we cannot cover every conceivable possibility.

Cost/Value Analysis

Whenever you shop for a product or service, you are faced with various levels of quality and price. In deciding what product or service to buy, you make a cost/value analysis on the basis of your willingness to pay and the quality you desire.

When buying a car, you decide whether you want transportation, comfort, status, or sex appeal. Accordingly, you decide among such choices as a Neon, a Lincoln, a Rolls Royce, or a Porsche. Before making a decision, you usually weigh the merits of each option against the cost.

When you get a headache, you can take a pain reliever (such as aspirin) or visit a medical specialist for a neurological examination. Given this choice, most people, of course, take a pain reliever, since it costs only pennies; whereas a medical examination costs hundreds of dollars and takes a lot of time. This is usually a logical choice because it is rare to need anything more than a pain reliever for a headache. But in some cases, a headache may indicate a brain tumor and failing to see a specialist right away can result in complications. Should everyone with a headache go to a specialist? Of course not, but people treating their own illnesses must realize that they are betting on the basis of their cost/value analysis of the situation. They are taking the most logical option.

The same cost/value analysis must be made when deciding to do one's own legal work. Many legal situations are very straight forward, requiring a simple form and no complicated analysis. Anyone with a little intelligence and a book of instructions can handle the matter without outside help.

But there is always the chance that complications are involved that only an attorney would notice. To simplify the law into a book like this, several legal cases often must be condensed into a single sentence or paragraph. Otherwise, the book would be several hundred pages long and too complicated for most people. However, this simplification necessarily leaves out many details and nuances that would apply to special or unusual situations. Also, there are many ways to interpret most legal questions. Your case may come before a judge who disagrees with the analysis of our authors.

Therefore, in deciding to use a self-help law book and to do your own legal work, you must realize that you are making a cost/value analysis. You have decided that the money you will save in doing it yourself outweighs the chance that your case will not turn out to your satisfaction. Most people handling their own simple legal matters never have a problem, but occasionally people find that it ended up costing them more to have an attorney straighten out the situation than it would have if they had hired an attorney in the beginning. Keep this in mind if you decide to handle your own case, and be sure to consult an attorney if you feel you might need further guidance.

Local Rules

The next thing to remember is that a book that covers the law for the entire nation, or even for an entire state, cannot possibly include every procedural difference of every county court. Whenever possible, we provide the exact form needed; however, in some areas, each county, or even each judge, may require unique forms and procedures. In our *state* books, our forms usually cover the majority of counties in the state, or provide examples of the type of form that will be required. In our *national* books, our forms are sometimes even more general in nature but are designed to give a good idea of the type of form that will be needed in most locations. Nonetheless, keep in mind that your *state*, county, or judge may have a requirement, or use a form, that is not included in this book.

You should not necessarily expect to be able to get all of the information and resources you need solely from within the pages of this book. This book will serve as your guide, giving you specific information whenever possible and helping you to find out what else you will need to know. This is just like if you decided to build your own backyard deck. You might purchase a book on how to build decks. However, such a book would not include the building codes and permit requirements of every city, town, county, and township in the nation; nor would it include the lumber, nails, saws, hammers, and other materials and tools you would need to actually build the deck. You would use the book as your guide, and then do some work and research involving such matters as whether you need a permit of some kind, what type and grade of wood are available in your area, whether to use hand tools or power tools, and how to use those tools.

Before using the forms in a book like this, you should check with your court clerk to see if there are any local rules of which you should be aware, or local forms you will need to use. Often, such forms will require the same information as the forms in the book but are merely laid out differently, use slightly different language, or use different color paper so the clerks can easily find them. They will sometimes require additional information.

Changes in the Law

Besides being subject to state and local rules and practices, the law is subject to change at any time. The courts and the legislatures of all fifty states are constantly revising the laws. It is possible that while you are reading this book, some aspect of the law is being changed or a court is interpreting a law in a different way. You should always check the most recent statutes, rules and regulations to see what, if any changes have been made.

In most cases, the change will be of minimal significance. A form will be redesigned, additional information will be required, or a waiting period will be extended. As a result, you might need to revise a form, file an extra form, or wait out a longer time period; these types of changes will not usually affect the outcome of your case. On the other hand, sometimes a major part of the law is changed, the entire law in a particular area is rewritten, or a case that was the basis of a central legal point is overruled. In such instances, your entire ability to pursue your case may be impaired.

Again, you should weigh the value of your case against the cost of an attorney and make a decision as to what you believe is in your best interest.

INTRODUCTION

The number of patent applications filed in the Patent and Trademark Office (PTO) has increased dramatically over the past decade. Giant companies like IBM have obtained thousands of issued patents and spend millions in obtaining new ones each year. News reports persistently tell us that stock prices of a company climbed due to the issuance of some new patent.

Clearly, patents are of great importance to large corporations and investors. But patents are equally important to small businesses or individual inventors who want to protect a new invention. In fact, patents may even be more important to small businesses and individual inventors since they probably do not have the resources to market and develop their invention, and need to protect their invention so that it can be licensed or sold to others. With patent protection, one can truly compete with the Goliaths of the world.

This book will show you, simply and step-by-step, how to go about obtaining a patent on your invention. It is divided into three sections. Section 1 will help you decide if obtaining a patent is right for you. To this end, Chapter 1 discusses the advantages and disadvantages of patent protection, as well as other forms of intellectual property protection you should consider. Chapter 2 explains the statutory requirements that you must address in order to obtain a patent. Chapter 3 will show you how to efficiently search for other patents and literature related to your invention in order to see if your invention is, in fact, new and unique. Projecting the success of your patent application up front may save you the money and time it takes to try and obtain a patent.

In Section 2 you will learn how to draft and file a patent application. Chapter 4 will show you how to draft the disclosure of your invention, and Chapter 5 will show you how to characterize your invention by drafting claims. Chapter 6 then explains how to fully prepare your application to send to the PTO.

In Chapters 7 and 8, the book will take a small but necessary diversion to explain other types of patent applications that you may need to file. For example, Chapter 8 devotes itself to how to protect foreign rights by filing what is called a "PCT" application, where you can designate a whole host of countries that you intend to seek patent protection in later on.

Section 3 discusses the various transactions that occur between you and the PTO after you file your application. Chapter 9 discusses how to reply to the PTO's initial questions and speeding up the process. I will then show you how to change your patent application in Chapter 10 through the use of an "amendment." The final chapters of the book will explain the possible rejections that you may encounter from the PTO. They will also supply strategies and tips for overcoming each type of rejection.

I have included a flowchart on the opposite page that will help you see the big picture of the patent process from start to finish. You will learn about all these steps in the chapters to come. The flowchart shows you where each is discussed.

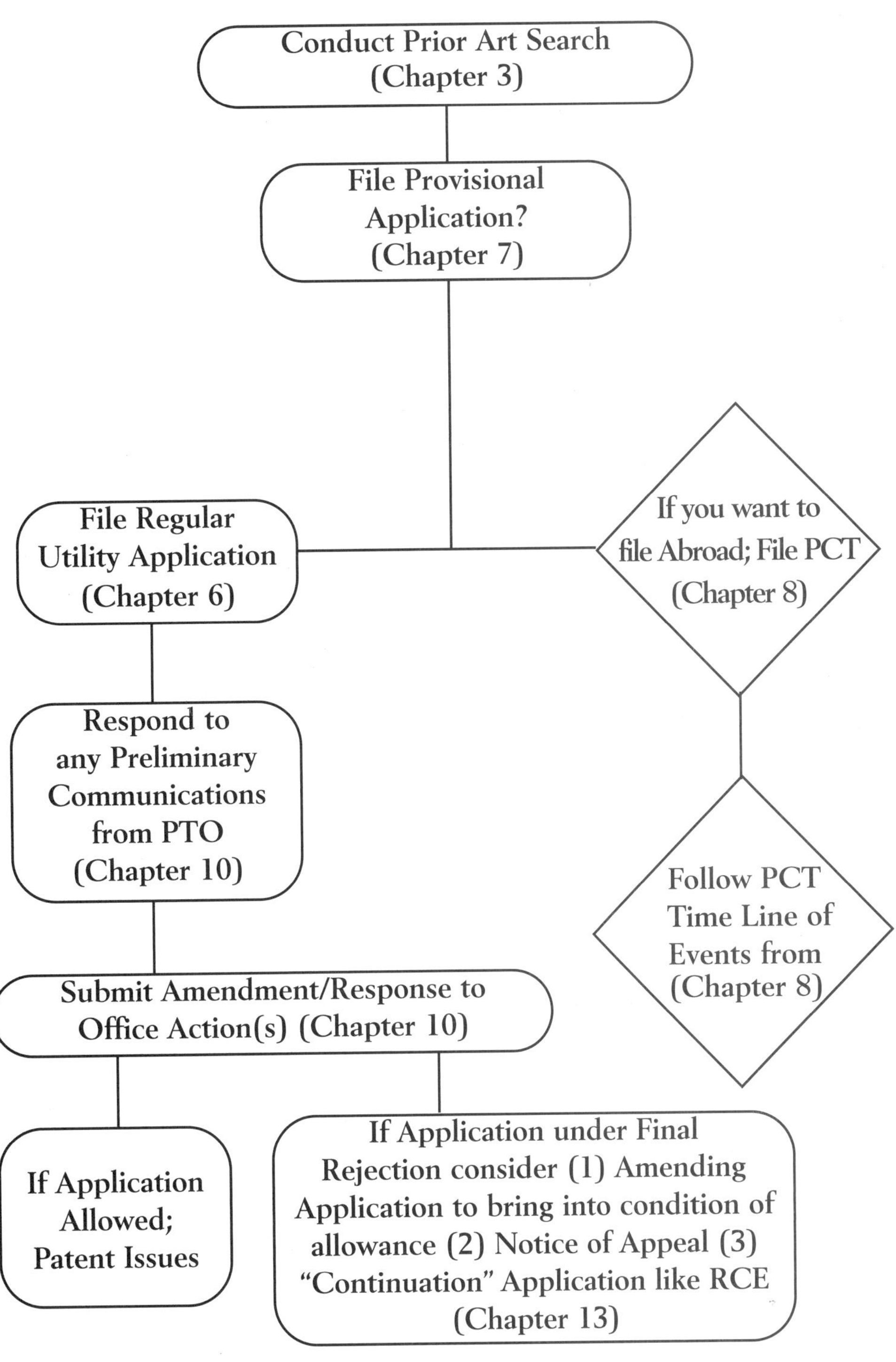
THE PATENT PROCESS
FROM START TO FINISH
Conduct Prior Art Search
(Chapter 3)
File Provisional
Application?
(Chapter 7)
File Regular
Utility Application
(Chapter 6)
If you want to
file Abroad; File PCT
(Chapter 8)
Respond to
any Preliminary
Communications
from PTO
(Chapter 10)
Follow PCT
Time Line of
Events from
(Chapter 8)
Submit Amendment/Response to
Office Action(s) (Chapter 10)
If Application
Allowed;
Patent Issues
If Application under Final
Rejection consider (1) Amending
Application to bring into condition of
allowance (2) Notice of Appeal (3)
"Continuation" Application like RCE
(Chapter 13)

Various readers with different objectives will read this book. Perhaps you are a student of patent law and want a reference that can break down a complicated subject into an easy and logical manner. You might be a company executive or venture capitalist who feels that learning more about the patent process will be to your advantage. Maybe you are using the book to draft a patent application and obtain a patent for your own invention.

Whatever the reason, I have strived to put together a book which contains everything I have learned about the patent application process over the years. I hope that you will find it not only clear and easy to use, but comprehensive as well.

I welcome your feedback, questions, or concerns. Feel free to contact me at my website:

www.Ypatent.com.

Section 1:
Before You File Your Application

Overview of the Patent Process

1

A *patent* gives you, the inventor, the exclusinve right to make, use, or sell your invention. The entire rationale for granting inventors patents is "to promote the progress of science and useful arts, by securing for limited times to authors and inventors the exclusive right to their respective writings and discoveries," as stated in Article 1, Section 8 of the U.S. Constitution.

The Purpose of Patents

By giving inventors an exclusive right to their discoveries, such inventors have a greater incentive to pursue their inventions since there is a greater likelihood that they may see a return on their investment. Patents are, in effect, a valuable reward given to inventors for all of their hard work in creating something new. By giving you a type of monopoly on your invention for a certain term, it is believed that you will more likely make sacrifices and investment to invent.

Another rationale for patents is that there is a much greater incentive for inventors to make public their inventions through the patenting system. If you know that as soon as you disclose your invention someone could steal it and start using it as their own invention, then you are probably going to be hesitant about disclosing your invention. In fact you are probably going to want to keep your invention secret. By giving you protection against such stealing as soon as you file your patent application, it is believed that you will be more likely to tell the outside world about your invention. In the eyes of patent law, disclosing your invention to the world adds to the wealth of information in your field. This, in turn, leads to future technological improvements and advances in your field.

Considering Obtaining a Patent

Deciding whether you should seek patent protection on your invention involves a variety of factors. No one factor is likely to answer this question for you, so here are some of the factors that you should consider.

Drawbacks to Applying for a Patent

On the negative side, be aware that obtaining a patent is not an inexpensive process. Even if you go it alone, there are some pretty hefty fees associated with the patent process itself. For example, the fee just to file a basic application in the United States Patent and Trademark Office (PTO) is $370 for the small inventor. Even if you are able to obtain a patent, you will need to pay what are called *maintenance fees* to keep your patent in force. If you hire a patent attorney or agent to handle your application process, your fees will be considerably more expensive, ranging in the thousands of dollars just for their representation alone.

Another thing that you should keep in mind is that obtaining a patent is not an easy process. Your success in obtaining a patent will depend on a host of factors such as the novelty (a term that will be defined for you in Chapter 2) of your invention.

Another factor that you should consider is that having a patent on your invention does not necessarily mean that you have anything of value. What will be important instead is whether your invention has any value to someone else. If your invention has no value to anyone, then your patent is going to be basically worthless. However, do not let uncertainty about this second factor deter you right now.

There have been plenty of inventions that someone may not have considered valuable when invented but later turned out to be worth a lot of money. One reason for this is that times change. What may not seem very valuable today could be valuable to someone in months or years from now.

Benifits to Applying for a Patent

The most significant benefit of a U.S. Patent is that it will give you the right to exclude others from making, using, selling, or offering for sale or importing your invention within the United States, its territories, and possessions.

The right to exclude others in this manner can be a formidable right. By having a patent on your invention, your invention is going to be worth considerably more to someone else then if you do not have a patent. The reasons for this are simple. Any person who might be interested in your invention will not only have to spend money to purchase your invention, but will also most likely need to spend a lot of money to get your invention to the market place. Since the purchaser will need to spend a couple hundred thousand dollars to do this, he is going to be much more interested in a market place that is not already infiltrated with competitors. You can feel more confident about the marketability of your invention, and can obviously charge a lot more and also sell a lot more copies of a product that is not already out in the market place.

In addition to creating barriers in the market place, there are many other possible factors why patents are obtained. To name just a few, patents can create value in and of themselves. A patent can be licensed, sold, and even put up for collateral. Patents will probably also lend you credibility if you ever need to obtain financing for your company. For example, you may have an easier time obtaining financing from a venture capitalist for a start-up company with a patent in hand.

Who Can Apply for a Patent

A patent can only be applied for in the names of the real persons (the "inventors") who have conceived the invention that you claim in your patent application. If any person has made any contribution towards the conception of any element in any claim listed in your patent application claims, then that person must be listed as an inventor in your patent application. It does not matter whether you have contributed 99.9% towards the conception of your invention. If another person has contributed the remaining .1% towards the invention, then you must apply for the invention with that person if that .1% is part of any *claim* in your application.

Ordinarily, there must at least be communication, direct or indirect, between those claiming joint inventorship. Where two persons are totally unaware of each other's work, even if they are employed by the same company, there is no joint inventorship. The conception of each joint inventor need not have occurred at the same time, however.

You may be wondering how any future proceeds of your invention will be split among co-inventors. The answer is that each inventor will have an undivided one-half interest in the patent. This could lead to unfair results if one inventor has done most of the conceiving of the invention while a co-inventor has made only a small contribution. In such a case, it is recommended that you have an agreement between yourself and your co-inventor so that any future proceeds are divided according to your respective contributions.

Types of Available Patents

Utility Patent

There are three types of patents that you can obtain from the PTO. The first and most common patent is called a *utility patent*. A utility patent protects the way an article is used and works. (U.S.C., Title 35, Sec. 101.) A utility patent is the most common type of patent. Unless otherwise noted, the chapters of this book are written on the assumption that you are interested in preparing a utility patent.

Design Patent The second type of patent you can obtain is called a *design patent.* A design patent protects the way an article looks. By and large, most of what applies to utility patents in this book will also be applicable to design patents. You will learn more, however, about some specific rules about design patents in Chapter 7.

Plant Patent The last type of patent you can obtain is called a *plant patent,* which, as the name suggests, protects the discovery of new varieties of plants. This is a specialized type of patent that is not too common and is beyond the scope of this book.

What is Patentable

There are four categories of inventions that Congress deemed to be the appropriate subject matter of a patent: processes, machines, manufactures and compositions of matter. (U.S.C., Title 35, Sec. 101.)

Process means a process, art, or method, and includes a new use of a known process, machine, manufacture, composition of matter, or material. Process inventions consist of a series of steps or acts to be performed, namely a model of treating certain materials to produce a given result. It is an act, or a series of acts, performed upon the subject matter to be transformed and reduced to a different state or thing. A process requires that certain things be done with certain substances, and in a certain order.

Example: If you were to develop a new business method for allowing mutual funds to pool their assets, you could seek a patent for this process. (*State Street Bank & Trust Co. v. Signature Financial Group, Inc.*, 149 F.3d 1368 (Fed. Cir. 1998).)

AUTHOR'S NOTE

A set of steps or rules for manipulating symbols, including numbers, characters, money, and other data, typically by a computer, to accomplish some end is called an algorithm. (*In re Iwahsahi*, 88 F2d 1370 (Fed. Cir. 1989).) The famous State Street Bank case in the example on the previous page put the definitive word in on whether algorithms are patentable. The definitive word was yes. In that case, the Federal Circuit upheld the patentability of a computerized algorithm used to manage a mutual fund investment structure. The only thing transformed by the algorithm was intangible: data, representing discrete dollar amounts.

This famous case effectively eliminated any barrier to patenting computer software. All that is required is that the algorithm lead to some practical and useful result. The useful result in the *State Street* case was the new mutual fund business method. (One would probably not be able to patent, for example, an algorithm that merely results in the addition or subtraction of numbers and no more.)

The last three categories—machines, manufactures, and compositions of matter, all define *things* rather than actions.

A *machine* is defined as a concrete thing consisting of parts or certain devices and combination of devices. Examples of machines include cars, telephones, and computers.

A *manufacture* is the production of useful articles from raw or prepared materials by giving to these materials new forms, qualities, properties, or combinations. This category is sometimes also referred to as an *article of manufacture.* Examples include such things as desks, cabinets, and screwdrivers. You can distinguish an article of manufacture from a machine because manufactures do not have working parts as their primary feature.

A *composition of matter* is a composition of two or more substances and all composite articles, whether they be the results of chemical union, mechanical mixture, or whether they be gases. In biotechnology, composition of matter includes chemical structures and formulations of drugs, genes, and proteins.

The types of things that you can seek to patent are really very broad. In fact, the Supreme Court has stated that Congress intended statutory subject matter to "include anything under the sun that is made by man." (*Diamond v. Chakrabarty*, 447 U.S. 303 (1980).)

WHAT IS NOT PATENTABLE

While the Supreme Court stated that "anything under the sun that is made by man is patentable," this famous quotation does have limits. First, the United States Code requires that the subject matter sought to be patented be a "useful" invention. (U.S.C., Title 35, Sec. 101.)

Second, you cannot patent things that you find as they exist in nature. For example, if you discovered a new mineral in the earth, you would not be able to patent the mineral unless you made some type of alteration to it (such as by genetic engineering.) Similarly, while you would not be able to obtain protection on a new, naturally occurring protein or chemical compound, a patent could be obtained on *purified* forms of the protein or chemical compound. This is the reason that in patents to such compositions you will see words like "a purified," "an isolated," "a substantially pure," or "a biologically pure" product or compound to distinguish them from naturally occurring, non-statutory subject matter.

Akin to not being able to patent things that exist in nature, courts have also held that you cannot patent ideas, laws of nature, and natural phenomena. Thus, scientific ideas like Einstein's $E=mc^2$ would not be patentable, nor would Newton's law of gravity. However, while the idea itself is not patentable, a new device by which it may be made practically useful would be.

Printed matter per se is not proper subject matter for protection by patent. An exception exists, however, where the printed matter has physical significance and is incorporated appropriately into a claim. For example, layout marks on a headband or physical demarcations on magnetic storage media have been held to constitute statutory subject matter.

NOTE: *Descriptive material such as music, literature, art, photographs and arrangements or compilations of facts or data that are merely stored so as to be read or outputted by a computer without any functional relationship to the computer is not a process, machine, manufacture or composition of matter.*

Length of a Patent

If you obtain a utility or plant patent on your invention, your patent will last for a period of twenty years from the earliest effective U.S. filing date of your patent application. The term for design patents is a shorter, fourteen years.

The earliest effective filing date of your application will be the date that you file your first regular U.S. patent application, even if you file an earlier *provisional application* or subsequent *continuation applications*. Both of these types of applications will be discussed in later chapters.

When You Should Apply for a Patent

Assuming that you have weighed all the factors and have decided that it is worthwhile to seek patent protection on your invention, you should apply for your patent before you disclose your invention to the public. While you will learn that in the U.S. you can disclose your invention (such as by publishing it in your favorite journal or marketing it) for up to a year prior to the time you file for a patent application, the laws in foreign jurisdictions are usually not going to be as kind. Most foreign jurisdictions bar you from obtaining a patent once you have disclosed your invention to the public. Unless you want to forgo patent rights in foreign countries, I recommend that you apply for your U.S. patent as soon as possible and *before* you disclose your invention to the public.

The Work Involved with Obtaining a Patent

You will read the term *patent prosecution* or simply *prosecution* of your patent application in this book many times. This is different from the prosecution that you might associate with the police, trial, or any breaking of the law. In the world of patents, the term *prosecution* has to do with not only preparing and filing your patent application, but also what occurs after such filing. It is *all* the work that is involved with obtaining a patent.

After you file your patent application, there will be a type of exchange between you and the patent office regarding your application. For example, the patent office may send you what is called an *office action* in which they reject some or all of the claims in your application and then set out a list of their reasons. You will then have to respond to this action in the form of a letter in which you provide reasons why the PTO is wrong. Alternatively, you will have to amend your claims to bring them in line with what the PTO wants. This type of exchange between you and the PTO is referred to as *prosecution.*

Hiring an Attorney or Agent

As we will see in the chapters to come, probably the toughest job in the patent process is going to be dealing with all of the scientific literature (called *prior art*) that already exists relating to your invention. A knowledge of this prior art and how your invention differs from it will be very important as you distinguish your invention from this prior art. The best person to deal with distinguishing an invention from what others have written in the field is the inventor herself rather than a patent attorney or agent who is less familiar with the field pertaining to your invention. In that respect, I think that you not only can, but are, perhaps, the best person suited to write your own application.

Choosing a Patent Attorney or Agent

Even if you later decide that you are running into problems with the prosecution of your application, you can always consult a patent attorney or agent for advice, probably reducing your costs by doing a lot of the work yourself. In fact, if you decide to obtain an attorney or agent to write and prosecute your application even after finishing this book, you will still be that far ahead in learning about the process of prosecuting your application. This knowledge will keep you better informed about the patent process so that you can make decisions more wisely in assisting your attorney or agent.

Both patent attorneys and agents are registered with the PTO and are legally capable of representing you before this office and handling the prosecution of your application. The difference between the two is that patent attorneys are also registered to practice law in at least one state. This means that patent attorneys have a qualification that agents do not—they have been prepared in areas of law such as contracts and the like that are offered by U.S. law schools.

Given that a considerable amount of prosecution of your patent application involves dealing with laws, rules, and regulations, this could give a patent attorney an advantage over an agent when it comes time to argue legal points regarding your application. However, there are also some excellent patent agents who are considerably more versed, particularly in patent law, than most patent attorneys.

Whether you choose a patent attorney or an agent to assist you, you should choose one who has familiarity with your scientific discipline. Thus, if your invention relates to the chemical field, it would be better to choose an attorney or agent who has a chemical scientific background and experience in the chemical arts rather than one who say has a mechanical background.

You should also inquire into their level of experience with obtaining patents in your field. Legitimate questions to ask are the following:

- How many patent applications have you written in my field?
- How many patents have you obtained?

You should also look at the cost of your patent attorney or agent. Patent attorneys will generally cost more than agents. Also, a patent attorney or agent with considerable experience in obtaining patents will be more expensive than one with less experience.

Obtaining a patent involves more than just writing your application. It also involves a lengthy process with the PTO. The length of time will depend on each individual case, which means that even if an agent or attorney can offer you a ball park figure of how much the process will cost, you must remember that this will be only an estimate given the uncertainty of what type of obstacles you are going to incur as your attorney or agent prosecutes your application.

Further Information

There are several main sources of laws that you should be able to find so that you can consult them when you have questions regarding patent prosecution of your application. These are the following:

- *Title 35 of the United States Code.* These are the broad based laws enacted by Congress that guide the PTO in enacting more detailed laws governing patent prosecution. They are sometimes referred to as the *Patent Laws*. You can find the patent laws on the PTO website at:
  www.uspto.gov/web/offices/pac/mpep/patlaws1214.pdf

- *Title 37 of the Code of Federal Regulations.* These are often referred to as the *Patent Rules* and are somewhat more detailed than the patent laws. These rules can be found on the PTO website at:

  www.uspto.gov/web/offices/pac/mpep/patrules0322201.pdf

- *Manual of Patent Examining Procedure.* This is referred to as the "MPEP" for short and is a detailed rule book that you will inevitably consult as you prosecute your application. This is, in effect, the bible of the PTO. If your examiner needs guidance, he or she will consult the MPEP. Therefore, it also makes sense for you to consult the MPEP. This book is so important that I would recommend you go online now and start to familiarize yourself with its organization. The MPEP can be found online at:

  www.uspto.gov/web/offices/pac/mpep/mpep.htm

REQUIREMENTS FOR OBTAINING A PATENT 2

This chapter introduces the most important statutory restrictions that can bar you from obtaining a patent on your invention. These requirements are absolutely vital for you to understand. They will also be somewhat foreign to you at this point in time. The requirements are:

- novelty;
- obviousness;
- written description requirement;
- enablement;
- best mode; and,
- utility.

NOVELTY

As the name suggests, *novelty* has to do with whether your invention is new. If your invention is an old concept, then it makes sense that the government will not give you an exclusive monopoly in the form of a patent. This is because patents are granted to inventors in return for the exchange of new information that can advance the technological body of knowledge in this country. The government is not interested in giving away patents in exchange for information that is already known.

If all else fails, you can think of novelty as requiring that your invention must not have been known before. However, as you will learn, patent law is much more specific about what this term means. You will be at an advantage if you can start thinking about this in terms of patent law.

Under patent law, novelty requires two things:

- *prior art* and,
- *anticipation* of your invention by that prior art.

Prior art is discussed below. You can also find a detailed discussion on each of the prior art sections in Chapter 3. For now, you can limit your understanding about prior art to what I will have to say below. But if you get a rejection of your patent application on the basis of one of the prior art sections, you will appreciate the more detailed discussion in Chapter 12 as well as the tips contained there for overcoming such rejections.

PRIOR ART

Prior art can include printed material like patents and publications, or it can include things like public knowledge and use or sale of your invention. Prior art can be a patent or publication that discusses an invention similar or related to yours. It also can be general public knowledge, public use, or public sale of such an invention.

PATENTS

A **U.S. or foreign patent** is prior art if it is

- issued before your *date of invention*, or
- issued more than one year before your U.S. filing date.

A **U.S. patent issued to "another"** is also prior art if its *U.S. filing date* precedes your date of *invention*, even if it does not issue until after the filing date (or patent issue date) of your claims under examination.

PUBLICATIONS

A **printed U.S. or foreign publication** is prior art if it is

- published either before your *date of invention*, or

- published more than a year before the *filing date of your application.*

A **U.S. published patent application** is also prior art if its

- *U.S. filing date* precedes your *date of invention.*

The PTO takes the position that Internet materials are printed so long as they include publication dates (MPEP Sec. 2128)

PUBLIC KNOWLEDGE, USE, OR SALE OF YOUR INVENTION

Any knowledge or use of your invention by others in the U.S. before your invention date constitutes prior art. Any public use or sale of your invention more than one year before the date of your patent application also constitutes prior art. (Chapter 3 will fully explain how to search for prior art.)

ANTICIPATION

As stated, the only time that prior art may bar your invention from being patented is when anticipation is directly related to how you draft your claims. Lack of novelty is when such prior art *anticipates* your invention.

You define your invention in the *claims* sections of your patent application. You will learn how to define your invention by writing claims later on in Chapter 5. For now, all you really need to know is that each of your claims sets the boundaries of your invention.

For example, if your invention is a table, you might have one claim that claims the table with legs and a top. In such a case, you are claiming a table made up of legs and a top. The legs and top are said to be "elements" or "limitations" of your claim because they are the features that you list in your claim. If you were to have a second claim to the table having legs, top, and an enamel surface, then this claim would have an additional limitation—the enamel surface.

You look at claims individually for *anticipation* purposes. A claim is anticipated only if each and every element as set forth in your claim is found, either expressly or inherently, in a prior art reference. In other words, anticipation requires that a piece of prior art (a patent, publication, sale, or use) disclose each and every limitation of your claimed invention. The invention described by the prior art must be shown in as complete detail as is contained in your claim..Although the elements must be arranged as required by your claim, identical terminology is not required. (MPEP Sec. 2131.)

It is permissible for your examiner to find that a prior art reference *inherently* discloses an element of your claim, even though the disclosure does not come right out and explicitly state the element. To do this your examiner must provide a basis in fact and/or technical reasoning to reasonably support his or her decision.

Claim Charts

In considering whether your claims are anticipated and therefore invalidated by prior art, it is helpful to develop a *claim chart*. In a claim chart, you make two columns, one for the invention as described in your patent claim and one for the reference you are considering. When you write the claim in the left column, you divide it into its "elements" or "limitations." On the right side of your chart, you can list the elements that are disclosed in your prior art reference. If your claim *reads on* the prior art in that it contains all of the elements disclosed in the prior art reference, it is invalid. Reading on means that there is a 1:1 correspondence between the items in the two columns of the chart.

If you uncover a prior art reference that has a 1:1 correspondence with your claimed invention, you will need to think of an element to add to your claimed invention that is not contained in the prior art reference in order to differentiate your claimed invention and thereby negate such anticipation. If you find it impossible to this, then your invention is not patentable the way it is. You will therefore want to reconsider whether you should even try to obtain a patent on it at this point in time.

Obviousness

In addition to a lack of novelty discussed above, a claimed invention is unpatentable if the differences between your claimed invention and the prior art are such that the subject matter as a whole would have been *obvious*, at the time your invention was made to a person having *ordinary skill in the art* (a person skilled in your field). In short, the PTO can take anything that qualifies as prior art, combine it with any other prior art, and then reject your claimed invention on the basis that it is an obvious invention—even though neither one of such references alone would anticipate your invention.

Obviousness is a potent tool for the examination of your application because the examiner does not have to find that each particular reference, such as one individual science report, anticipates your claim. The examiner *would* have to do this if rejecting your invention on the basis of a lack of novelty. Instead, the examiner here need only find that all of the references combined teach or suggest your invention.

Any reference that your examiner uses as prior art, however, must be analogous to the art of your invention. A reference is considered *analogous*, and, therefore, available for use in an obviousness rejection, if it is either:

- within the field of your endeavor, or
- reasonably pertinent to the particular problem with which your inventor was involved.

This is not a requirement for anticipation. With anticipation, reference may be from an entirely different field than that of your invention or may be directed to an entirely different problem from the one addressed by you, yet the reference will still anticipate if it explicitly or inherently discloses every limitation recited in your claims.

You will learn much more about obviousness in Chapter 12. Note that just because you may not find any one reference that alone does not anticipate your invention, this may end your inquiry for novelty but not for obviousness purposes. Keep both novelty and obviousness in mind as you do your patent searching in Chapter 3.

WRITTEN DESCRIPTION REQUIREMENT

The *written description requirement* is the first of three requirements under the first paragraph of U.S.C. Title 35, Sec. 112. The second and third requirements, "enablement" and "best mode" will be discussed in the next two sections.

The written description requirement prevents you from claiming subject matter that was not described in your patent application as filed. In fact, it prevents you from doing anything to your claims of your patent application that are not supported by your written description in your application as you file it.

The essential goal of the written description requirement is to clearly convey the subject matter that you have invented. The requirement for an adequate disclosure ensures that the public receives something in return for the exclusionary rights that are granted to you by a patent. The government will give you a patent, but in return, wants you to disclose your invention to the public. This disclosure will add to the scientific body of knowledge that will advance technology.

To satisfy the written description requirement, your patent application must describe the claimed invention in sufficient detail that one skilled in the art can reasonably conclude that you have possession of your claimed invention. This is done by describing your invention with all of its limitations using such descriptive means as words, structures, figures, diagrams, and formulas that fully set forth your invention.

Possession can be shown by describing an actual reduction to practice of your invention. You could do this, for example, by showing that you constructed an embodiment or preformed a process that met all the limitations of your claimed invention and determined that your invention would work for its intended purpose.

Possession can also be shown by proving your invention was "ready for patenting" such as by the disclosure of drawings or structural chemical formulas that show your invention was complete, or by describing distinguishing identifying characteristics sufficient to show that you were in possession of your claimed invention.

Enablement

Enablement is another requirement, and becomes an issue in more unpredictable fields like biology and chemistry. The test for enablement is whether one skilled in your art would be able to practice your claimed invention without an undue amount of experimentation. The state of the art that is considered is based on the art as it exists at the time you file your application. The fact that the state of art latter changes so that one is enabled to practice your invention does not eliminate this rejection if one skilled in your art was not enabled to practice your invention at the time your application was filed.

For some types of inventions, particularly computer-related inventions, it is not unusual for the claimed invention to involve more than one field of technology. For such inventions, the disclosure must satisfy the enablement standard for each aspect of the invention.

Example: To enable a claim to a programmed computer that determines and displays the three-dimensional structure of a chemical compound, the disclosure must enable a person skilled in the art of molecular modeling to understand and practice the underlying molecular modeling processes. The disclosure must also enable a person skilled in the art of computer programming to create a program that directs a computer to create and display the image representing the three-dimensional structure of the compound.

As long as your specification discloses at least one method for making and using your claimed invention that bears a reasonable correlation to the entire scope of your claim, then the enablement requirement is satisfied.

Determining Enablement

There are many factors that are considered when determining whether there is sufficient evidence to support a determination that a disclosure does not satisfy the enablement requirement and whether any necessary experimentation is "undue." These factors include, but are not limited to:

The breadth of your claims. If your claims are narrow in scope, then it will be easier to satisfy the enablement requirement. This is because it is more likely that someone can practice your narrowly-defined invention without undue experimentation.

The nature of your invention. This is the subject matter to which your claimed invention pertains. The nature of your invention will become a backdrop to determine the state of the art and the level of skill possessed by one skilled in your art.

The state of the prior art. This is what one skilled in your art would have known, at the time you filed your application, about the subject matter to which your claimed invention pertains. The state of the prior art will provide evidence for the degree of predictability in the art.

The level of one of ordinary skill. This refers to the skill of those in your art in relation to the subject matter to which your claimed invention pertains.

The level of predictability in the art. The more predictability in you art, the more likely it is that someone can practice your invention without undue experimentation. If one skilled in the art can readily anticipate the effect of changes within your invention's field or subject matter, then there is predictability in the art.

On the other hand, if one skilled in the art cannot predict how your invention's topic matter would react to a change, then there is lack of predictability in the art. For example, in fields like chemistry, there may be times when the well-known unpredictability of chemical reactions will alone be enough to create a reasonable doubt as to whether an invention enables others in your field.

The amount of guidance or direction provided by you. This refers to that information in the application, as originally filed, that teaches exactly how to make or use your invention. The amount of guidance or direction needed to enable your invention is inversely related to the amount of knowledge in the state of the art as well as to the predictability in the art. The more that is known in the prior art about the nature of your invention—how to make it, how to use it, and the more predictable the art is, the less information needs to be explicitly stated in your specification. In contrast, if little is known in the prior art about the nature of your invention, and the art is unpredictable, your specification will need more detail as to how to make and use your invention in order to be enabling.

The existence of working examples. A working example is based on work that has actually been performed. The more working examples there are, the more likely someone can easily practice your invention.

The quantity of experimentation. Obviously, the quantity of experimentation needed to make or use the invention based on the content of the disclosure also effects the ease at which someone can practice your invention.

Enablement will also bar your application where any features critical or essential to your claimed invention are missing from your claim(s). Such essentiality will be determined by looking at your application to see if you have recited any feature as being critical to the practice of your claims. If this feature is missing from you claims, then those claims fail the enablement test. This is discussed further in Chapter 13.

Example: Where the only mode of operation of a process disclosed by Joe in the Specification involved the use of a cooling zone at a particular location in the processing cycle, the examiner made a proper rejection of Joe's claims because they failed to specify either a cooling step or the location of the step in the process. (*In re Mayhew*, 527 F.2d 1229 (CCPA 1976).)

Biotechnology Inventions and Enablement

The Manual for Examining Patent Procedure (MPEP) Section 2402, paragraph 1 states that "where the invention involves a biological material and words alone cannot sufficiently describe how to make and use the invention in a reproducible manner, access to the biological material may be necessary for the satisfaction of the requirement for patentability under U.S.C., Title 35, Sec. 112."

Thus, a deposit of biological material is necessary when the material is essential for the practice of the invention and

- the material is not known and readily available to the public, or
- when the material cannot be made or isolated without undue experimentation.

Although it may not be necessary to deposit host cell lines or plasmids containing heterologous DNA even where such DNA sequences and proteins expressed by the DNA sequences are claimed, such deposits should nevertheless be considered. If an error in either the DNA and/or protein sequence is discovered after an application is filed, amendment of the claims and/or specification to correct such an error in the absence of such a deposit may be considered new matter. (*Ex parte Maizel*, 27 U.S.P.Q.2d 1662 (1993).)

However, if an application as filed includes sequence information and references a deposit of the sequenced material made in accordance with the requirements of C.F.R., Title 37, beginning with Sec. 1.801, corrections of minor errors in the sequence may be possible based on the argument that one of skill in the art would have resequenced the deposited material and would have immediately recognized the minor error.

It may also be useful to deposit essential biological materials if the material is only referred to in a publication but is not commercially available. The MPEP states that "those applicants that rely on evidence of accessibility other than a deposit take the risk that the patent may no longer be enforceable if the biological material necessary to satisfy the requirements of U.S.C., Title 35, Sec. 112 ceases to be accessible." (MPEP Sec. 2404.01.) If at some point during the patent term the material becomes unavailable and cannot be obtained without undue experimentation, the patent would become unenforceable.

You must also make reference to your biological deposit in your specification by indicating:

- the name and address of the depository institution with which the deposit was made;

- the date of deposit of the biological material with that institution;
- the accession number given to the deposit by that institution; and,
- to the extent possible, a taxonomic description of the biological material.

While no specific, universally applicable rule exists for recognizing an insufficiently disclosed application involving computer programs, the failure to include either the computer program itself or a reasonably detailed flowchart that delineates the sequence of operations the program must perform are subject to challenge by your examiner.

Moreover, as the complexity of functions and the generality of the individual components of a flowchart increase, the basis for challenging the sufficiency of such a flowchart becomes more reasonable because the likelihood of more than routine experimentation being required to generate a working program from such a flowchart also increase. (MPEP Sec. 2106.02.)

Best Mode

The *best mode* requirement is the third requirement of The United States Code. (U.S.C. Title 35, Sec. 112 (1).) The best mode requirement does not permit inventors to disclose only what they know to be their second-best embodiment, while retaining the best for themselves. In other words, if you know of a preferred way of using and making your invention, you cannot conceal this from the public by leaving it out of your patent application.

There are two factual inquiries to be made in determining whether a specification satisfies the best mode requirement. First, there must be a subjective determination as to whether at the time your application was filed, you knew of the best mode of practicing your invention. Second, there must be an objective determination as to whether the best mode was disclosed in sufficient detail to allow one skilled in the art to practice it. (*Fonar Corp. v. General Electric Co.*, 107 F.3d 1543 (Fed. Cir. 1997).)

UTILITY

Utility is a patentability requirement that makes sure your claimed invention has an actual real-world use. In most cases, this will not be a concern to you as most novel inventions are useful to *someone* in this world. However, utility becomes an issue in the less predictable arts.

Consider biotechnology as an example where this requirement has barred applicants. You may have heard in the news that the PTO has been using this as a bar to patentability to many applicants who are trying to claim naked DNA sequences that have no known function. In the past, companies would present DNA sequences of human genes in order to exclude others from using those genes in the market place. The thing that stirred up the public was that the companies did not even know anything about those sequences. It is much harder or impossible to do this now and even those past patents claiming such naked sequences may be invalid based on lack of utility.

Some types of inventions that plainly lack utility are inventions that do not operate to produce the results claimed. Such inventions are called *inoperative* and if an invention does not work, it cannot be said to have any utility. These cases are rare, however, and usually revolve around inventions that are incredible, such as speculative claims that some uncharacterized composition cures a wide range of cancers. The PTO may establish a reason to doubt your asserted utility when the written description suggest(s) an inherently unbelievable undertaking or involve(s) implausible scientific principles. (*In re Eltgroth*, 419 F.2d 918, (CCPA 1970).)

While an invention that is inoperative is not useful according to the law, the Federal Circuit has stated that a claimed device must be totally incapable of achieving a useful result in order to have no utility. (*Newman v. Quigg*, 877 F.2d 1575 (Fed. Cir. 1989).) If an invention is only partially successful in achieving a useful result, a rejection of the claimed invention as a whole for lacking utility is not appropriate. (*In re Gardner*, 475 F.2d 1389 (CCPA 1973).)

Special PTO Guidelines in Assessing Utility

The PTO has set out guidelines that an examiner will address in determining whether your invention has utility. The first step in the analysis is to identify what an applicant claims as her invention. For example, if the claim states, "a cDNA consisting of the sequence as set forth in SEQ ID No. 1," the applicant is claiming a cDNA.

The next question to ask is whether there is a "well established utility" for that claimed invention. An invention has a "well-established utility" if

- a person of ordinary skill in the art would immediately appreciate why the invention is useful based on the characteristics of the invention (e.g., properties or applications of a product or process) and,
- the utility is specific, substantial, and credible as will be explained below.

If a well established utility exists—utility exists.

Example: Alec's application teaches the cloning and characterization of the nucleotide sequence of the well-known protein, insulin. Since those skilled in the art at the time Alec files his application knew that insulin had a well-established use, it would be improper to reject Alec's claimed invention as lacking utility on the basis that Alec did not include in his application any statement as to a specific and substantial utility.

If there is no well-established utility, the PTO will look to see whether you have made any assertion of utility for your invention. If there is no such assertion, a rejection under Section 101 is made.

If any assertion is found in your application, the PTO asks whether such assertion identifies a specific utility. A *specific utility* is specific to the subject matter claimed in contrast to a general utility that would be applicable to a broad class of the invention.

Example: Melissa claims a cDNA and asserts in the specification that it can be used as a probe to obtain the full length gene that corresponds to the cDNA. Melissa also asserts that each full

> length gene can be used to make the corresponding protein that can then be used to study the mechanisms in which the protein is involved.
>
> This use would not be considered by the PTO as specific because it would be applicable to the general class of cDNAs. Any partial nucleic acid prepared from any cDNA may be used as a probe in the preparation and or identification of a full-length cDNA. Melissa's invention would be rejected for a lack of utility.

Even assuming that a specific utility exists, the PTO will next ask whether the asserted utility identifies a substantial utility. A *substantial utility* is a utility that defines what the PTO defines as a *real world* use. Although the PTO does not specifically define this term itself, the PTO gives examples of what does and does not constitute real world uses. The following are examples of real world uses:

- a therapuetic method of treating a known or newly discovered disease; and,
- an assay method for identifying compounds that themselves have a real world context of use.

The following are examples that do *not* have a real world use:

- basic research—such as studying the properties of the claimed product itself or the mechanisms in which the material is involved (the cDNA example above);
- a method of treating an unspecified disease or condition (in contrast to specific diseases or conditions);
- a method of assaying for or identifying a material that itself has no specific and/or substantial utility;
- a method of making a material that itself has no specific, substantial, and credible utility; or,

- a claim to an intermediate product for use in making a final product that has no specific, substantial and credible utility.

Assuming that your invention does have a specific and substantial utility, the final question that the PTO will ask is whether the assertion of specific and substantial utility is credible.

An assertion is credible unless the logic underlying the assertion is seriously flawed, or the facts upon which the assertion is based are inconsistent with the logic underlying the assertion. Basically, the asserted utility must be believable to a person of ordinary skill in the art based on the totality of the evidence and reasoning provided.

An assertion that a claimed invention is useful in treating a symptom of an incurable disease may be considered credible by a person of ordinary skill in the art on the basis of a fairly modest amount of evidence or support. In contrast, an assertion that the claimed invention will be useful in "curing" the disease may require a significantly greater amount of evidentiary support.

UTILITY IN THE PHARMACEUTICAL ARTS

In the pharmaceutical arts, practical utility may be shown by adequate evidence of any pharmacological activity. Simply identifying a pharmacological activity of a compound relevant to an alleged pharmacological use provides an immediate benefit to the public and therefore meets the requirements of Section 101. (*Nelson v. Bowler*, 626 F.2d 853 (CCPA 1980).)

Example: A compound's modulation of blood pressure in rats and its stimulation of smooth muscle tissue of gerbil colons constituted sufficient utility. The court stated that "practical utility" is a shorthand way of attributing "real-world" value to claimed subject matter. In other words, one skilled in the art can use a claimed discovery in a manner which provides some immediate benefit to the public.

Knowledge of the pharmacological activity of any compound is obviously beneficial to the public. It is inherently faster

> and easier to combat illnesses and alleviate symptoms when the medical profession is armed with an arsenal of chemicals having known pharmacological activities. Since it is crucial to provide researchers with an incentive to disclose pharmacological activities in as many compounds as possible, the court concluded that adequate proof of any such activity constitutes a showing of practical utility. (*Nelson v. Bowler*, 626 F.2d 853 (CCPA 1980).)

Generally, pharmacological activity refers to the properties and reactions of drugs, especially with relation to their therapeutic value. (*Cross v. Iizuka*, 753 F.2d 1040 (Fed. Cir. 1985).)

Courts have routinely found evidence of structural similarity to a compound known to have a particular therapeutic or pharmacological utility as being supportive of an assertion of therapeutic utility for a new compound. (*In re Brana*, 34 USPQ2d 1436 (Fed. Cir. 1995).)

Example: Tom presented evidence in his Specification that his claimed compounds had a close structural relationship to daunorubicin and doxorubicin, both of which were known to be useful in cancer chemotherapy. Joe also presented evidence demonstrating substantial activity of his claimed compounds in animals customarily employed for screening anticancer agents. The claimed compounds were found to have utility.

If reasonably correlated to the particular therapeutic or pharmacological utility, data generated using *in vitro* assays, or from testing in an animal model or a combination thereof, almost invariably will be sufficient to establish therapeutic or pharmacological utility for a compound, composition, or process. (MPEP Sec. 2107.03.)

Example: Where a Japanese priority application disclosed an *in vitro* utility, (i.e., the inhibition of thromboxane synthetase in human or bovine platelet microsomes), and where the disclosed *in vitro* utility was supplemented by the similar *in vitro* and *in vivo* pharmacological activity of structurally similar

> compounds, (the parent imidazole and 1-methylimidazole compounds), the in vitro utility was sufficient to comply with the practical utility requirement of Section 101. (*Cross v. Iizuka*, 753 F.2d 1040 (Fed. Cir. 1985).)

Evidence of a therapeutic or pharmacological utility also does not have to be in the form of data from an art-recognized animal model for the particular disease or disease condition to which the asserted utility relates. Data from any test that you can reasonably correlate to your asserted utility may be provided.

There is also no requirement that you wait to file your application until you have initiated human clinical trials for a therapeutic product or process. However, if you have initiated human clinical trials for a therapeutic product or process, the PTO should presume that you have established that the subject matter of that trial is reasonably predictive of having the asserted therapeutic utility. This is because before a drug can enter human clinical trails, you must provide a convincing rationale to those skilled in the art (the FDA) that the investigation may be successful. (MPEP Sec. 2107.03.)

Utility versus Enablement Requirement

The requirement of utility under U.S.C. Title 35, Sec. 101 is different from the requirement of how to use the invention under U.S.C. Title 35, Sec. 112, first paragraph. The requirement of utility is that some specific, substantial, and credible use be set forth for the invention. On the other hand, enablement requires an indication of how the use (required by utility) can be carried out (i.e., how the invention can be used).

SEARCHING FOR PRIOR ART 3

A *patentability search* is used to seek for patents and publications that constitute prior art with respect to your invention. There are a number of very important reasons why you should do this.

THE IMPORTANCE OF A PRIOR ART SEARCH

First, the search may uncover prior art that is identical to your invention being considered for patenting (i.e., such prior art anticipates your invention) as stated above. If this is the case, you should not waste the time and money that goes into the patenting process.

Second, even if the prior art that you uncover does not anticipate your invention, the prior art may be so close to your invention that any patent you might obtain would be so limited as not to be worth anything.

Third, if you do decide to go ahead and draft a patent application and engage in the patent process, the patents and other prior art uncovered by you during your search will help you develop technical prose for writing your own application and refine the scope of your claims to be presented.

The next two chapters will show you how to write a patent application. Reading through prior art patents relating to your field of art now will help you write a better application, later.

Simple Searches for Free

The use of other patents as references is not limited to what patentees describe as their own inventions or to the problems that they address. Patents are part of the literature of the art, relevant for all they contain and what follows from them. Therefore, the search for prior art patent references should not only be a big part of your search, but you should pay attention to everything that is contained in the patents (not just the claims).

Use the PTO Site

Probably the best way to search for and access U.S. patents for free is by going to the PTO website and searching for U.S. patents. You can do this by following these steps:

- Go to the PTO home page at **www.uspto.gov**.
- At the PTO website, you then click on "Patents," which will bring you up to a page under the title "Patents."
- Select "Search Patents" under the heading "Services." This will then bring you up to a Web page where you will see the heading "Patent Grants" on the left side and "Patent Applications" on the right.

You will also notice on this last web page that there are three options for your patent search. You can either do a "quick search," "advanced search," or "patent number search."

If you click on "quick search," you will bring up a page where you can input two terms and thereby search for those two terms in all U.S. patents. This is a "Boolean" search. You will notice that your search can be limited by "fields."

You will notice that you can search all fields or limit your search of your two terms to particular fields such as the title, assignee name, inventor name, as well as a host of other fields. You will also notice that you can select specific years or *all* years dating back to 1790 for your search.

Look at the patent in Figure 1 on the following page (p.34). This is an example of what your search might produce. You will notice on the front page of the patent a heading called "current U.S. class" followed in bold by the numbers 43/139. The 43 represents the class of this U.S. patent and the 139 represents the subclass. The class/subclass is in bold to indicate that the PTO considers this class/subclass to be the most on target for this particular invention. However, you can see that other classes and subclasses are also listed to which this invention may also belong. For example this patent has also been assigned the class/subclass of 43/107. Class/subclass classifications become particularly important if you are conducting your own search at the PTO, something that I will shortly discuss next.

AUTHOR'S NOTE

You can save any of the pages that you bring up by hitting "File" at the top of your browser and then "Save as." You can also save any image by right clicking on your mouse and then hitting "Save as." This will allow you to return to your pages on disk later on while you continue your search.

Your last search option on the PTO website is to do a "patent number search." This requires you to know the number of the patent that you want to find. This will probably be of less use to you as you are searching for prior art relating to your invention and are probably not aware of any patent numbers concerning your invention. However, if you do know the patent number that you want to look up, this is the quickest way to obtain that patent.

One disadvantage of using the PTO website is that although your search option gives you the choice to search all years, it is somewhat deceiving. Patents prior to 1976 can only be searched for by patent number or current US classification. Thus, when you enter your Boolean terms you are only really searching patents from 1976 to the present. This is a serious limitation that you should be aware of since old patents are just as good prior art as more recent patents. By searching only the PTO database you might leave gaps in your search. Nevertheless, the PTO database is the best starting site for your money—its free!

figure 1

United States Patent: 6,145,243

US Patent & Trademark Office

Patent Full Text and Image Database

Home Boolean Manual Number Help

Hit List Bottom

View Shopping Cart Add to Shopping Cart

Images

United States Patent	6,145,243
Wigton, et al.	November 14, 2000

Method and device producing CO.sub.2 gas for trapping insects

Abstract

An insect trapping device generates its own insect attractants of carbon dioxide (CO.sub.2), heat and water vapor through catalytic conversion of a hydrocarbon fuel in a combustion chamber. The hot insect attractants generated in the combustion chamber are diluted and cooled to a temperature above ambient temperature and below about 115. Degree. F. by mixing with air, and then the mixture is exhausted downward through the exhaust tube. A counterflow of outside air is drawn into the trap through the suction tube that concentrically surrounds the exhaust tube. Biting insects are captured in a porous, disposable bag connected to the other end of the suction tube. A thermoelectric generator, including thermoelectric modules coupled to the combustion chamber generate power for fans that provide the exhaust flow and the suction flow. Additional chemical attractants may be used with the device to make the trap even more effective. The trap may be adapted for trapping different types of insects by adjusting airflow velocities and attractants.

Inventors: **Wigton; Bruce E.** (Jamestown, RI); **Miller; Mark H.** (Hope, RI)
Assignee: **American Biophysics Corporation** (East Greenwich, RI)
Appl. No.: **009950**
Filed: **January 21, 1998**

Current U.S. Class:	43/139; 43/107
Intern'l Class:	A01M 001/06; A01M 005/08
Filed of Search:	43/113,139,107

References Cited [Referenced By]

U.S. Patent Documents

1693368	Nov., 1928	Cherry	
2893161	Jul., 1959	Reid	43/139.
3196577	Jul., 1965	Plunkett	43/139.
4506473	Mar., 1985	Waters, Jr..	

NOTE: *As you uncover prior art patents, read the entire disclosure of the patent to see whether it anticipates your invention. Be careful not to fall into the trap of thinking that only the claims of a patent can by used to anticipate your invention. You may be particularly inclined to do this after reading Chapter 5, which states that claims define your invention. For anticipation purposes, however, your examiner is free to use everything he or she finds in a patent or any other prior art reference.*

U.S. Published Applications

U.S. non-provisional utility and plant applications are published eighteen months from the earliest filing date for which benefit is sought. (U.S.C., Title 35, Sec. 122(b).)

Benefits. Having your application published is actually beneficial because you are entitled to receive a reasonable royalty dated back to your publication date, with respect to any claims that are infringed as of the publication date so long as those claims have been substantially unaltered from the publication date to your patent issuance date.

Your application will normally be published in the form it exists at the time that you file your patent application. Amendments that you make to your application will generally not be reflected in your published application unless you supply an electronic copy of your application containing the amendment within one month from the date you file your application or within fourteen months from the earliest filing date for which benefit is sought, whichever is later. (C.F.R. Title 37, Sec. 1.215.)

Early Publishing. You may request early publication of your U.S. patent application. If you make such a request, you must submit an early publication fee (currently $300) at the time that you submit your application.

Requesting early publication will usually speed up the publishing of your application a couple of months before the normal eighteen months publishing date. This could be advantageous because your reasonable royalty for infringement of your claims may then extend back several months. However, requesting early publishing is your call. If you want to make the request, you need to indicate this in your *application data sheet* (see Chapter 6) and pay the required fee.

Searching for a U.S. publication. Published applications will become the predominant form of prior art used by examiners. Therefore, you absolutely must include a search for both U.S. and foreign published applications during your search. You can search foreign published applications from March 15, 2001. You will see that the PTO writes this as 15 March 2001, which is the same way that you will see dates abroad written (the day followed by the month and the year).

FOREIGN PATENTS

Let's restate our definition of what constitutes prior art with respect to patents:

A *U.S. or foreign patent* is prior art if it is

- issued before your *date of invention,* or
- issued more than one year before your U.S. *filing date.*

A *U.S. patent issued to "another"* is also prior art if its

- U.S. *filing date* precedes your *date of invention,* even if it does not issue until after the filing date (or patent issue date) of your claims under examination.

This definition includes foreign patents, so you must include a search for foreign patents during your search. As with U.S. patents, your examiner is not restricted to the information conveyed by the patent claims but may use any information provided in the specification that relates to the subject matter of the patented claims. So you will need to read the entire patent.

The free PTO website explained in the previous section for finding U.S. patents will not be useful for you to find foreign patents. One free database where you can search is at **ep.espacenet.com**.

INTERNATIONAL APPLICATIONS

You will learn more about foreign filing in Chapter__; however, a typical way to file foreign applications is through the Patent Cooperative Treaty (PCT). These applications are published eighteen months from their priority date in the *PCT Gazette,* which can be accessed electronically through the Intellectual Property Digital Library website (**ipdl.wipo.int**) of the World Intellectual Property Organization. This can serve as yet another useful free website to search for prior art on your invention.

FEE-BASED SEARCHING

In addition to the USPTO free website, there are various fee-based search engines. One website that you may find helpful is **www.delphion.com** (formerly **http://www.patents.ibm.com**). To use most of the best features on this site, you must become a paid subscriber.

A very powerful fee-based search engine is called *Dialog*, which you can find at **www.dialog.com**. The fees can be considerable based on your usage. However, Dialog is probably the most powerful search tool around for intellectual property. You can search for everything from patents to literature concerning your invention. Dialog takes some time to learn, but their customer assistance is very good. If you do learn Dialog, you will be equipped to do some of the most powerful prior art searching possible.

PAYING ANOTHER TO DO A SEARCH FOR YOU

Another option that you have is to pay someone to do a prior art search for you. You can find such searchers by looking for them on the Internet or in various intellectual law journals and magazines. One such magazine is called *Intellectual Property Today* which you can also find at **www.iptoday.com**. Another popular journal among patent agents and attorneys is called the *Journal of the Patent and Trademark Office Society* which you can find at **www.jptos.org**.

If you do not have the time to do a search yourself, you should consider paying someone to do a search for you. However, you should keep in mind that you not only can do a search for prior art yourself, but you are perhaps the best person to conduct the search.

EXTENSIVE PATENT SEARCHING AT THE PTO

If you have the time and the means to get to the PTO in Washington D.C., then you may want to also consider going physically to the PTO to conduct a search regarding your invention. There are several advantages to doing such a search.

- You can review patents much quicker when you have all of the pages right in front of you. You may have also noticed above in doing your free PTO database search that you will have to click on an "image" icon at the top of your page in order to view the drawings. This can be a slow process particularly if you do not have a high speed connection.
- Your search at the PTO will be more thorough because you can search all years, whereas your free PTO database search will only allow you to do Boolean searches from 1976 onwards.
- You may has its opportunity to ask employees questions regarding your search if you run into any problems.
- The PTO has its patents arranged by class/subclass, which means that related inventions are grouped together. When you pull out a sleeve that contains all the patents in a class/subclass, you will be seeing every patent related to that class/subclass all at once.

The PTO houses all of its patents in Arlington, Virginia at a place known as "Crystal City." The address is Crystal Plaza 4, South 23rd Street and U.S. 1 (Jefferson Davis Highway). At this address, there is a public search room where patents are contained in sleeve-like folders by class/subclass number.

Finding the Class/Subclass for Your Invention

Since all of the patents are arranged by class/subclass, your first step in locating patents pertaining to your own invention is to know the classes/subclasses that pertain to your own invention. You can determine this at the PTO, using their *Index to the U.S. Patent Classification System* and *Manual of Classification* books. However, you should look at these books and determine these classes *before* you go to the PTO to save time.

You should be able to find both the *Index to the U.S. Patent Classification System* and the *Manual of Classification* books at your local library. If you cannot find them there, you certainly can find them at a Patent and Trademark Depository Library (PTDL). This is a library designated by the PTO to receive and house copies of U.S. patents and trademark materials. These libraries are usually found in major cities. A list of their locations can be found on the PTO website.

By following the same type of procedure with respect to the *Index to the U.S. Patent Classification System* and the *Manual of Classification* with your own invention you should be able to come up with at least several classes/subclasses most relevant to your invention.

You may also be able to obtain the class/subclass for your invention by visiting the PTO web site at **www.uspt.gov**. When you get to the home page you can click on the index and then hit "i" to find the *Index to the U.S. Patent Classification System*.

You can find more information on any classes/subclasses for your invention by also looking at *Classification Definitions,* which are usually contained on CD ROMs at your library. Alternatively, you can again go to the PTO website at **www.uspto.gov**, hit the index and then hit "c" to find "Classification Index, Patents."

Conducting Your Search at the PTO

Once you have located one or more class/subclass for your invention, you are ready to go into the public search room at the PTO and start looking for patents in those classes/subclasses that you have found. As you review the various patents, make a list of the classes/subclasses on those patents most relevant to your own invention. Search any new classes/subclasses that you do find.

Any type of list that you want to use to keep track of your patents and search results is fine. You might, for example, divide your notebook in the following way:

INVENTION			
Class/Subclass	Patent #	Date of Application	Description

You then might have a separate page in a notebook to record all of the classes/subclasses that you have found.

While at the PTO, get a pass from the front desk to go upstairs and search the examiner search files. This area also contains foreign patents as well as the U.S. classified patents that you find in the public search room. In other words, you get more upstairs. If you are lucky, you may even be able to find an examiner who works in your field of art who can give you valuable information as to the type of prior art that exists in your field. Be persistent. Searching is a tough job. Most of all, be polite and you should come from the PTO having done a day or two worth of work that will not only be invaluable to you in evaluating your own invention, but also in writing your application and responding to office actions later on.

NOTE: *Be sure to search articles published in your field, company brochures, and catalogs as well. These things can also be used against you as prior art.*

File Wrappers

File wrappers refer to the contents of everything that a patent applicant has filed with the PTO with respect to his or her application. There is the possibility that you may want to view everything that is contained within the file wrapper of a patent application. Such file wrappers will give you information as to exactly what occurred during the prosecution of a patent application, which can be useful to you if you want to simply see how someone else went about the prosecution of their own application.

In general, a patent application is required by law to be kept confidential, and the PTO will not allow inspection of an application by a member of the public. However, there are a few exceptions to this rule.

After a patent has been issued, you can obtain copies of all papers contained in the file wrapper for that patent application. The PTO will also provide to you an abandoned or pending published application upon written request and payment of a specified fee. The only exception to this is where the patent applicant submitted a *redacted copy* of the patent application. Redacted means that portions of the published application are marked off by the patent applicant as confidential and not subject to public inspection. Redacted applications are rare.

However, patent applicants do have the right to do this in certain circumstances. For example, if an applicant files foreign patent applications on an invention that are less descriptive than an application filed in the U.S. for the same invention, an applicant has the right to request that the portions not described in the foreign applications be redacted in the U.S. application if the rules of C.F.R., Title 37, Sec. 1.217 are followed.

If you do want to obtain the file wrapper of a patent application, you must contact a search company who will physically go to the PTO and make such a copy for you unless you live near the PTO and wish to make the copy yourself. Again, you can find such companies in various patent journals.

Documenting Your Search

As you conduct your prior art search and you run into any reference that you feel is related to your own invention, you should incorporate such reference into a typed master list. You do not need to do this right away, but I would recommend doing this list before you move onto the next chapter. It may be easier to keep this list on a word processor so that you can manipulate it later on. All references that may have a bearing on the patentability of your own invention must be disclosed to the PTO in an *Information Disclosure Statement* (IDS). By compiling a list of any such references now, your job of submitting an IDS will be much easier later on.

Your master list should have the following 4 headings:

- *U.S. Patents*—Place only U.S. Patents that you find during your search under this heading;
- *Foreign Patents*—Place only foreign patents that you uncover during your search;

- *Publications*—Under this heading, place your science publications as well as any published patent applications that you find; and,
- *Other References*—Use this heading to place any miscellaneous references that you find such as company brochures or anything else that does not fit into one of the other headings.

Section 2:
Filing Your Application

Drafting Your Patent Application: Specification and Drawings

At this point, you should have completed your prior art search from Chapter 3. You are hopefully starting to get a feel for what must be included in a patent. If this is the case, you are off to a good start with drafting your patent application, since issued patents contain the information that is included in the application. The only difference between an issued patent and a patent application is the order of the information.

Parts of Your Application

The recommended ordering of your application is stated at C.F.R., Title 37, Sec. 1.77(a) and is also stated in the MPEP at Sec. 601 and Sec. 608.01(a). According to these sections, your application should include the following parts:

- utility application transmittal form;
- fee transmittal form;
- application data sheet;
- specification;
- drawings; and,
- executed oath or declaration.

This chapter will discuss your specification and drawings.

Drafting Your Specification

As provided by C.F.R., Title 37, Sec. 1.77(a), your specification consists of the following parts in the following order:

- title of the invention;
- cross-reference to related applications;
- statement regarding federally sponsored research or development;
- reference to a "sequence listing", a table, or a computer program listing appendix on a compact disc and an incorporation by reference of the material on the compact disc;
- background of your invention which includes both
  - the field of your invention, and
  - a description of related art;
- brief summary of your invention;
- brief description of the several views of your drawings;
- detailed description of your invention;
- claim(s) that must commence on a separate sheet (see Chapter 5);
- abstract; and,
- DNA sequence listing (only applicable to biotechnology invention)

NOTE: *In addition to these sections, you will sometimes see a "Copyright Notice" section that you can place right after the title of the invention. The notice is required if you use copyrights anywhere in your specification. Your section heading and notice should look like the following:*

> COPYRIGHT NOTICE
>
> A portion of the disclosure of this patent document contains material to which a claim for copyright is made. The copyright owner has no objection to the facsimile reproduction by anyone of the patent document or the patent disclosure, as it appears in the Patent and Trademark Office patent file or records, but reserves all other copyright rights whatsoever.

You should make the above items the section headings of your specification. Each one of these section headings should be in uppercase and without underlining or bold type. If one of the listed sections is not relevant to your invention, you can simply write "Not Applicable" next to the section heading or simply leave out the section altogether.

➲*Appendix C contains a sample patent application.* You will notice that various section headings that are not applicable to the particular patent have been left out.

Your specification should be written using 1.5 spacing or double spacing. You must use paper which is either 8 1/2-by-11 inches or size A4. You should also number your pages, preferably centered at the bottom of the page.

➲*Look again at the sample patent application contained in Appendix C.* You will also notice that the paragraphs of the specification other than the claims and abstract are numbered. By numbering your paragraphs, you will find it much easier later on to make any amendments to your specification by replacement paragraphs.

The paragraph numbers should consist of at least four numerals enclosed in square brackets, including leading zeros (e.g., [0001]). The numbers and enclosing brackets should appear to the right of the left margin as the first item in each paragraph and should be highlighted in bold. A gap of four spaces should follow the number. You do not consider section or paragraph headers as part of your paragraph for numbering purposes, nor would you consider any tables or formulae.

AUTHOR'S NOTE

Although I am presenting this material in step order fashion according to how you arrange your patent application under the MPEP, you should realize that the order you draft your application is not etched in stone. In fact, many patent drafters find that drafting some claims first before they do any other part of the application is much easier. I think this can actually be helpful because claim drafting really focuses your thoughts on what is essential to your invention. Once you have focused on writing a few claims, you can then come back to the other parts of your application such as the detailed written description and fill in the details. Details are required as you might recall from Chapter 2 to fulfill all of your disclosure requirements such as the written description requirement.

Whether you proceed to write your claims first or draft your application in the order presented here, I would suggest that you read both this chapter and the following one first before you start doing any work on drafting your application. You should have a good idea of what is required for your application before you start drafting.

Let's now go through each part of your specification in the order you would write them.

STEP 1: TITLE OF THE INVENTION

The title of your invention should appear at the top of the first page of your specification unless your have included it in your application data sheet (discussed in Chapter 6). The title should be as short and specific as possible. It should be general in scope but not so general that it fails to describe broadly the invention claimed.

The title of the invention has been used by the Federal Circuit to assist in claim interpretation. Thus it is important that the title capture the gist of your invention.

Step 2: Cross-Reference to Related Applications

You should include a cross-reference to any related applications that you may have filed unless you have included this information in your application data sheet (discussed in Chapter 6).

Examples of related applications that you might cross-reference are any other U.S. or foreign applications from which you are claiming priority.

➲*The sample patent in Appendix C has no cross-reference to related application section because the patent upon which this application is based had no cross-reference to any related applications.*

Step 3: Statement Regarding Federally Sponsored Research and Development

If your invention is sponsored by the federal government, you must include any necessary statement required by contract or by the governmental agency sponsoring the work. This is one of those sections that will probably not apply to you. ➲*If it does not, you can leave this section heading out of your application.*

Step 4: Reference to a "Sequence Listing," a Table, or a Computer Program Listing

A computer program listing, a nucleotide and/or amino acid sequence listing submitted under C.F.R., Title 37, Sec. 1.821(c) or a table that has more than fifty pages of text may be submitted on compact disc. A computer program listing which is over 300 lines *must* be submitted on compact disc.

A computer program listing is defined as a printout that lists in appropriate sequence the instructions, routines, and other contents of a program for a computer. A compact disc is defined as a Compact Disc-Read Only Memory (CD-ROM) or a Compact Disc-Recordable (CD-R).

If you decide to or are required to submit a compact disc with your application, you must follow the requirements set forth in C.F.R., Title 37, Sec. 1.52(e). One such requirement is that your specification must incorporate-by-reference the material on the compact disc, which is done in this section heading.

Again, if none of this is applicable to your own invention, you can simply leave out this section heading. ➲*The sample application contained in Appendix C has no such heading.*

Step 5: Background of The Invention

Technical Field

This is a statement of the field of art to which your application belongs. If you have problems drafting the *technical field*, the PTO states that you can simply paraphrase the applicable U.S. patent classification definitions of your invention's subject matter. So, if you have determined the most relevant class/subclass for your invention, you can use the class definitions to help you draft your field of invention.

➲*Look at the "Field of Invention" for the sample patent application contained in Appendix C on page 272.* The statement starts off with the words "the present invention relates" followed by the words "more particularly." This is a good example of how you should write your statement.

The first part of the statement after "relates" is a broad characterization of your invention and the second part after "more particularly" characterizes the most important feature of your invention. In other words, you start off your statement with a broad characterization which is similar to the class of your invention and then you end your statement with a more specific characterization that is equivalent to the subclass of your invention. If your invention relates both to a device *and* method, both should be included in the technical field.

Description of Related Art

The next part of the background section should be a *description of related art* including any prior art references that you have uncovered in your prior art search from Chapter 3. (This section can also be entitled "Background Art.") This section should begin by showing the prior art, namely the type of product or method that your invention will be better than. You should then address the problems associated with this prior art product or method and the fact that there exists a need to overcome these problems.

Example: You have just come up with a way to label nucleotides non-radioactively, and you believe this will be of great use to the scientific community in using such non-radioactive nucleotides for assays due to their increased safety.

You could start off your *Description of Related Art* section by introducing radioactive nucleotides of the past and their various uses by the scientific community. You would then describe the associated problems of using such radioactive nucleotides by explaining that their use is often very hazardous. You might also explain that because of this their use in the laboratory is often very slow and cumbersome. You would want to keep emphasizing that there exists a need for safer nucleotides which is just crying out to be solved.

If you follow this format of identifying all of the problems of any prior art invention, you can really start making an argument for the nonobviousness of your invention over the prior art (non-obviousness will be discussed at length in Chapter 12). The reader should come out of your background section with the feeling that the prior art has lots of problems. Your reader will then be impressed when she moves on to the rest of your specification and finds out that your invention has solved all these problems.

The length and detail of your background section will really depend on how much prior art you wish to discuss as well as the scope of the claims that you are trying to patent. If you are presenting very broad claims to an invention, then you should prepare a rather detailed background section explaining many of the deficiencies and problems of the prior art. However, if you are claiming a very narrow invention, then you can get right down to business and simply note the specific problem of the prior art that your invention is going to solve.

➲*Take a look at the "Description of the Prior Art" for the sample application in Appendix* C. You can see that this section is very short. This most likely means that the claims are going to be narrowly drawn to an invention that solves the problem of carriers that have not been very easy to ship and store in the past .

Incorporating Material by Reference Into Your Background

When you refer to other patents, scientific journals and the like to indicate the background art, you can rewrite what was said in those references directly into your background section. In the alternative, you can incorporate the reference directly into your specification without having to rewrite everything that has been said in the reference. This is known as *incorporation by reference*. The information that you incorporate by reference into your application becomes as much a part of your application as if the text was repeated directly into your application.

Any reference that you are using to indicate the background of the invention or the state of the art is considered to be nonessential subject matter by the PTO. You are allowed to incorporate-by-reference such nonessential subject matter from a wide range of sources including both patents and non-patent publications.

To incorporate by reference, you must make sure that you include an identification of the reference (e.g., patent, publication or application). If you want to incorporate only specific parts of the reference, you must also identify just those parts.

Example: "The details of the handle assembly are set forth in column 5, lines 62-100, of U.S. Patent 4,133,196, the disclosure of which is incorporated by reference."

The preferable method of incorporating a *co-pending application* by reference is to provide the names of all the inventors, the title of the application, and its filing date.

Step 6: Brief Summary of the Invention

Your *brief summary* (sometimes called the *disclosure of invention*) should be comparable to the scope of your broadest claim. (Drafting your claims is discussed more thoroughly in Chapter 5.) However, your brief summary should be written in clear prose rather than in the patent-like language that you will use in drafting your claims. In other words, your summary should be written in a way that a non-technical person, who may have difficulty interpreting claim language, can easily understand.

One technique that you can use in writing the summary of your invention is to take the broadest claim that you draft and then rewrite that claim into plain English. You can then also include any of your dependent claims as aspects of your invention.

You will often also see the objects of the invention listed in the brief summary. These objects correspond to the advantages of your invention. If you include any objects of your invention in your summary, you should try to draft objects that are not so narrow that they might be construed to limit your invention. The objects that you list should relate to the advantages of your invention with respect to overcoming the problems you discussed in the background section.

Since drafting your brief summary is often done in conjunction with or after you draft your broadest claims, you can save this section for later and complete it after you have drafted your claims if you prefer.

Step 7: Brief Description of the Several Views of the Drawing

You must briefly describe each figure of the drawing. Each figure should be described in a separate paragraph.

➲*Look again at the sample application in Appendix* C. Since the invention is relatively easy to picture in that patent, there are not very many different views or figures presented. However, it is better to be over inclusive than under inclusive. You will shortly learn that your drawings work with your detailed description section and must provide enough detail and clarity so that someone skilled in your art can make and use your invention.

Step 8: Detailed Description of the Invention

The first thing that you should know about your *detailed description* (often referred to as the *description* or *best mode for practicing the invention*) is that it must be complete and detailed enough so that a person who is skilled in your field (or your "art") can make and use your invention without extensive experimentation. This requirement is referred to as the *enablement requirement*. (U.S.C., Title 35, Sec. 112, paragraph 2.)

Author's Note

To insure that you have met the enablement requirement for computer software inventions, you should include a computer program listing (you will also need to comply with the requirements of Step 4 regarding the submission of your listing.) At a minimum, you should include a detailed flowchart so that a person skilled in your field would be able to write your program without undue trial-and-error.

As stated earlier, the enablement requirement demands that your invention be described in such full, clear and concise terms as to enable a person skilled in your field to practice your invention. This does not mean that you have to detail what is already well known in the art concerning your invention.

In fact, MPEP specifically states that "where elements or groups of elements, compounds, and processes, which are conventional and generally widely known in the field of the invention described, and their exact nature or type is not necessary for an understanding and use of the invention by a person skilled in the art, they should not be described in detailed." (MPEP Sec. 608.01 (h).) However, the MPEP goes on to state that "where particularly complicated subject matter is involved or where the elements, compound, or processes may not be commonly or widely known in the field, the specification should refer to another patent or readily available publication which adequately described the subject."

Example: Suppose that you have just come up with a protein in the biological field. Part of your invention involves the cloning of the gene that expresses that protein. Since the cloning of a gene is now well-known in the biological field, you would not need to provide instruction on the steps of cloning. You could simply state that cloning techniques are well known by persons skilled in the biological arts. However, it would still be safer in this case to incorporate-by-reference some texts that teach how to clone.

NOTE: ***Remember to be cautious.*** *If you are not sure whether some feature of your invention is well known in your field, you should either incorporate-by-reference patents that adequately describe this feature or write into your detailed description an adequate disclosure of this feature. It is extremely important that you provide a complete and adequate disclosure of features that are necessary to enable your invention.*

If you do not incorporate such necessary material into your application now, you will forever be barred from putting such material into your application later and still rely on your application's filing date for prior art purposes. This is because the PTO will not allow you to add new matter to your patent application later on. Your claims will also fail for lack of enablement if such claims are directed to any subject matter for which you have not provided a full disclosure on how to make and use your invention.

Incorporating-by-Reference Essential Material

Just as with your background section, it is permissible to incorporate references into your detailed description without actually stating everything that is contained in the references. But if the material that you want to incorporate by reference is considered to be *essential material,* the PTO limits the types of references that you can incorporate by reference.

If the material that you want to incorporate-by-reference into your specification is necessary to describe your invention; provide an enabling disclosure of your invention; or, describe your best mode, such material is considered essential material by the PTO. (MPEP Sec. 608.01(p).)

The PTO will only allow you to *incorporate-by-reference* essential material from U.S. patents or patent publications. You may also incorporate-by-reference certain U.S. patent applications (those that do not incorporate essential material by reference), but not foreign applications, patents, or publications.

You do not, however, need to worry too much about improperly incorporating essential material into your specification space. You can later amend your disclosure to include the material incorporated by reference directly into your specification. The amendment must be accompanied by an affidavit or declaration stating that you mistakenly tried to incorporate the amendatory material by reference into your application.

However, the consequence of failing to incorporate material (or write such essential material directly into your specification) that is necessary to enable your invention is much greater. Your claimed invention may be invalid. Do not be afraid to incorporate references into your specification. Make your description as complete as possible.

Just as with incorporating-by-reference material into your background section, you must make sure that you properly identify the referenced patent, application, or publication that you want to incorporate-by-reference. You must also specifically state that you hereby incorporate such specified reference either in its entirety or by identifying the parts that you want to incorporate-by-reference (see the discussion about incorporation-by-reference in your background section for the specific language that you can use). Mere reference to the other application, patent, or publication is not enough. You need to use the specific language discussed in your background section.

Specific Issues Regarding Your Detailed Description

While you must be complete in your detailed description, you should *not* discuss why your invention works. There is no requirement that you provide an explanation of the underlying mechanism of your invention.

An important issue with respect to your detailed description relates to what is referred to as the *written description requirement*. Under this requirement, your detailed description must provide clear written support for all of the terms that you use in your claims. In other words, your detailed description section is like a dictionary for your claims.

The reader must be able to find information about any features that you mention in your claims by looking through your detailed description. If the reader cannot find any such information, then you have not provided a sufficient basis for your claims and they will fail for lack of written description. You can help to avoid written description problems by writing as complete and full disclosure of your invention as possible in your detailed description section.

Enablement and written description issues can be some of the toughest issues to overcome later on with your patent application. Another important issue that does not come up as often is referred to as the *best mode requirement*. The best mode requirement simply means that your description must disclose the embodiment of your invention that you consider to be the best mode for practicing your invention. In other words, you are not allowed to hide from the public the best way to carry out your invention. For example, if you are aware of a specific material that will make possible the successful reproduction of your invention but do not disclose it, speaking instead in terms of broad categories, the best mode requirement has been violated.

You should also include statements in your application as to why you believe your invention is useful. *Statements of utility* are particularly important in the more unpredictable arts such as biotechnology and chemistry. In fact, if your application relates to such arts, it would be a good idea to read about the utility requirement in Chapter 2 so that you are forewarned now about some of the problems that you could encounter later on if you do not assert a specific and credible utility in your application.

WRITING YOUR DETAILED DESCRIPTION

Having discussed the requirements of enablement, written description, best mode and utility, let's take a look at the actual mechanics of writing your detailed description. Your description should be written in easy-to-understand English. Short paragraphs are better than long ones. Also particularly in mechanical inventions, your description section must work in conjunction with your drawings.

➲*Look at the sample application contained in Appendix* C. You will see the format of a typical written description for mechanical inventions. (A mechanical invention is used as an example because these types of inventions are very common in patent law. The style and format of writing your description will vary depending on the type of art to which your invention pertains. The best thing you can do is to look at a lot of patents relating to your invention to get a feel for a standard format.)

➲*Examine the detailed description in Appendix* C *on page 273.* The detailed description refers to the different views of the drawings by specifying the numbers of the figures and the different parts by use of reference numerals. For example, the description starts off with a reference to the entire inventive part (the folding carrier) and assigns it the number 12.

You may also notice that the sample application not only details many physical characteristics of the folding carrier, but also includes cooperative relationships, functions performed, and results attained. For example, after supporting member 18 is described, there is an explanation of how the carrier works (how it is attached to the car, how the carrier is moved from an extended to a collapsed position, etc.). This helps satisfy the requirement of sufficiency of disclosure and provides a basis for broad claim coverage.

NOTE: *It is typical and advisable to start the numbering of your parts with a number such as 10 (or in this case 12) or a number that is as least larger than the number of figures contained in your drawings in order to avoid any confusion between your reference number and the figure numbers in your drawings. It is also advisable to skip numbers as you sequentially identify parts of your invention. If you look at the sample patent, you will see that the numbers increase by 2 (14, 18, 20). Skipping numbers in this manner will leave you some unused numbers (the odd numbers in this case) to assign to any parts that you want to add later.*

If your invention has any alternate embodiments of your invention, you should discuss these in your detailed description.

Example: You invent an improved latch that slides by the use of a handle. If alternative embodiments exist (the handle takes on different shapes that are used for sliding the latch) you should include these in your detailed description. Instead of assigning completely different reference numbers for the alternate embodiments of the handle, you could give your main embodiment of the handle the number 20 and then identify the second embodiment with the number 20(a), the third embodiment of the handle with 20(c), and so on.

If any parts or features of your invention are critical to the operation of your invention, then you must set forth all such elements. Be careful about emphasizing the importance of any characteristic of your invention unless it is truly a critical aspect of your invention. If you emphasize any feature of your invention as critical to your invention, you will have to include such feature later on in your claims. As you will learn in Chapter 5, adding limitations to your claims actually narrows the scope of your claims.

You can include tables, chemical and mathematical formulas in your detailed description, or your can submit such material as formal drawings. You are not allowed to include graphical illustrations, diagrammatic views, flowcharts, or diagrams in your detailed description, but must instead submit such material as formal drawings.

The detailed description usually ends with some type of statement that the embodiments of your invention that you have disclosed are not intended to be *limiting* features. ➲*Look at the sample application in Appendix* C *on page 277.* It states that "Since certain changes may be made in the foregoing disclosure without departing from the scope of the invention herein involved, it is intended that all matter contained in the above description and depicted in the accompanying drawings be construed in an illustrative and not in a limiting sense." You can use this same language in your own patent application or any similar type of language that you find in your review of other patents during your prior art search.

Good Drafting Techniques: There is a general trend within the PTO toward using your detailed description in construing the terms of your claims. Keep this in mind as you draft your detailed description.

- Avoid closed-ended phrases like "the invention" or "all embodiments of the invention." These phrases have been interpreted to expressly limit the claims. (*SciMed Life Systems v. Advanced Cardiovascular Systems,* 242 F.3d 1337 (Fed. Cir. 2001).)
- Use open-ended phrases instead, such as "one embodiment of the invention, among others." Also, use permissive language like "may" or "can."

- Disclose alternative embodiments of your invention. Disclosing only one embodiment in a consistent manner serves to "implicitly define" claim terms.
- Be careful that your alternative embodiments do not themselves limit alternative structures. This can happen when your alternative embodiments limit your invention to the commonalities found among your different embodiments.
- Keep in mind that when you discuss prior art elements, you may be excluding those prior art elements from your claimed invention.

Step 9: Claims

This section of the specification is discussed in detail in Chapter 5.

Step 10: Abstract of the Disclosure

Your *abstract of disclosure*, or simply *abstract*, should start on a separate page in your application and should be limited to a single paragraph, not to exceed 150 words. This is the place where you let your reader quickly ascertain the nature of the subject matter of your invention. (The abstract will not be used for interpreting the scope of your claims.)

Your abstract should include everything that is new in the art to which your invention pertains. If your invention is an improvement of an old apparatus, process, product, or composition, your abstract should include the technical disclosure of the improvement.

Where your invention pertains to a machine or apparatus, your abstract should include its organization and operation. However, extensive mechanical details should not be included. In fact, your abstract should not be any more limiting than your broadest independent claim. This is because some courts have used the abstract in limiting your claims. The MPEP provides an example of an abstract as stated below:

Example: "A heart valve which has an annular valve body defining an orifice and a plurality of struts forming a pair of cages on opposite sides of the orifice. A spherical closure member is held within the cages and is moved by blood flow between open and closed positions in check valve fashion. A slight leak or backflow is provided in the closed position by making the orifice slightly larger than the closure member. Blood flow is maximized in the open position of the valve by providing an inwardly convex contour on the orifice-defining surfaces of the body. An annular rib is formed in a channel around the periphery of the valve body to anchor a suture ring used to secure the valve within a heart."

Author's Note

I actually find it easier to draft my abstract after drafting at least my broadest claim in the application. Your broadest claim is your claim that is broadest in scope (i.e., has the fewest number of elements). Your abstract should be no broader than your broadest claim as some courts have used abstracts in limiting claims (although they are not supposed to do this).

Step 11: Sequence Listing

If your patent application contains a nucleotide and/or amino acid *sequence listing,* then you must include a paper or compact disc copy disclosing it in the sequence listing section. (C.F.R., Title 37, Sec. 1.821(c).) You should consult these rules if you are required to provide a sequence listing with your application.

Also, you should go to the PTO website and download a program on their site called "PatentIn." (The 3.1 version of this software was the most current version at the time of publication of this book.) You can find the software and its user manual on the PTO site. The "PatentIn" software will create a sequence listing that you can print out and attach to your application. Remember to copy the sequence listing onto a 3.5 floppy disc.

As before, if this is not applicable to your invention, you can simply leave out this section heading in your application or write "Not Applicable" underneath the heading section.

Drawings

You are required to provide drawings of your invention where such drawings are necessary to understand your invention. (U.S.C., Title 35, Sec. 113.) If you file your application without drawings, and the PTO considers that drawings are necessary for an understanding of your invention, your application will be considered incomplete and you will not obtain a filing date.

In most cases you will need to prepare drawings for your invention. The rules that govern the formalities of your drawings are specified in C.F.R., Title 37, Sec. 1.84. If your drawings do not conform to all of these rules upon submission, your drawings will be considered *informal.* You will be notified of such informalities in a *Notice of Draftspersons Patent Drawing Review,* which is a form usually attached to the first *Official Office Action* that you receive from the PTO. This notice will list all of the defects in your drawings.

You can wait to correct such defects right up to the time when or if your application is allowed. However, once you receive a *Notice of Allowance,* you must correct such defects within three months. This is an absolute cutoff date. No extensions are allowed. (A notice of allowance is a paper from the PTO that tells you that your patent application has been approved and that a patent will soon be issued.)

FORMAL DRAWINGS

You can take a chance and submit informal drawings with your application and wait to see if your application is allowed before spending the money to provide formal drawings. However, I would recommend that you submit formal drawings with your application for the following reasons:

- Your application will be published eighteen months from the time you file your application unless you have certified that you are not filing abroad and do not want your application published (something I do not recommend), your drawings must now be of sufficient quality for publication. If your drawings are not of sufficient quality, examination of your application will be delayed. Submitting formal drawings will insure that your drawings are fit for publication;
- Formal drawings will make a better impression on your examiner.
- Drawings are a very important part of your obligation to teach persons skilled in your art how to make and use your invention without undue experimentation (enablement) and also your obligation to provide a written description for your claimed invention. By submitting carefully prepared drawings now, you are less likely to make costly errors later. Remember that you will never be able to add features to your drawings later on that are not disclosed in your specification. This is because the PTO will consider it "new matter." You are *never* allowed to add new matter to your application later on and still rely upon your earlier application filing date.
- If you wait to submit formal drawings until after you receive a notice of allowance, you will have only three months to do it. Doing it initially will save you the stress and time.
- The PTO will issue your patent a few months sooner if you have already filed formal drawings before a notice of allowance.

Unless you have some specialized drafting experience, you will most likely need to hire a professional draftsman to complete formal drawings for your invention. In practice, even most patent attorneys and agents hire professional draftsman to complete the drawings for a patent application. You can find a professional draftsman by doing a search on the internet or by consulting technical journals such as the *Journal of Patent Office Society* or *Intellectual Property Today*.

DRAWING RULES

Even after you receive formal drawings back from your draftsman, you should check them for accuracy. Check to make sure they meet the following important requirements for drawings. (C.F.R., Title 37, Sec.1.74.)

Views. You should provide as many views of your invention as are necessary to make the understanding of your invention clear. The views may be plan, elevation, section, or perspective views. Detail views of portions of elements, on a larger scale if necessary, may also be used. Having too many views (figures) can never hurt.

All views on the same sheet of your drawings should stand in the same direction and, if possible, stand so that they can be read with the sheet held in an upright position.

The figures or views on the sheets of your drawings should be labeled in consecutive Arabic numbers (FIG.1, FIG. 2, FIG 3, etc.). You should not crowd your figures all onto one page. Use as many sheets as you need to keep your figures spaced apart enough so they do not look crowded. If you do place more than one figure per sheet, you should arrange such figures so that the numbers increase from top to bottom. Of course, the numbers should also increase from sheet to sheet.

Drawing Sheets. Your drawing sheets must be on paper that is flexible, strong, white, smooth, non-shiny, and durable. Only one side of the sheet may be used for the drawing. The sheets must be either 8.5 by 11 inches or size A4. The sheets that contain the figures of your drawings should be labeled in consecutive Arabic numbers followed by a forward slash and then the total number of sheets you are submitting. Therefore, if you are submitting six sheets of drawings, you would label the first sheet as "1/6" and the second as "2/6" and so on.

These numbers should appear on the top center of each sheet, just outside the margin. The drawing sheet numbering must be clear and larger than the numbers used as reference characters to avoid confusion. Your draftsman should do this for you if you are having your drawings professionally prepared.

Identification of Drawings. It is a good idea to identify each sheet of your drawings so that if any of your sheets become disorganized, the PTO can easily put the sheets back together. You should place this identification on the front of each sheet, centered within the top margin. The identification should include the title of your invention, inventor's name, and *application number* or *docket number* if an application number has not been assigned to the application. One way to create a docket number is to use your last name (or first couple of letters of your last name) followed by a number that corresponds to how many applications you have filed.

You can type the identifying information onto a label and then affix this label directly to your drawing sheets. If you type directly onto your drawing sheets, you may damage your sheets. For example, if your name is Susan Smith, you might include the following information on a label and then affix it to your sheet.

Applicants: Susan Smith
Serial No.: Not Yet Assigned
Title: SLIDING LATCH
Docket No.: SMITH1

Reference Numbers. You should include reference numbers specifying where on your drawings each of the parts or features are located that were introduced in your detailed specification. These numbers must match the numbers which you used in your detailed description. As stated before, these numbers should start at 10 or a number larger than your highest figure number and increase by two or more so that if you ever need to add a reference number in between later on you will be able to do so without having to place such added on reference number out of incremental sequence.

You should draw a line from each of your reference numbers to the feature or part that you are designating. The line should start just off (not touching) each reference number from about the imaginary center of the reference number and then extend and touch the part of feature or part that you are identifying. The lines that run from your reference numbers can be straight or curved but should never run into each other. ➲*You can see this by looking at Fig. 2 from the sample patent application contained in Appendix C on page 284.* The only time that the line extending from a reference number should not touch the part it is referring is where the reference number is used to designate an entire assembly of parts as with reference number 12 in Fig. 2. You will notice that the line extending from 12 also has an arrow pointing to the assembly and any line that you use to designate such an assembly should also have an arrow.

If you place more than one figure on a drawing sheet, you may be tempted to draw two lines from one reference number to the same feature. Although this may be convenient, you should not do this but rather use two of the same reference numbers with two separate lines since the figures should be self-contained.

Photographs (black and white). Photographs are not usually submitted in drawings unless there is some special reason for doing so, such as where the photographs are the only practicable medium for illustrating your invention. Photographs are typically submitted, however, in biological inventions for electrophoresis gels, blots, autoradiographs, and the like.

Color Drawings or Photographs. Because of reproduction problems, the PTO sets down quite a few rules that you must follow if you want to submit either color drawings or color photographs. This rules are contained in C.F.R., Title 37, sec 1.84(a) for color drawings and C.F.R., Title 37, Sec. 1.84(b) for color photographs. In each case you are required to submit a petition to the PTO.

Copyright Notices. A copyright notice (e.g., "© 1983 John Doe") may be placed adjacent to copyright material in your specification. Remember to include an additional separate section heading at the start of your specification as discussed previously.

If your copyright notice appears in your drawing, the notice must be limited in print size from 1/3 inch to 1/4 inch and must be placed within the "sight" of the drawing immediately below the figure representing the copyright material.

5 The Most Important Part of the Application: Claims

This chapter covers the claim section of your specification. I have devoted a separate chapter to explain how to draft your claims because it is a lengthy and important topic.

Claim Format

Your claims section must begin on a separate sheet of paper, and it must start with one of the following phrases:

- "I claim" (use this if you are the sole inventor);
- "We claim" (use this if you are filing an application where there are more than one inventors); or,
- "The invention claimed is" (this can be used whether you have one or more inventors).

On the next line of your claims portion, number your claims using Arabic numerals (ie: 1, 2, 3…). If you have just one claim, you would see just the number 1 followed by the claim. If you have more than one claim, you would see 1, 2, 3…. ➲*Look at the sample application in Appendix C for the format of your claims*. You should see that there are 12 claims in the sample patent 4,518,108.

A claim contains three separate parts:

- the preamble;
- a transition phrase; and,
- the body of the claim.

Following is a detailed explanation of each of the three parts.

PREAMBLE

Following the appropriate numeral, start your claim with a capital letter (typically "A" or "An") and then the product or method that you are claiming. This portion of your claim is known as the *preamble*.

The preamble of a claim is an introductory statement, usually in single paragraph form, that should recite at least the statutory class of the invention (e.g. apparatus, composition, process), but it may recite more. ➲*Look at claim 1 of the sample patent application in Appendix* C. You will see that the claim starts off with the phrase "A folding carrier mountable on an automobile or the like." This is the preamble. The phrase starts off with the word "A" and then cites an apparatus ("a folding carrier"), which is the statutory class of the invention.

If the body of your claim (discussed below) fully sets forth all the limitations of your claimed invention, and your preamble merely states, for example, the purpose or intended use of your invention, then your preamble will not be considered a limitation and will be of no significance in construing your claim. However, any terminology in your preamble that limits the structure of your claimed invention must be treated as a claimed limitation.

TRANSITIONAL PHRASE

The *transitional phrase* is an introductory clause between the preamble and body of the claim. It indicates where the background ends and where the body begins, and defines how to interpret the claims. The commonly used phrases are "comprising," "consisting essentially of," and "consisting of." Each one of these phrases is important to understand because its use determines how broad your claim will be. Each phrase defines the scope of your claim with respect to what unrecited additional components or steps, if any, are excluded from the scope of your claim.

NOTE: *Sometimes you will see "comprising," "consisting essentially of," and "consisting of" in the body of your claim. When such phrases appear in a clause of the body of your claim, rather than as a transition phrase immediately following the preamble, they limit only the element set forth in that clause; other elements are not excluded from your claim as a whole. (Mannesmann Demag Corp. v. Engineered Metal Products Co., 793 F.2d 1279 (Fed. Cir. 1986).)*

Open-Ended Transitional Phrases. The word "comprising" is frequently used because it is open-ended in that it does not exclude additional, unrecited method steps or elements. *Comprising* is a term of art used in claim language that means that the named elements are essential, but other elements may be added and still be within the scope of the claim. Such an open-ended claim is infringed if all the recited elements are found in the infringing product, even if additional elements are also found. In other words, an accused product or method will infringe upon product or method claim having the transitional phrase "comprising" even if it employs additional steps.

Example: A claim that recites a device as comprising elements A,B, and C, would be infringed by a device having elements A,B,C, and D. The claim is interpreted as "my invention is at least the following, but it may include more."

Sometimes you will see the word "including" or "which comprises" instead of "comprising." All are equivalent to each other. The use of the transition phrases "comprising" or "including" are the best types of transition phrases that you can use in drafting your patent claims because your coverage is broadest.

However, sometimes the PTO will not give to the broad coverage that you normally get by using the transition clause "comprising." For example, your detailed description may not enable such broad coverage. Also, it is easier for prior art to anticipate a broad claim than a claim with more elements. So if you write a claim comprising only two elements hoping to capture potential infringers whose products contain those two elements, it will be easier for a prior art reference to anticipate (teach each and every element) elements A and B rather than elements A, B, and C.

Closed Transitional Phrases. *Consisting of* is a transitional phrase that is much more limiting when it comes to what you are claiming. The use of the word "consisting" when used as a transitional phrase excludes any element which you have not specifically claimed. Thus if your claim is to a gadget "consisting of" elements A and B, any potentially infringing product must contain only elements A and B or their *equivalents* and nothing else.

Author's Note

You might be asking me what do I mean by "equivalents" in the above paragraph. This brings up a very important concept in patent law called the *Doctrine of Equivalence*. This doctrine comes into play if and when it comes time for you to sue someone for infringement of any one of the claims of your patent.

In essence, the doctrine says that not only can you sue someone for infringing upon the literal meaning of a limitation in your claim, but also for any *equivalents* of that limitation. By equivalents the law means insubstantial differences of that limitation. This is deemed fair because it is difficult for mere language to capture every type of minor variation.

Partially open ended transitional phrases. A third type of transitional phrase that can be used in claim drafting is the phrase *consisting essentially of.* This transition phrase is used to denote a partially open claim. It occupies a middle ground between closed claims that are written in *consisting of* format and fully open claims that are drafted in a *comprising* format.

This transition phrase is sometimes seen preceding a list of ingredients in a composition claim or a list of steps in a process claim. By using the term *consisting essentially of,* you signal that the invention necessarily includes the listed ingredients or steps and is open to unlisted ingredients or steps that do not materially affect the basic and novel properties of the invention

An ingredient or step has a material effect if the effect is of importance or consequence to those persons having the typical and ordinary skill in your art. For example, if your invention is to a chemical composition, then you might ask whether the addition of some other element to that composition would have any importance in respect to the properties of that composition. If the answer is no, then a claim using "consisting essentially of" would encompass that additional element. If the answer is yes, then the element would be outside the scope of the claim and escape literal infringement of that claim.

Although *consisting essentially of* is typically used in the compositions of matter, there is nothing wrong with using this term as modifying language for method steps. In such a case, the claim can only include steps that do not materially affect the basic and novel characteristics of the claimed method.

Example:

1. A process of producing a completely hardened metal structural element provided with a fracture of an intended course consisting essentially of:

   (a) subjecting the surface of the completely hardened structural element at least along a portion of the intended course of the fracture and in traverse limitation thereto to a high energy radiation to selectively embrittle the metal, and

   (b) splitting the elements along the intended course of the fracture.

While a *consisting essentially of* may help you to capture potential infringers who try to include steps that do not materially affect the basic and novel characteristics of your invention, this type of claim can sometimes run into problems with prior art just as with the broader *comprising* format.

To see this, say there is prior art that has the additional elements of (c) and (d), so that the prior art contains elements (a,b,c,d). So long as (c) and (d) do not affect the basic and novel characteristics of the process, you would not be able to argue that your claimed invention is different from the prior art for anticipation purposes. You *would* be able to argue this if you had written the claim in the *consisting of* claim format.

By writing a claim with *consisting essentially of,* you are in effect saying "I'm claiming my listed steps, plus any other steps that do not affect the basic and novel characteristics of my method." You would need to amend your claim in such a situation to the more restricting transition phrase of *consisting,* or else you would be infringing upon this prior art and the PTO would reject your claim.

For purposes of searching for and applying prior art, if you do not spell out clearly in your specification what the basic and novel characteristics are, *consisting essentially of* will be construed as equivalent to *comprising.* (MPEP Sec. 2111.03.) Moreover, if you contend that additional steps or materials in the prior art are excluded by the recitation of *consisting essentially of,* you have the burden of showing that the introduction of additional steps or components would materially change the characteristics of your invention.

Author's Note

Although I cannot give you a definitive answer as to which transition phrase to use, it would be rare for a patent application not to contain at least one claim having the broadest "comprising" transition phrase. Broad is better from the standpoint of the number of possible infringers that you can capture later on.

Sometimes the choice to use the broadest transition phrase simply will not be yours. To see this, you need to understand the following: While using a broad transition phrase like "comprising" will indeed capture more potential infringers of your claim, it will also make it easier for your examiner to find prior art that anticipates your claim.

Body of Claim

The third part of your claim is called the *body of your claim.* This is where you set out either the process steps (if you are claiming a method or process) or the structural limitations (if what you are claiming is a structure). These steps or limitations are what define and make up your invention for which you seek protection. ➲*Look again at claim one of the sample patent application on p.278.* I have reproduced the start of this claim for you below and have put in italics the start of the body of the claim.

1. A folding carrier mountable on an automobile or the like, said carrier comprising:
   (a) a frame;

   (b) a carrying member pivotally mounted to said frame said carrying member movable about a first axis between an operative extended position and a collapsed position, said carrying member and said frame being in a substantially side-by-side relationship when said carrying member is in its collapsed position, a foot of said carrying member positioned to contact the automobile when said carrying member is in its operative extended position;

In this claim, there are structural limitations set out in the form of (a), (b), etc. To make the reading of these limitations easier, each of the elements or limitations is set out in a separate paragraph.

You should also notice that the structural elements making up this folding carrier are not set out alone but are rather interrelated to the other structural elements set out in the claim. Your claim must end with a period, and you may not use a period in your claim anywhere except at the end of your claim.

Types of Claims and How to Draft Them

You read in Chapter 1 that U.S.C., Title 35, Sec. 101 allows for four categories of inventions; namely, processes, machines, manufactures and compositions of matter. For ease of discussion, I will divide the classes of claims into the following headings: Apparatus, Compound, Composition, and Process claims. All of these types of claims come within the scope of U.S.C., Title 35, Sec. 101. (I divide them up this way because this is how I have seen most patent attorneys refer to them over the years in this business.)

The thing that you must keep in mind as your write your claims is that each claim must fall into a separate statutory class. Think of claims as an individual oasis. Claims are separate and distinct from each other. When it comes time for your examiner to examine your application, he or she will look at each of your claims independently for patentability purposes. Similarly, when it comes time for you to enforce your claims for infringement purposes, you will look at each one of your claims separately to determine whether infringement exists.

While you can include more than one statutory class of claims in a patent application, you cannot include two separate classes within the same claim. The only exception to this rule is a *product-by-process* claim. This claim has been determined to be a separate statutory claim class. (This class of claim is discussed more fully later in this chapter.)

APPARATUS CLAIMS

Apparatus claims are one type of product claim that covers a device. For example, the following would be considered an apparatus claim.

1. A decorative figure assembly, comprising:

a) a non-fluid filling, material;

b) a plurality of individual closure means each for closing a bag;

c) a plastic torso bag containing a first portion of said filling material and having an open end being closed by a first of said plurality of closure means;

d) a plastic head bag containing a second portion of said filling material and having an open end being closed by a second of said plurality of closure means;

e) two plastic arm bags containing third and fourth portions, respectively, of said filling material and each having an open end being closed by a third and a fourth of said plurality of closure means, respectively; and

f) a plurality of coupling means for coupling said torso bag to said head bag, to said arm bags, and to said legs bags,

wherein said head bag, said arm bags, and said leg bags are coupled by said plurality of coupling means to said torso bag and form a figure proportioned to a costumed human.

A claim to an apparatus covers what a device is. As you can see from claim 1 above, there are elements or limitations (a-f) that define the structure of the decorative figure assembly. The claim in this case ends with a *wherein* clause. Such *wherein* or *whereby* clauses are typical in apparatus claims and usually tie in the important elements of the apparatus and state the advantage or what is accomplished by the apparatus.

Claims directed to an apparatus must be distinguished from the prior art in terms of structure rather than function. You should claim an apparatus in terms of its structure, not by what it does.

The only time that you are allowed to come close to describing something by its function is when you use a special type of claim drafting format called a *means-plus-function clause*. The reason for this one exception is that there is a special statute that states that an element in a claim for a combination may be expressed as a means for performing a specified function, without recital of the structure, material, or acts disclosed in the specification.

The apparatus claim above had the following elements in means-plus-function format—

(b) a plurality of individual closure means...

(f) a plurality of coupling means for coupling said torso bag...

As stated, if you use a means-plus-function format in your claim, you must remember to always include more than one element in your claim. In other words, you cannot write your claim with a single means plus a statement of function and nothing more. This rule comes from the statute that authorizes means-plus-function claims.:

> An element in a claim for a *combination* may be expressed as a means or step for performing a specified function without the recital of structure, material, or acts in support thereof, and such claim shall be construed to cover the corresponding structure, material, or acts described in the specification and equivalents thereof. (U.S.C., Title 35, Sec. 112.)

The key word above is "combination." If your claim with a means-plus-function clause is not a combination of more than one element, then the claim will be rejected.

A means-plus-function element can be incorporated in the preamble of a claim, as well as in the body as above. It can appear in combination with other means-plus-function elements or in combination with non-functional elements. If you are using more than one "means" clause in your claim, it is often helpful to distinguish between the clauses by stating "first means" to refer to the first means clause and "second means" to refer to the second means clause and so on. (More detailed information about means-plus-function clauses is discussed later in this chapter.)

Again, in order to make sure that your apparatus claim is not "anticipated" by prior art, you must recite at least one feature that structurally differentiates your apparatus from any prior art apparatus. You cannot avoid anticipation by claiming some novel *function* that your apparatus does.

Example: Evan's claims were drawn to a disposable diaper having three fastening elements. A prior art reference disclosed two fastening elements that could perform the same function as the three fastening elements in Evan's claims. Evan's claims would not be anticipated by the reference since the reference did not disclose the separate third fastening element.

Compound Claims

If you are claiming a chemical compound, a typical way to phrase your claim is to say, "A compound of the formula:" and then draw the formula that you are claiming. Such claims are commonly referred to simply as *compound claims*. The format of this claim is exactly like a conventional format except that it lacks a transitional phrase like "comprising."

If you do not know the formula or structure of the compound that you are claiming, you may claim your compound by listing its physical and chemical characteristics. This is sometimes referred to as *fingerprinting*.

A second way that you may claim a compound of unknown formula is by claiming it in terms of the process by which it is made. (ie: your product-by-process claim). For example, it would be proper to claim "A chemical compound produced by a process comprising the steps of:" and then list all of the steps.

COMPOSITION CLAIMS

Composition claims define a composition as a combination of chemical components. Such claims may not be directed to naturally occurring substances because such substances are unpatentable under U.S.C., Title 35, Sec. 101. Claims directed to *newly* discovered compositions of matter that are products of nature must be prefixed with the phrases such as "a purified," "an isolated," "a substantially pure" or "a biologically pure," product or compound (such as a "purified" protein) to distinguish them from naturally occurring, unpatentable subject matter.

You will often see ranges cited in a composition claim. One thing that you need to keep in mind is that such ranges are anticipated by prior art that intersects anywhere within your cited range. Thus if your claim cites 02–0.4% molybdemum (Mo) and 0.6–0.9% Nickel (Ni) as your composition, this claim will be anticipated by a reference that discloses 0.25% by weight Mo and 0.75% Ni. (*Titanium Metals Corporation of America v. Banner,* 778 F.2d 775 (Fed.Cir. 1985).)

If your claimed composition is physically the same as the composition cited in prior art, and you are simply stating some new property or use of the composition,the prior art will render your claim unpatentable. Thus, you would not distinguish yourself from prior art merely by citing the glass transition temperature of a copolymer that was not cited in the prior art since this is merely citing a new physical property of the same composition. (*In re Spada,* 911 F.2d 705 (Fed.Cir. 1990).)

PROCESS CLAIMS

There are two types of *process claims*. The first type is a claim that defines how to make something such as an apparatus, composition or compound. Such a process claim may consist of a single step or many steps.

The second type of process claim is one that defines how a machine operates or how to operate on a composition, material or article to make it do something. The second type of process claim is commonly referred to as a "method" claim although the word "process" is good form because it is the word used in the relevant statute.

Warning: Process claims can be somewhat inconvenient to enforce because the infringer may be the end user of the device and thus often a customer rather than a competitor. Also, the claim must be operated, or the composition, material, or article operated upon in the U.S. in the same manner as required by the claims. You should try to include other types of claims in your application in addition to process claims if possible.

Example:

1. A purified polynucleotides having a nucleic acid sequence selected from the group consisting of SEQ ID NO:1, SEQ ID NO:2 and SEQ ID NO:3.
2. An expression vector comprising the polynucleotide of Claim 1.
3. A host cell transformed with the expression vector of Claim 2.
4. A process for producing and purifying a polypeptide, said process comprising the steps of:

    (a) culturing the host cell of Claim 3 under conditions suitable for the expression of the peptide; and

    (b) recovering the polypeptide from the host cell culture.

This last claim, a process claim, is taking the host cell which was claimed in Claim 3, and performing process steps on the cell to obtain a protein.

AUTHOR'S NOTE

A *Markush Group* is a group of related items joined by the word "and." Inventions in metallurgy, refractories, ceramics, pharmacy, pharmacology and biology are most frequently claimed under the Markush format. However, purely mechanical features or process steps may also be claimed this way.

A Markush group, incorporated in a claim, should be "closed," i.e., it must be characterized with the transition phrase "consisting of," rather than "comprising" or "including." The Markush group can be broadened somewhat, however, by the transitional phrase "consisting essentially of" to include traces of materials outside the specified group.

You can see that the transitional phrase "consisting of" is used. Look at Claim 1 that states, "SEQ ID NO:1, SEQ ID NO:2 and SEQ ID NO:3." While Claim 1 could have been made into three separate claims by claiming each sequence separately, the use of a Markush Group does the trick itself with one claim.

In a process claim you must set forth all the active steps with verbs ending in "-ing" or else your process claim will be rejected as being vague and indefinite.

Example: Alison wrote two of her claims as follows:

6. A process for using monoclonal antibodies of Claim 4 to isolate and purify human fibroblast interferon.
7. A process for using monoclonal antibodies of Claim 4 to identify human fibroblast interferon.

These claims are properly rejected under U.S.C., Title 35, sec 112 on the basis that they cite a use without the reciting of any active "ing" process steps. (*Ex parte Erlich*, 3 U.S.P.Q.2d 1011 (1986).)

Product-by-Process Claims

There is one type of hybrid between a product and process claim that is authorized, called a *product-by-process* claim. In this type of claim, the process referred to is the process of *making* a product, not the process of *using* a product.

While a product-by-process claim format may appear to cross the line between improperly combining two statutory classes of invention, it is acceptable because a product-by-process claim merely uses one statutory class of invention (e.g., process limitation) to define or fingerprint another statutory class (i.e., the product). (*Ex parte Lyell*, 17 USPQ2d 1549 (1990).)

If you include a product-by-process claim in your application, you should also include a product claim if possible. There are some disadvantages of a product-by-process claim when compared with a product claim:

- Product by-process claims are easier to infringe than a product claim alone. This is because a product-by-process claim is infringed only by the claimed product made through a substantially identical process as the process recited in your product-by-process claim. However, if you have a product claim, your product claim will be infringed by the same product made by a different process. In other words, the process serves as an added limitation of a product-by-process claim when it comes to infringement analysis.
- Even though product-by-process claims are defined by a process, determination of patentability is based on the product itself. If the product in the product-by-process claim is the *same as* or *obvious from* a product of the prior art, the claim is unpatentable even though the prior product was made by a different process.

If you include a product-by-process claim and your process is itself novel and non-obvious, you should also include a claim directly to your process in your application. If your product claim is not allowed, you will be able to patent your process claim.

Special Claim Format

Drafting Dependent Claims

A dependent claim is a claim that refers back to and further restricts a single preceding claim. There are many reasons for including dependent claims in your application. Here are several of them:

- A dependent claim saves you from repeating all of the elements of the main claim (the claim from which the dependent claim depends).
- A dependent claim shall be presumed valid even though dependent upon an invalid claim. (U.S.C., Title 35, Sec. 282.) Dependent claims are a good way to add additional claims to your application if you want to add some significant element or feature to a claim that you have previously written. If your main, broader claim is held invalid, your dependent claim will be evaluated on an independent basis and is presumed valid until proven otherwise.

Thus if a potential infringer finds a prior art reference that anticipates your broad main claim and is successful in invalidating it (but not your narrower dependent claim), you will still be able to enforce your narrower dependent claim.

Of course, independent claims also stand on their own and you would be able to achieve the same result by writing your independent claims as dependent claims. However, you are charged an extra fee for each independent claim that you file in excess of three independent claims. Filing dependent claims will therefore not only save you from repeating all of the elements of an independent claim but it will also save you money;

- By further restricting your invention with the use of dependent claims, there is greater likelihood that one of your dependent claims has all of the features in an accused infringer's product. Although the accused product will also infringe the broader independent main claim in your application from which your dependent claim depends, you may gain a psychological advantage with a judge or jury who is able to clearly see how the accused product matches up to your claim.

A dependent claim may depend from an independent claim or from another dependent claim. There is no limit to the length of a chain of dependent claims. However, you should group all claims dependent from the same independent claim directly after that claim. Also, any dependent claim that you write must further restrict the claim(s) on which it depends.

Example: Inventor Joe claimed an electrical circuit in the following manner:

I claim:

1. *An electrical circuit comprising, in series, a 10-20 amperes DC current source of variable content, an 8-10 ohm resistor, and a 3-8 uf capacitor.*
2. *An electrical circuit according to claim 1, wherein the resistor is a 5-10 ohm resistor."*

The second dependent claim is rejected by the PTO since it broadens rather than restricts claim 1 (The ohm range of the resistor is increased from a 8–10 range to a 5–10 range). The PTO will be this detailed regarding your claims.

When you draft a dependent claim, your dependent claim is considered to include all of the limitations that you have placed in the claim from which your dependent claim depends as well as any additional limitations that you add in your dependent claim. This has the practical effect where any time the main claim is not infringed, then your dependent claim will never be infringed. In fact, the PTO defines a dependent claim as one that shall not conceivably be infringed by anything that would not also infringe the basic claim. This makes sense because main claims are less restrictive and therefore more encompassing than dependent claims.

Since the transition phrase *consisting of* is a closed ended phrase, if you use it in the main claim, you are not allowed to add new elements to its dependent claim. You are allowed to add new information to your dependent claim that further defines a pre-existing element contained in the prior claim, but you cannot go as far as to add a new feature to your dependent claim.

There is no rule against using a dependent claim that is in a different statutory class from the main independent claim. For example, if your main independent claim is a product claim, you are allowed to use a dependent claim that is a process of using the product of your main claim.

Multiple Dependent Claims. Sometimes, but not often, you may want to refer back to not only one preceding claim, but to several other claims. When you do this, you are creating what is called a *multiple dependent claim*. As with dependent claims, a multiple dependent claim must further restrict the claim(s) on which it depends.

While multiple dependent claims are permissible, you must always refer to the prior claims in the alternative. Examples of properly wording multiple claims are:

> "A gadget according to Claims 3 or 4, further comprising" or,
> "A gadget as in any one of the preceding claims, in which..."

Examples of unacceptable multiple dependent claim wording are:

> "A gadget according to Claim 3 and 4, further comprising.." or,
> "A gadget according to Claims 1-3, in which..."

You should avoid using multiple dependent claims, as there is a multiple dependent claim surcharge. The number of claims upon which the filing fee is based increases considerably as a result of multiple dependency.

NOTE: *A multiple dependent claim* may not *depend on any other multiple dependent claim. (For more information on multiple dependent claims, see MPEP Sec.608.01(n).)*

Means-Plus-Function Clauses

When you use a means-plus-function clause, the PTO (or a court later on in an infringement suit) will look to your specification for structures that you have listed that carry out the function of your means-plus-function clause. Structures that you have disclosed in your specification that are clearly linked or associated to your cited function will be considered as corresponding structures. After you obtain a patent on your claims, any infringer who uses a corresponding structure to the one that you have cited in your specification will be an infringer of your means-plus-function claim. The reverse side of this that any corresponding structure in the prior art will also anticipate your means-plus-function formatted claim.

If you read the statute closely, you will see that it also speaks about "equivalents thereof." This means that the PTO (or a court later on an infringement analysis) will not only look to the corresponding structures that you have disclosed in your specification, but also any equivalents.

Factors that the PTO will look to in order to determine whether a prior art element is an equivalent include:

- whether the prior art element performs the identical function specified in your claim in substantially the same way, and produces substantially the same results as the corresponding element disclosed in your specification;
- whether a person or ordinary skill in the art would have recognized the interchangeability of the prior art element for the corresponding element disclosed in your specification; and,
- whether there are insubstantial differences between the prior art element and the corresponding element disclosed in your specification. (MPEP Sec. 2183.)

The reason that you are given equivalents is so that you do not have to fill up your patent specification with a laundry list of everything you can think of that might be an equivalent to your invention. This prevents a would-be infringer from using your invention later just because they thought of some equivalent structure that can carry out your means-plus-function clause. Again, the reverse side of this is that the PTO can look for equivalents to anticipate your claimed element.

Using a means-plus-function clause can actually be more limited than simply writing your claims without such clauses. When you use a means-plus-function clause, equivalents are determined with respect to the actual means that you have shown in your specification. In determining the equivalents of an element not written in means-plus-function format, however, any and all equivalents of that element are looked at.

If you use a means plus-function-clause, an equivalent structure cannot embrace technology developed after the issuance of your patent, whereas you can use such equivalents to find infringement under the doctrine of equivalents. For these reasons, if you include some of your elements in means-plus-function format, it is wise to include other claims where your elements are not in such a format, if possible.

General Claim Drafting Rules and Techniques

The Number of Claims You Should Draft

Your specification must include at least one claim that states with precision what you consider to be your invention for which a patent is sought. However, in practice, your specification will always include more than one claim. It would be very risky to include just one claim because if that one claim were to be held invalid later on in litigation, you would have nothing to enforce. If you include other claims in your specification—even if some of your claims were to be held invalid later on—you would still have other claims to rely on. The fact that one or more claims may be held to be invalid does not mean that other claims are automatically invalid. Claims stand or fall on their own and each claim is considered separate from the other claims.

Although there is no particular rule, an application ordinarily will have at least one or two independent claims characterizing the invention as an apparatus, at least one independent claim directed to the anticipated commercial embodiment of your invention, another one or two as a method, if appropriate, and a sufficient number of dependent claims to comprise a claim total of at least twenty.

After twenty claims, you will be charged an extra fee for each additional claim that you submit. (The fee was $9.00 per claim in excess of twenty at the time publication.) You are also charged an extra fee for each independent claim in excess of three that you submit. (The fee was $42.00 per claim for a small entity at the time of publication.) Often you will see only three independent claims in an application unless your invention is particularly complex or some other reason justifies adding more.

How to Draft Broad Claims

If you draft broad claims, it is harder for someone's invention to avoid infringing on your claims, meaning that you have a broader scope of protection. To do this, you should use an open-ended transition phrase such as *comprising* if it is possible to do so. As stated above, by using an open-ended transition phrase, you will capture an infringer whose product has elements A, B, C, D even if your claim recites only elements A, B, C.

Another way that you can make sure a claim is written as broad as possible, is to include as few elements in your claim as possible. This may seem counter-intuitive. You do *not* make claims broader by adding detail. Adding more elements or limitations to a claim will actually limit the claim in as far as the types of products that it can encompass.

NOTE: *Infringement of a claimed combination requires the presence in the accused structure of each claimed element or its equivalent.*

Another way to make your claims as broad as possible is to pay attention to the language that you use to describe features in your claim. You should use language that is broad rather than limited. ➲*Look at the sample patent in Appendix* C. One could recite "a folding bicycle carrier" rather than simply a "folding carrier," but you can probably see that by including the word "bicycle" your patent protection might be limited only to bicycle folding carriers. This could be a problem if your potential infringer comes along and uses your folding carrier to carry their suitcases.

To find the language that you want, go to dictionaries and other patents in your field to see if you can pick up better terms for your words. The use of words like "about," "approximately," and "substantially" are also a wise choice instead of reciting specific parameters such as dimensions.

NOTE: *Your broadest claim (the one that restricts your invention the least) should appear as* Claim 1. *In other words, as you add claims, you must add limitations that further restrict what exactly you are claiming as your invention. You should never place such further restricted claims above any prior less-restricted claims.*

Make sure Your Claims are Not Anticipated

While you should write broad claims, you should also draft them so that they are not *anticipated* by the prior art. As stated in Chapter __, a claim is anticipated by a prior art reference only if each and every element as set forth in your claim is found, either expressly or inherently described, in that prior art reference.

In times past, patent attorneys and agents would often write very broad claims and then let the PTO worry about whether such claims were anticipated by any prior art. This was a convenient way to draft claims because you could let the PTO do a lot of your work in as far as uncovering prior art. You could also push the limits of the PTO in your quest to obtain the broadest claims possible.

This is no longer recommended due to a federal circuit court decision which states that if you amend any element of your claim for any reason related to patentability (this includes avoiding the prior art), then you give up any equivalents as to that element(s) that you amended. (*Festo Corp. v. Shoketsu Kinzoku Kogyo Kabushiki Co.*, 56 USPQ2d 1865 (Fed. Cir. 2000).)

In other words, you will be entitled to absolutely no range of equivalents as to element(s) that you have amended during prosecution. All a potential infringer needs to do to get around your amended claim element is to substitute something equivalent for that element. This would not have been possible if you had not amended your claim element during prosecution.

Given that amending your claims can now have adverse consequences, your prior art search has become all the more important (See Chapter__.) You should be aware of the prior art concerning your invention and draft claims so that they are not over-broad, or anticipated by this prior art. If you *do* want to draft overly-broad claims that really push the limits, then you should also include claims that are narrower in scope. This way if you are forced to amend your overly broad claims later on, you still might be allowed your narrower claims that you have not amended, and will thereby be entitled to a range of their equivalents.

Drafting claims is, in effect, a balancing act. While you do not want to draft overly broad claims that will likely force you to make amendments to the claim, you do want to draft claims as broad as possible without reading on or being anticipated by the prior art. By drafting your claims as broad as possible in this manner, you will be able to capture as many potential infringers as possible. At the same time, by drafting your claims so that they do not read on the prior art, you will be less likely have to amend your claims during prosecution and will not give up any equivalents to any element(s) that you have amended.

USING ANTECEDENT BASIS

Make absolutely sure that all of the terms and phrases that you use in your claims have *antecedent basis* (support) in your detailed description. If your claims do not have support, then your claims will be rejected for a lack of written support.

Another issue that frequently arises with respect to lack of antecedent basis is when you state a phrase like "said lever" or "the lever" in your claim but you have never previously introduced "lever" into your claim. To avoid this problem, use words like "a" and "an" when you are first introducing elements that you are citing in a claim. After you have introduced an element by the words "a" or "an," you then typically refer back to the previously introduced element using the word "the" or "said."

If you try to introduce an element or limitation in your claims with the word "said" your claim will fail for indefiniteness. Fortunately, the problem can be easily cured by amending your claim to include the proper antecedent article.

ESSENTIAL FEATURES

If you have stated in your specification some feature that is critical to your invention, you must include this critical feature somewhere in your claims. Such essential matter may include missing elements, steps, or necessary structural cooperative relationships of elements described by you as necessary to practice your invention.

In addition to including all the essential features of your invention in your claim(s), you should interrelate all these essential elements or your claim may be rejected as being vague and indefinite.

AVOID NEGATIVE LIMITATIONS

You should avoid drafting your claim(s) by excluding what you *did not* invent rather than by particularly and distinctly pointing out what you *did* invent. Such phrases are known as *negative limitations* and can lead to problems in your claims. Statements in your claim that try to sum up your invention by saying what it does *not* constitute are likely to lead to a rejection as being vague and indefinite. You should always state what you are claiming in the positive.

Use of Trademarks in Your Claims

The use of trademarks to identify the source of materials is permitted in claims so long as the trademark is in all capital letters. However, avoid using a trademark alone to describe anything in your claim.

Draft from Broad to Narrow

The whole idea to drafting claims is to obtain the broadest coverage for your invention as possible. You can do that as previously explained by drafting broad claims. But what if your broad claims are rejected by your examiner? Where are you left after that? The answer is that you will have to make an amendment to your claim to restrict or narrow its scope. By making amendments to your claims, you will give giving up the possibility of suing anyone for using any equivalents of your amended elements.

Include a Variety of Claim Types

The way around this is to draft a variety of claims with varying degrees of scope. Again, you should place your broadest claims at the beginning and your narrower claims at the end. It is also wise to include a variety of claim formats if possible. If you have a new product, you should also include any possible process claims relating to that product.

Useful Technique for Drafting Good Claims

While there is no one right way to go about drafting your patent claims other than by putting time and care into writing your claims and studying the way others have written claims, here is one technique that may assist you.

As stated before, you will want to start your claims with your broadest claim. As a first step in drafting you broadest claim, list all of the fundamental elements of your invention. You should include enough such elements to just distinguish your invention over the prior art, but no more. Decide which elements of your invention are absolutely necessary for operability and clear it against the prior art.

Example: Suppose that you are the first person to come up with the idea of a table. Your essential elements would probably be 1. a top (since tables need tops), 2. legs (since tables probably need legs), 3. some way to secure your legs to the top (you would not want to specifically delineate rivets or some other specific means at this time). Having listed all of the appropriate necessary elements, you could now write an independent claim that might go as follows.

1. A table, comprising:

(a) a top portion or surface; and

(b) one or more legs which are secured to said top portion or surface.

You could then proceed to further limit your broad claim by adding dependent claims that add limitations corresponding to the different embodiments of your table. For example, you might want to specify how the top portion is attached to the legs. You might also want to specify the shape of your elements in Claim 1. Some possible dependent claims you might write are the following:

2. The table of Claim 1 wherein said one or more legs are secured to said top portion or surface by a hinge.

3. The table of Claim 1 wherein said top portion is substantially rectangular.

Although this is a very simplified example, it serves to show you that you need to think broadly with the fewest elements possible to begin. You then add more limitations in your dependent claims. After you have finished this, you can write additional independent claims. As stated above, your additional independent claims might cover any novel process that you can also claim. It is also a good idea to write an independent claim that covers the embodiment of your invention that you are going to actually use commercially.

6 Completing Your Application

In Chapter 4 you learned that your application has the following parts:

- utility application transmittal form;
- fee transmittal form;
- application data sheet;
- specification;
- drawings; and,
- executed oath or declaration.

At this point, you have completed drafting your specification and your drawings. This chapter will cover how to complete the remaining parts of your application. You can take pride that you have already prepared your application for all practical purposes. The rest of the work that follows is more akin to procedural matters, but is important nevertheless.

In addition, this chapter will discuss how to complete your *Information Disclosure Statement* (IDS). Although an IDS is not a formal part of your application, I recommend that you complete your IDS now and submit it along with your application for reasons that will be discussed in this chapter.

To get started, the very first thing that you will want to include in your application materials is a cover sheet in which you tell the PTO exactly what you are enclosing in your envelope. Your cover sheet should look like the one contained in Appendix E. Next, you should complete the *Utility Application Transmittal Form,* described below.

Utility Application Transmittal Form

- The utility application transmittal form should be downloaded from the PTO website in order to ensure that you are using the most recent version. Information on this can be found in Appendix E. At the upper right corner, fill in your docket number (this is your own internal reference number which you create to keep track of your application), your name as the inventor, the title of your invention, and the express mailing number you will use to send your application. (See the section on "Sending Your Patent Application" on page 107.)
- You should check item (1), fee transmittal form, to indicate that you are including this form with your application.
- You should check item (2) if you are claiming *small entity status.* If you are filing your application as an individual inventor and have not yet assigned your application, then you will check this box.

  By claiming small entity status, you will be entitled to half the regular fee that the PTO charges to file an application. This reduced fare is available for three types of inventors:

  - an independent or sole inventor;
  - a small business that is defined as a business that employs 500 or fewer employees; and,
  - a non-profit organization either in this country or abroad.

  Neither of these three classes of inventors can have assigned or be under any obligation to assign their invention to an entity that does not classify as a "small entity" in order to qualify for this special fee status.

- You should check item (4) if you are including drawings with your application and indicate how many sheets of drawings you are submitting.
- You should check the applicable box to indicate that you are submitting a declaration. If this is your original application and not a continuation, you should check the box labeled "newly executed."
- Check box (6) indicating that you are submitting an application data sheet.
- Boxes (7–8) will only apply if you are submitting a CD-ROM, CD-R or sequence listing.
- If you have assigned your application, you can send in the assignment papers with your application and would correspondingly check box (9).
- You should check box (12) if you are submitting an *information disclosure statement* (discussed later in this chapter on p.102) as well as the box labeled "copies of IDS citations" to indicate that you are submitting copies of your listed references.
- You should check box (14) to indicate that you are submitting a return postcard.
- If you are making any priority claim to a previously filed foreign patent application that you have filed for your invention, you will need to submit a certified copy of the foreign application and check box (15).
- If for some reason you are requesting that your application not be published, you should check box (16).
- If this is your original or first application in the U.S., you do not have to worry about box (18).
- Fill in the information concerning your correspondence address unless you have a customer number in which case you would simply affix your customer number label to the area indicated on the form.

You can obtain a *customer number* by going to the PTO website and filing out Form PTO/SB/125 ("Request for customer number"). Within a few weeks after you send in the form to the PTO, you will receive small bar-code stickers that have your customer number. You can use these labels on all future filings with the PTO.

- Print your full name and sign the form.

Fee Transmittal Form

Include a fee transmittal form in duplicate after your utility transmittal form. A copy of this form can be found on the PTO website. You can also fill out a Patent Application Fee Determination Record (also reproduced in Appendix E) and attach it behind your fee transmittal form.

- In item (1) you should check the box authorizing the Commissioner to charge any indicated fees and credit any overpayments to your deposit account number if you have such an account set up with the PTO.
- You should also check the box labeled "charge any additional fee required under C.F.R., Title 37, Sec. 1.16 and 1.17," which will notify the PTO that you want any other fees that you may incur with respect to your application to be charged to your deposit account.

Deposit Accounts

Provisions exist where you can establish for a small fee ($10), a *deposit account* with the PTO in order to cover fees associated with the handling of your application. However, a minimum amount of $1,000 is required to establish such an account and a monthly service charge is incurred for balances below the $1,000.

Deposit accounts are very convenient because you can charge any fees associated with the prosecution of your application to your account. If you so authorize at the time you pay your fee, the PTO will also charge any deficiency or credit any overpayment to your account. If at any time, you authorize any fee to be charged against your account and there are insufficient funds to cover such a fee, then the PTO will charge you a surcharge in addition to the fee.

If you are an individual inventor who is planning on filing a single application, then the trouble of setting up a deposit account will probably not be worth obtaining one. However, if you plan on filing additional applications in the future, a deposit account may be worth setting up with the PTO.

- You should check the box labeled "small entity status" if you qualify as a "small entity."
- Under item (2) you should indicate the type of payment you are making if you are submitting your payment to the PTO along with your application (i.e. not charging your deposit account). If you check the box labeled "credit card" you should fill out a credit card payment form PTO-2038. This form is listed in Appendix E. You should attach this form directly behind your fee transmittal. This form should be pretty much self-explanatory. If you need further help with the form, there are instructions on the PTO website. Under the "Request and Payment Information" heading, you should state "basic filing fee" as a description of request and payment information.

FEE CALCULATION

This is the section of your fee transmittal where you calculate out how much money you owe the PTO for various fees.

- Under item (1) you should enter the appropriate fee next to the "utility filing fee" box. (This fee was $370 for small entities at the time of publication of this books.) You should carry that figure over to the subtotal box.
- Under item (2) you will need to figure out your total number of claims in your specification, the total number of independent claims, and the total number of multiple dependent claims.

- Each independent and dependent claim in your application will count for one claim. If you have included any multiple dependent claims, you will need to count up all of the claims to which the multiple dependent claim refer to in order to figure out how many claims to add to your total.

Multiple Dependent Claims. If you have used any multiple dependent claims in your application, you should submit a separate form provided by the PTO called a "Multiple Dependent Claim Fee Calculation Sheet." Download this form as instructed in Appendix E. This is to ensure that you are using the most recent PTO version. You should attach it after your Patent Application Fee Determination Record.

Claims in proper multiple dependent form are considered to include all of the claims to which they refer. If you have any other claims that depend on a multiple dependent claim, those claims also count for the number of claims referred to in your multiple dependent claim.

- In Item (3) you will see several boxes where you can request an extension of time. Extensions of time will only become relevant for you after you file your application and you need additional time to respond to various actions which the PTO makes concerning your application.

EXTENSIONS OF TIME

Automatic extensions are paid for in packages of one month, two months, three months, four months and five months. (C.F.R., Title 37, 1.136(a)) Five months is the maximum amount of time that you can buy. No cause or reason is needed to make an automatic extension of time. The PTO is very liberal on granting you such extensions as long as you pay the necessary fee.

Extensions of time can and usually are made retroactively. Thus you are allowed to wait until the final day necessary to respond with your extension of time before sending in your response.

One thing that you should keep in mind with extension of time is that you are never allowed to request an extension that will take you past six months from the mailing date of an office action from the PTO that requires you to do something. (There is a statute that says you must make your response within six months from the mailing date of the office action.)

Another thing that you should keep in mind is that extensions of time are not available for the following more obscure types of things that you could get involved with during the prosecution of your application:

- reexamination;
- interference proceedings;
- reply briefs;
- requests for an oral hearing in an appeal;
- response to a decision by the Board of Patent Appeals and Interferences; and,
- any action from the PTO that specifically states that you cannot seek an automatic extension of time.

Application Data Sheets

If you go to the PTO website at **www.uspto.gov** and look under "p" using the index at the top of the home page, you will find information on how to prepare your *patent application data sheet*. This form is simply a sheet where you list out various information concerning your application. A blank form that you can use as your application data sheet is provided in Appendix E.

Not all of the various parts of the data sheet will apply to your situation. If a various section does not apply, you are permitted to simply leave that section blank. In other words, you only need to fill in the various situations that are applicable to your own application.

You should consult the PTO website for a detailed explanation about how to fill out this sheet. At the end of the information packet on the PTO website are various examples on completing your sheet. You may also consult C.F.R., Title 37, Sec. 1.76.

Oath or Declaration

An *oath* is a statement signed before a notary, while a *declaration* is a statement warning you about willful false statements. While you do not have to file an oath or declaration at the precise time you file your application to obtain a "filing date," it is highly recommended that you complete your oath or declaration now. If you wait to file it, you will receive a "Notice Missing Parts" and you will also incur a surcharge for late filing.

The Information Disclosure Statement

Each individual associated with the filing and prosecution of a patent application has a duty of candor and good faith in dealing with the PTO, which includes a duty to disclose all information known to that individual to be material to patentability. (C.F.R., Title 37, Sec. 1.56.)

The way that you comply with your duty to disclose information to the PTO is through an *Information Disclosure Statement* (IDS). There is no limit to the number of IDS submissions that you can make. For example, you could submit an IDS now with your current application and then if you later discover a material reference, you can include that reference in a second IDS, which you would simply call a *Supplemental IDS*.

It is very important to be diligent in forwarding to the PTO any information that you believe may be material. When a failure to meet the disclosure duty is found to be a result of fraud, bad faith, or other misconduct on your part, the failure will prevent your patent from being granted. Alternately, if your patent is granted before such misconduct is discovered, the courts can hold all of your patent's claims to be invalid and your patent unenforceable if such misconduct can be shown later on.

In order to comply with your disclosure duty, you should submit the most recent IDS form that the PTO has available. Instructions on how to download this form from the PTO website are in Appendix E.

Behind your IDS, you should also submit a form that the PTO provides to list all of your references (*Information Disclosure Statement Cover Letter*), which is reproduced on pages 304–305. Again, because you will not know your examiner's name or Group Art Unit at this point, you can simply state "Not Yet Assigned."

If you have met all of the requirements for your IDS, your examiner will consider each of the references that you have listed on your citation list form and initial next to each of the references which the examiner has considered. Your examiner will send you a copy of the citation list with his or her initials next to the references considered in the next office action that you receive from the PTO. Any items that have not been considered by your examiner will have a line drawn through the citation.

TIME TO SUBMIT YOUR IDS

I recommend that you submit your IDS now along with your application because the longer your wait after submitting your application, the more you must do in order to get the PTO to consider your IDS and the more you are going to have to pay. The following four stages in your prosecution illustrate this.

1. If you submit an IDS within three months from the date you file your application or prior to the mailing date of the first Office action on the merits (not procedure) by the PTO, whichever is later, the PTO will consider your IDS without any charge.

2. If you file your IDS after the time in (1), but prior to a final action or notice of allowance, you must either provide a certification or pay a fee specified in C.F.R., Title 37, Sec. 1.17(p).

   If you opt for the certification instead of paying the fee, you must certify (and this means it must be true) that the references you are submitting to the PTO became known to you or anyone else involved with the prosecution of your application no more than three months prior to the time you are submitting these references (i.e., the mailing date of your IDS).

In the alternative, you can certify that such references were cited in a *counterpart foreign application* (such as in an international search report you receive during the prosecution of your foreign application) no more than three months prior to your submission.

A counterpart foreign patent application means that a claim for priority has been made in your U.S. application and foreign application based on it, or that the disclosures of your U.S. and foreign patent application are substantively identical.

NOTE: *Under this certification, it does not matter whether you actually knew about any information cited before receiving a piece of information like a search report. What matters is what is stated in the search report.*

You can use either one of the certification statements below. Simply place the applicable certification statement into your IDS, and you can thereby avoid paying the required fee.

(a) "I hereby state that each item of information contained in the information disclosure statement was first cited in any communication from a foreign patent office in a counterpart foreign application not more than three months prior to the filing of the information disclosure statement" or,

(b) "I hereby state that no item of information contained in the information disclosure statement was cited in a communication from a foreign patent office in a counterpart foreign application, and, to the knowledge of the person signing the certification after making reasonable inquiry, no item of information contained in the information disclosure statement was known to any individual designated in Section 1.56(c) more than three months prior to the filing of the information disclosure statement."

In situations where some of the references that you list were cited in a communication from a foreign patent office not more than three months prior to the filing of your IDS whereas others were not known more than three months prior to filing your IDS, then you can simply create two lists in your IDS and make each certification under its appropriate list of references.

3. If you file your IDS after a final office action or a Notice of Allowance, but before paying the issue fee, then you must submit both the required certification under (2) as well as the fee set forth in C.F.R., Title 37, Sec. 1.17(p). You are no longer permitted a choice at this stage. If you are unable to make the certification because it is not true, then you should file a *Request for Continued Examination* (RCE) of your application.

4. If you want to submit an IDS after paying your issue fee, your only option is to withdraw your application from issue so that you can file your IDS in a continuing application.

WHAT YOU SHOULD INCLUDE IN YOUR IDS

Your IDS must include the following:

- A list of all U.S. and foreign patents, U.S. patent applications, publications, and any other information submitted for consideration by the Office (hereinafter individually or collectively referred to as documents or references);

Example: The duty of disclosure requires reporting to the PTO any co-pending US applications that contain information material to the examination of the application in question. A copy of the relevant co-pending application (or a copy of the relevant parts of that application) must be provided in your IDS. (C.F.R., Title 37, Sec. 1.98(a)(2)(iii).)

- Each U.S. patent listed in your IDS must be identified by patentee, patent number, and issue date.
- Each foreign patent or published foreign application must be identified by country or patent office that issued the patent or published the application, an appropriate document number, and the publication date indicated on the patent or published application.

- Each publication must be identified by author (if any), title, relevant pages of the publication, date, and place of publication. The date of the publication must include at least the month and year of the publication unless you point out in your IDS that the year of publication is sufficiently earlier than the effective filing date of your application so as not to raise any prior art issue (in which case you can simply specify the year).

- A legible copy of each submitted document. However, when the disclosure of two or more patents or publications listed in your IDS are substantively cumulative, a copy of just one of the patents or publications may be submitted provided that you state that the other patents or publications are cumulative; and,

- A concise explanation of relevance for any documents listed that is not in the English language. You have quite a bit of flexibility in your explanation, and you may simply point out similarities as well as differences between the reference and your claims. However, you must bring to the examiner's attention the reference's relevant teaching.

Your explanation can also be fulfilled by submitting an English-language version of any search report or action that cites such non-English reference and that indicates the degree of relevance found by the foreign office.

Other Things to Include with Your Application

Cover Letter

It is a good idea to include a cover letter that simply tells the PTO what they are receiving from you. A sample cover letter that you can fill out is included in Appendix E. Your cover letter should appear at the top of your stack of papers. None of your papers should be stapled. However, it is a good idea to place a clip around all of your papers so that they do not become disorganized either en route to the PTO or while at the PTO.

POSTCARD

It is also a good idea to include a self-addressed prepaid postcard with your patent application. Your self-addressed and stamped postcard is useful because it can serve as evidence of what you have sent to the PTO.

On the front of the postcard, print your name and address and place a stamp on it. On the back of your postcard, list each document that you are including in your package to the PTO. The back of your post-card can be organized as follows:

Serial No.: Not yet assigned	The following papers have been received:
Filed: Herewith	(1) Utility Application Transmittal
Title: (Insert title)	(2) Fee Transmittal Form (in duplicate)
	(3) Fee Determination Record
Inventor(s): (Insert names)	(4) Multiple Dependent Fee Worksheet
	(5) Declaration (executed)
	(6) Information Disclosure Statement
Docket No.: (insert #)	(7) IDS Citation List (2 pages)
Express Mailing #: (insert #)	(8) Postcard

SENDING YOUR PATENT APPLICATION

USE EXPRESS MAIL TO SEND YOUR PATENT APPLICATION

People are in the patent arena to protect their inventions. One of the simplest ways to protect your invention is to obtain the earliest effective filing date for your invention. For that reason alone, I recommend that you use Express Mail to send your patent application and no other type of delivery.

While it is possible to send your application by first class mail, your filing date will be the date that your PTO actually receives your application. However, if you send your application by Express Mail, your filing date will be the date that you actually deposit your application with the United States Postal Service.

To obtain the advantage of express mail, make sure that you fill in the "date in" box on your express mailing label. You should also include somewhere on your correspondence to the PTO an express mailing form where you certify the date that you have deposited your papers with the post office. This statement appears on all of the forms that you will use in Appendix E.

You can use Express Mail for any other type of paper you send to the PTO during the prosecution of your application.

Final Checklist

- ❒ Cover letter
- ❒ Utility Application Transmittal
- ❒ Fee Transmittal Form (After you complete this form, make a copy of it so you can submit it in duplicate.)
- ❒ Fee Determination Record Form
- ❒ Multiple Dependent Fee Worksheet (If you have any multiple dependent claims, you should complete this worksheet.)
- ❒ Specification (Include the number of pages.)
- ❒ Drawings (Indicate in your cover letter whether your are submitting formal or informal drawings.)
- ❒ Declaration (Indicate in your cover letter whether your drawings are executed or unexecuted; since there is really no reason why your drawings should be unexecuted unless you have not been able to obtain a co-inventor's signature at this time, you will most likely indicate "executed.")
- ❒ Information Disclosure Statement
- ❒ IDS Citation List (Indicate the number of pages you are sending.)
- ❒ Postcard (Be sure to place a stamp on the front of the card.)

Before you put all of your papers into a legal size Express Mail envelope to send, make sure that you copy all of your papers, including your postcard (front and back) and your completed Express Mail label. File each of these copied papers into a separate folder. Most patent attorneys and agents use a three-part folder, and I recommend that you do the same. Use one part of the folder for your copied application, one part for correspondence that you will receive from the PTO, and the third pocket for correspondence that you send to the PTO.

Your patent application should be sent to the following address:

Box Patent Application
Commissioner for Patents
Washington, D.C. 20231

7 Preparing Other Types of Applications

There are other kinds of applications you may file during the patent process besides utility and process patent applications. This chapter will discuss when, how, and why you would file these applications.

Design Patent Applications

There are three types of designs:

- a design for an ornament, impression, print or picture applied to or embodied in an article of manufacture (surface indicia);
- a design for the shape or configuration of an article of manufacture; and,
- a combination of the first two categories.

Note that each of the three types of designs has in common the embodiment of the design in an article of manufacture. This is an important distinguishing feature because a claim to a picture, print, impression, etc. per se, that is not applied to or embodied in an article of manufacture cannot be patented. (MPEP Sec. 1504.01.)

➲*Review U.S. Patent No. 296,039 in Appendix D on page 287*. You will notice that many parts are different from utility patents.

DIFFERENCES FROM UTILITY PATENTS

One of the first things you may notice is that design patents are much shorter than utility patents. The main reason for this is that there is no detailed written description in a design patent. In design patents, the drawings substitute for the detailed written description.

Another important feature is that a design patent includes only a *single* claim. This claim has a peculiar format that applies only to design patents. The single claim should normally be written as follows: "The ornamental design for (the article which embodies your design or to which the design is applied) as shown and described." One good thing about this is that you are not going to have to spend a lot of time drafting your claims for a design patent.

In addition to the above differences between a design and utility patent, you should note the following differences:

- the term of a design patent is fourteen years from the date of the patent grant whereas the term of a utility patent is twenty years from the effective U.S. filing date of the utility patent;
- utility patent applications may claim the benefit of a provisional application, but design patent applications may not;
- an RCE is not available for a design patent;
- design patent applications are not subject to the publication rules that are applicable to utility patent applications;
- an international application naming various countries may be filed for utility patents under the Patent Cooperation Treaty (PCT), but no such provision exists for design patents; and,
- foreign priority can be obtained for the filing of utility patent applications up to one year after the first filing. This period is six months for design patents.

DESIGN PATENT SPECIFICATIONS

For the most part, everything that you learned about utility patents is also applicable to the necessary sections of your design patent application. Your design patent specification should include the following sections.

- ***Title.*** Your title must designate the particular article on which your design is embedded and the title must correspond with your claim. ➲*For example, the design on the sample patent in Appendix D is embedded on a shoe sole, so this is the title of the patent.*

- ***Cross-reference to related applications.*** This is the same section as covered for a utility patent. You do not need to include a cross-reference to related applications if you include the cross-reference in your application data sheet.

- ***Statement regarding federally sponsored research or development.*** Just as with a utility patent, you must include this section if it is applicable.

- ***Description of the figure or figures of the drawing.*** This is the same as for your utility patent. (See p.65 for more information.)

- ***Drawings.*** Every design patent application must include either a drawing or a photograph of the claimed design. As your drawing or photograph constitutes the entire visual disclosure of your claim, it is of utmost importance they be clear and complete. (Photographs are only acceptable in applications in which the invention is not capable of being illustrated in an ink drawing or where the invention is shown more clearly in a photograph. You must also comply with C.F.R., Title 37, Sec. 1.84(b) if you want to submit photographs.)

  You should make sure that you include a sufficient number of views to disclose the complete appearance of the design, which may include the front, rear, top, bottom, and sides. In addition to all of the rules covered for a utility patent application, you should also look at the rules in MPEP Sec. 1503.02 for design patents.

- ***Single claim.*** As previously stated, your design patent has only one claim. The claim must be in the form "The ornamental design for (the article which embodies your design) as shown and described." ➲*Take a look at the sample patent in Appendix D for this format.*

Design Patent Application

You should include the following items for a complete design patent application.

- ***design application transmittal form.*** Instructions on obtaining the most recent version from the PTO website are included in Appendix E. One item that is new to you is item (14). You are entitled to obtain an expedited examination of your design patent application if you make the claim here and pay the specified fee in C.F.R., Title 37, Sec. 1.17(k), which was $900 at the time of publication of this book. If you want to claim expedited procedure, take a look at MPEP Sec. 1504.30. You will need to complete a request for expedited examination (Form PTO/SB/27) and a statement indicating that you have completed a pre-examination search concerning your design patent.
- ***fee transmittal form.*** Include a fee transmittal form. (See Chapter 6 for additional information.)
- ***application data sheet.*** Submit an application data sheet. (See Chapter 6 for additional information.)
- ***specification.*** Include your drafted specification.
- ***drawings or photographs.*** Include any drawings or photographs of your design that are necessary.
- ***executed oath or declaration.*** Include a completed declaration. (See Chapter 6 for additional information.)
- ***information disclosure statement and citation list.*** Complete an IDS just as you would for a utility patent application.

You should send your design patent application to:

Box Design
Commissioner for Patents
Washington, D.C. 20231

If you are requesting an expedited examination of your design patent application, then include the word "Expedited" before "Design" in the address above.

Provisional Applications

A *provisional application* is a U.S. national application for a patent filed under U.S.C., Title 35, Sec. 111(b). A provisional application can be filed for both utility and plant patent applications. However, you cannot file a provisional application for a design patent application.

A provisional application is considered expired twelve months after you obtain a filing date for the application, and it is not subject to revival after this time. If this twelve-month period falls on a Saturday, Sunday, or federal holiday, the provisional application will expire on the succeeding business day.

Claiming Priority to Your Provisional Application

Sometime within the twelve months before your provisional application is due to expire, you must file your regular utility patent application that claims priority to your previously filed provisional application. This way you will obtain an effective filing date for your regularly filed application, which dates back to the filing date of your provisional application.

You make this claim to priority in your application data sheet that you fill out for your regular U.S. filed application. If you do not make your claim in your application data sheet, you must specifically state in your regular application that you claim priority. To do this, write as the first sentence of your application, "This application claims the benefit of U.S. Provisional Application No. ___________, filed __________." I recommend that you do both, make a claim of priority in your specification as well as in your application data sheet, although it is not necessary.

Filing a Provisional Application

There are several reasons that either alone or in combination may make filing a provisional application a good idea.

- A provisional application is easier to complete than a non-provisional utility application because you do not need to submit any claims. You also do not need to file a declaration, nor do you file an IDS. Thus, if you are up against any immediate deadline to obtain your filing date, you will have an easier time completing a provisional application than a regular U.S. application.

- Provisional applications cost less to file than regular U.S. applications. Therefore, if there is the possibility that you may later decide to abandon your invention within a year after you file your provisional application, you could just let your provisional application expire.
- A provisional application's one year lifetime does not count in the twenty year lifetime of a patent. In effect, you are given a twenty-one-year period for the filing date of a provisional application before expiration of your patent.

Completing Your Provisional Application

You should submit the following items to complete the filing of your provisional application.

- a cover sheet identifying the application as a provisional application for patent. Use the downloading instructions provided in Appendix E;
- your filing fee as set forth in C.F.R., Title 37, Sec. 1.16(k) ($80.00 for small entities at the time of publication of this book);
- an application data sheet (see Chapter 6);
- a specification. However, you do not need to prepare claims for your specification. You can, however, submit claims if you want to and such claims will become part of your specification.

  NOTE: *Your provisional application specification should be as complete as possible (just as with completing your regular U.S. application.) The reason for this is that in order to obtain the benefit of the filing date of your provisional application later on, the claimed subject matter in your later filed regular U.S. application must have support in your provisional application.*
- any drawings necessary to understand your invention; and,
- a return postcard.

After your provisional application is complete, mail it to:

Box Provisional Patent Application
Assistant Commissioner for Patents
Washington, DC 20231

Continuation Application

A *continuation* is a second application for the same invention that was formerly claimed in a prior non-provisional application and filed before the prior application becomes abandoned or patented. You must have at least one inventor in common with your prior application in order to file a continuation from that prior application.

Filing a Continuation Application

Although your claims in a continuation are directed to the same invention as your previously filed non-provisional application, you can change the scope of your claims. It is not unusual to file a continuation application just prior to the issuance of a patent, so that prosecution based on the original disclosure will be able to be continued. This is valuable where a competitor may attempt to design around your patent in order to avoid literal infringement by adopting minor variants. In such a situation, it may be possible to revise the continuation application claims to cover the variant literally, considerably enhancing the scope of your protection.

A second situation where you may want to file a continuation is where your examiner has allowed some of your claims but rejected others. In such a situation it may be better to pursue the rejected claims in a continuation and take a patent now for your allowed claims. To do this you should cancel your rejected claims in your present application and file a continuation in which you pursue your rejected claims.

A third situation where you may want to consider filing a continuation is where all of your claims have been rejected by your examiner, and you wish to use a continuation to get in another shot.

NOTE: *What you can do after a final rejection can be quite limited. By filing a continuation, you can get your amendments entered into your new continuing application. However, also note that you can achieve this same purpose by filing an RCE, which is discussed on page 123. The filing of an RCE may also be less expensive because you do not need to pay for any excess claims which you previously paid for prior to the filing of the RCE.*

Example: Nicholi receives a Final Rejection from the PTO requiring a response by June 10, 1998. On August 10, 1998, Nicholi decides to file a continuation along with a one-month extension of time rather than responding to the outstanding action.

Since Nicoli obtained a one month extension of time, the continuation is co-pending with the original application and thus takes on the original filing date

A properly filed continuation contains the following parts:

- ***cover letter.*** Complete a cover letter for your continuation just as you would if you were filing a regular U.S. patent application.
- ***utility patent application transmittal.*** Complete this as you would for your original application. In Box 18, make sure that you check the box labeled "continuation." Also be sure to include the prior information about your parent application.
- ***fee transmittal.*** You will need to complete a fee transmittal just as you did with your original application.
- ***credit card payment form.*** If you are paying by credit card, you should complete this form just as explained in Chapter 6.
- ***application data sheet.*** You should complete another application data sheet just as you do for an original application.
- ***specification.*** Your disclosure in your continuation must be the same as your parent application. Usually what patent attorneys and agents do is to re-file an exact copy of the specification filed in the parent application, and then submit a preliminary amendment along with the continuation. (See Chapter 10 for more information on preliminary amendments.)

PRELIMINARY AMENDMENT

The preliminary amendment serves to update the specification with any changes made during prosecution of the parent application (changes that do not add any new matter). You must file an amendment to reflect the changes made during prosecution of your parent application because these changes do not automatically carry over in a Rule 53(b) application. The submission of a preliminary amendment is considered useful because it lets the examiner more clearly see the changes you are making to your specification. This often gives your examiner a greater comfort zone that you are not adding any new matter to your specification.

If you prefer, you can also rewrite your specification with all of the changes and simply submit it as your new continuation application without having to complete a preliminary amendment. This is easier than filing a preliminary amendment along with your application and I would recommend it at least with respect to your claims for the additional following reason.

Continuation-In-Part Application (CIP)

A continuation-in-part application (CIP) is filed during the lifetime of an earlier non-provisional application, repeating some substantial portion or all of the earlier nonprovisional application but adding matter not disclosed in it. (MPEP Sec. 201.08.) Thus, a CIP is a continuing application that discloses the same or a substantial part of the subject matter as the parent application, but also includes "new matter" not contained in the original or parent.

CIP applications are useful for updating an application with new technical developments that have arisen during prosecution. The original filing date is retained for subject matter common to the two applications—the "new matter" receives the later filing date of the CIP application.

A CIP must have at least one common inventor with the original parent application. This means that the parent application may have been filed by a sole applicant whereas the CIP is filed by that applicant along with other applicants. Vice versa, the parent applicant could be filed by joint inventors, whereas the CIP is filed by just one of those inventors.

FILING A CIP

All CIPs must follow the rules in C.F.R., Title 37, Sec.1.53(b). A properly filed CIP should contain the following parts:

- ***cover letter***. Complete a cover letter for your CIP just as you would if you were filing a regular U.S. patent application.
- ***utility patent application transmittal.*** Complete this as you would for your original application. In Box 18, make sure that you check the box labeled "continuation-in-part (CIP)." Also be sure to include the prior information about your parent application.
- ***fee transmittal.*** You will need to complete a fee transmittal just as you did with your original application.
- ***credit card payment form.*** If you are paying by credit card, you should complete this form just as explained in Chapter 6.
- ***application data sheet.*** You should complete another application data sheet just as you do for an original application.
- ***specification.*** As with a continuation, you have two choices here. You can file a duplicate copy of your original patent Specification and add your new matter, or any other changes, with a preliminary amendment. In the alternative, you can simply submit your CIP as a new rewritten patent application that reflects all of the changes that you want to make.

You should update your cross-references section of your specification so that you have made specific reference to your earlier filed application. (MPEP Sec. 201.09.)

- ***Declaration.*** Your CIP must be accompanied by a new oath or declaration executed by all of the inventors. (See Chapter 6 for information about how to complete a declaration).
- ***IDS.*** In any CIP application, there is an explicit duty to disclose all information known to be material to patentability which became available between the filing date of the prior application and the national or PCT international filing date of the CIP application. If any such references have come to your attention, you need to submit them on your IDS and also list them in your citation list.

DIVISIONAL APPLICATION

There is a good chance that you may have to file a *divisional application.* Such applications are necessary where you file your regular U.S. application, and the PTO determines that your application has claims directed to more than one separate invention. In such a case, the PTO will issue you a restriction requirement in your first office action. This requires you to elect one of your claimed inventions and file your other claimed inventions in separate patent applications. These separate patent applications are known as *divisional applications.* You must file these divisional applications while your parent application is still pending in order to take on the priority date of the parent application.

Divisional applications of utility or plant applications filed on or after May 29, 2000 are filed under C.F.R., Title 37, Sec. 1.53(b). As mentioned, this means that a divisional application is assigned a different file application number from its parent application. The filing of your divisional application will have no affect upon the prosecution of your parent application. Both applications can issue into separate patents.

FILING A DIVISIONAL APPLICATION

The following should be included in your divisional application.

- ***cover letter.***
- ***utility patent application transmittal.*** This is the same transmittal that you submit with a regular utility application. (see Chapter 6). In Box 18 of the transmittal check off the box labeled "divisional."
- ***fee transmittal.*** This is the same as for your regular application.
- ***credit card payment form.*** Include this form to pay by credit card just as you would for your regular application.
- ***application data sheet.*** This is the same data sheet covered in Chapter 6. Under the "application type" you should indicate "divisional" rather than "regular." You should fill in the appropriate

classification of your divisional application, which can be found in the Office communication of your parent application in which the restriction requirement was made.

- ***specification.*** The MPEP states that your divisional should set forth at least that portion of your earlier application that is germane to the invention that you are now claiming. Thus if a portion of your earlier disclosure is not relevant to the claimed invention of your divisional, you should delete that matter from your divisional application.

The MPEP also states that while you may rewrite your parent application using different phraseology, you are not allowed to depart in substance or variation from your originally filed application when writing for your divisional application. Therefore, patent attorneys and agents usually re-file an exact copy of their specification as filed in the parent application and delete claims or subject matter not pertinent to the divisional using a preliminary amendment. (see Chapter 10.) However, as with a continuation and CIP, you may decide that it is easier to simply re-write your specification on your word processor as a new application that incorporates the changes you want to make. This will save you from completing a preliminary amendment.

- ***drawings.*** You can use the drawings that you prepared for your regular application in your divisional.

- ***declaration.*** You can simply copy the declaration that you submitted in your prior application and submit it as your divisional declaration because you are not disclosing anything new from what you filed in your parent application.

However, if are you adding claims that are directed to subject matter described but not claimed in your prior filed application then you should file a supplemental oath or declaration. (C.F.R., Title 37, Sec. 1.67(b).) A supplemental declaration form should be downloaded from the PTO website to ensure the most recent version. See Appendix E for detailed instructions.

- ***information disclosure statement and citation list.*** You should submit another IDS with your divisional application. However, you do not need to make copies of any reference that was previously submitted and considered by the examiner in your earlier application. (C.F.R., Title 37, Sec. 1.98(d).) Simply alert your examiner in your IDS to the list of previous documents and state that since such documents were previously submitted, you are not resubmitting copies of the documents now. However, you should state that you still want the examiner to consider these previously submitted documents in your current IDS. You should also submit a citation list of these documents which your examiner will send you back with his or her initials indicating that these documents have been considered.

If you have learned of any new material references since you filed your original application, you should include these references in your current IDS, submit copies of these references, and include them on your citation list.

Request for Continued Examination (RCE)

A *request for continued examination* (RCE) is simply a request that your current application continues to be examined. You can file an RCE for a utility or plant patent application. However, you cannot file an RCE for a design or for a provisional application.

In order to file an RCE, prosecution of your application must be closed. Prosecution of your application is considered "closed" if you have been mailed a final office action, a *Notice of Allowance,* or your application is under appeal.

You file your RCE by filing a *submission* and the fee set forth in C.F.R., Title 37, Sec. 1.17(e), which was $740 at the time of publication of this book.

A *submission* includes such things as an amendment to your written description, claims, drawings, new arguments, or new evidence in support of patentability. A submission also includes the filing of an IDS.

An RCE is *not* a new application. Everything that occurred in the prosecution of your parent application will simply be carried over to your RCE. Your RCE is assigned the same application as your originally filed application. You can think of an RCE as a type of amendment in your current application. If you timely file your RCE, the PTO will withdraw the finality of your office action and your submission in the RCE will be considered.

FILING AN RCE

A properly filed RCE should include the following:

- ***Cover letter.*** Complete a cover letter for your RCE just as you would if you were filing a regular U.S. patent application.
- ***RCE Transmittal.*** Instructions for downloading a copy of this transmittal are included in Appendix E.

In Box 1 you must indicate what you are filing for your submission. This can be a submission (e.g., amendment) that you previously filed.

In Box 2 you will notice that you are allowed to request that prosecution of your RCE be suspended for a period of up to three months. I would not recommend that you request suspension unless you absolutely need the extra time. This is because your suspension period will be deducted from your patent term.

If you do request suspension of prosecution, you still must fulfill all of the requirements for your RCE. Therefore, do not expect to request a suspension of prosecution in your RCE with the hope that this will give you time to reply to a final office action. This will not happen.

In Box 3 you should check the appropriate box that indicates how you are paying your fee. If you need an extension of time to reply to a previous outstanding office action in your application, you should check the box for extension of time and pay the applicable fee.

NOTE: *You do not need to pay for a fee for any excess claims that you previously paid for prior to filing your RCE.*

COMPLETING AN RCE

Be sure to sign your RCE and also fill out the certificate of mailing.

- ***credit card payment form.*** Include this form if you are using your credit card to pay the required fee.
- ***your submission.*** This will normally include an amendment or reply to your previous final office action. However, a *submission* might also include other types of papers, even an IDS. For example, you might want the PTO to consider some reference after prosecution of your application has closed. You could use an RCE with an attached IDS to do this.
- ***information disclosure statement.*** If you are aware of any material references that you have not previously brought to the attention of your examiner, you should submit an IDS along with your RCE.

An IDS will be considered without you having to make a certification or pay a fee so long as your IDS is submitted prior to the mailing of a first office action on the merits in your RCE. You generally will receive your first office action within two months from the date that you file your RCE. The three month window period that you have to file an IDS in a Rule 53(b) application does not apply to an RCE. This means that it is even more important that you file any IDS along with your RCE now if you need to do so.

Claiming Priority to Your Earlier Filed Application(s)

One nice thing about continuing applications is that they can take on the effective filing date of their parent application. Thus if your original application was filed in June 1, 1999, and your file a continuing application in February 1, 2000, the effective filing date for your continuing application will be June 1, 1999, so long as you meet the rules for claiming priority.

Benefiting from an Earlier Application

There is no limit to the number of prior applications through which a chain of continuing applications may be traced to, but there are three main requirements that must be met in order for you to obtain benefit to an earlier filed application.

- there must be at least one common inventor between your current application and the application to which you seek benefit;
- your currently filed application must have copendency with your earlier filed application. Copendency means that your continuing application must have been filed before
  - the patenting, or
  - abandonment or other termination of your previously filed application; and,
- you must make a specific reference to your earlier filed application in the first sentence of your description in your continuing application following the title. You can also make this specific reference in your application data sheet (see Chapter 6).

Sometimes your pending application is one of a series of applications wherein your pending application is not copending with the first filed application in the series, but is copending with an intermediate application entitled to the filing date of the first application. If you desire your pending application to have benefit of the first filing date, you must make specific reference not only to the intermediate application but also to the first application. (MPEP Sec. 201.11.)

Your reference in your specification can state the following:

> "This is a _______(Insert the type of continuing application) of Application No. ______(insert the application Number of the parent application), filed ____.

You should also include the status of your previously field parent application (whether it is patented or abandoned) if you know it. For example, if your previously filed application is now a patent, you can state the following:

"This is a _____ of Application No. _____, filed _____, Patent No.____"

As another example, if your previously filed application was abandoned, you can state the following:

"This is a ____of Application No.___, filed__, now abandoned."

For utility or plant applications (including reissues) filed on or after November 29, 2000, any claim of priority must be made within four months from the actual filing date of your current application or sixteen months from the filing date of your prior application, whichever date is later. (C.F.R., Title 37, Sec. 1.78 and MPEP Sec. 201.11.)

There may be cases where you decide either not to claim priority of a prior application, or to cancel your claim to priority by amending your specification or submitting a new application data sheet to delete any references to prior applications. Remember that the term of the patent will be measured from the earliest effective filing date of your application. Thus, if you are making reference back to several continuing applications and an originally filed application, your effective filing date will be the date you filed your original application and your patent term will run from that date. However, if you refrain from making reference back to your earlier filed applications, then your patent term will start later.

While it is easy to say that you should consider not making a claim of priority to earlier filed applications in order to increase your patent term, you usually do not have this luxury. It is uncommon not to rely on an earlier filing date for prior art purposes because usually several years do not go by without prior art becoming a problem in your later filed application.

However, you may want to consider refraining from making a reference to an earlier filed application so as to extend your patent term if your invention is a pioneer in your field rather than just an improvement. This is because the pioneer invention presumably will encounter a minimum amount of relevant prior art. On the other hand, if the invention is an improvement, it may be better to claim an early priority date so as to limit its prior art exposure.

You can obtain the earlier filing date of a parent application only as to the subject matter that is common to both your continuing and parent application.

Another thing that you should note is that if your earlier filed application is fatally defective because of an insufficient disclosure (eg., lacks enablement, written description, etc.), then your current application is not entitled to the benefit of the earlier filing.

8 Filing Your Application Abroad

As stated in Chapter 1, a U.S. patent will give you the right to exclude others from making, using, selling, offering for sale, or importing within the United States, its territories, and possessions the subject matter that is covered by the patent. A patent will *not* give you the right to exclude others from these acts if they are carried out in foreign countries. Given the importance of the possible foreign market for your product, you need to consider the possibility of making foreign applications for patents abroad.

Patent Cooperation Treaty (PCT)

A well-known procedure to gain patent protection in many countries is a procedure under the *Patent Cooperation Treaty* (PCT). The PCT enables you to file one application called an *international application* in a standardized format in English with the PTO and have that application acknowledged as a regular national filing in as many member PCT countries that you designate.

Advantages and Disadvantages

There are many advantages of filing your application under the PCT to gain foreign protection. Some of the more important ones follow.

- By filing a PCT application, you will not need to hire foreign associates in each of the countries where you seek a patent right now. All you will need to worry about is meeting the requirements of filing your one PCT application.

- By filing a PCT application, you are given thirty months from your claimed priority date before you need to file national stage applications under the PCT (under U.S.C., Title 35, Sec. 371) in each of the countries that you want patent protection.
- The cost of filing your application is considerably cheaper than paying for the filing of individual patents in each country that you seek protection right at the start. You have up to thirty months to decide whether you want to file a national stage application in the foreign countries which you designate at the time you fill you PCT application. During this thirty month period, you can evaluate the potential strength of your patent application and evaluate financial, marketing, and commercial considerations.
- The PCT gives you the benefit of an international search report with respect to prior art on your invention. This can give you a good idea whether your invention will be patentable before you go to the considerable expense of patenting your invention in each of the foreign countries that you designate and even whether you should continue prosecution of your U.S. application.

Overview of the PCT Process

There are four divisions or conceptual entities that work together to process your PCT application. These divisions are conceptual because in reality, each of these four divisions can reside in as few as two actual governmental bodies—the PTO and World Intellectual Property Organization.

Receiving Office (RO)

The first division is called the *Receiving Office* (RO), which is the office where you file your PCT application. The PTO will act as a Receiving Office for your application so long as at least one of the applicants (this can include assignees) is a resident or national of the U.S. The RO grants an international filing date to your application, collects fees, handles any informalities in your application, and monitors all corrections.

The RO will transmit a copy of your application, called the *search copy* (SC), to the International Searching authority (ISA). The RO will also forward your original application, called the *record copy* (RC) to the International Bureau (IB). The RO will keep its own *home copy* (HC) of your application.

INTERNATIONAL BUREAU (IB)

The second division is called the *International Bureau* (IB). The basic job of the IB is to publish your application and act as a central coordinating body for your application. The function of the IB is actually performed by the *World Intellectual Property Organization* (WIPO) in Geneva, Switzerland.

After publication of your PCT application (between about eighteen and nineteen months from your priority date), the IB notifies each national office that you designate of your desire to proceed with a patent application in that designated country. The IB also forwards to each designated office a copy of your PCT application, a copy of the International Search Report, a copy of any amendments you have made under PCT Article 19, and a copy of any priority document.

INTERNATIONAL SEARCHING AUTHORITY (ISA)

The third division is called the *International Searching Authority* (ISA) whose job is to conduct a prior art search of your invention. You can elect the PTO as your ISA.

It is also possible to select the European Patent Office (EPO) as your ISA. Many PCT applicants have historically selected the EPO as their ISA since you can obtain a PTO search anyway later when you enter the national stage examination in the U.S.

By selecting the EPO to conduct a search for you now, you can obtain the benefit of having more than one search done for you. This can be beneficial to you in accessing the strengths of your patent application.

The ISA will search for relevant prior art pertaining to your invention and then present the results of this prior art in its *international search report* usually sixteen months from your priority date or nine months from the filing date of your PCT application. A copy of this report will be sent to you. A copy is also forwarded to the IB which will publish the report along with your PCT application eighteen months from your priority date.

Any patent documents that the ISA lists on your international search report are identified by a two-letter country code of the country issuing or publishing the document as well as a code for identifying the kind of patent document. The codes for identifying the kinds of patent documents can be found on the WIPO web site at:

www.wipo.int/scit/en

INTERNATIONAL PRELIMINARY EXAMINING AUTHORITY (IPEA)

The fourth division that can be involved with your PCT application is called the *International Preliminary Examining Authority* (IPEA). This entity will only become involved with your application if you make a demand for preliminary examination of your application. The PTO can serve as an IPEA for all applications filed in the PTO as an RO and also for those PCT applications filed in other receiving offices for which the PTO has served as an ISA. The job of an IPEA is to issue an international preliminary examination report. This report is then communicated to each of the elected offices by the IB.

PCT TIME LINE

The PCT process is very time sensitive and can best be understood in the form of a time outline. The process is divided into two stages. The first stage is the *international stage* (or Chapter I of the PCT) and the second stage is called the *national stage* (or Chapter II of the PCT). The national stage is the stage where you enter the actual individual filings in each of the countries you have designated to obtain a patent.

Let us start the discussion at time zero and work our way through Chapters I and II of the PCT process. Note that the time periods highlighted below are absolute cut-off dates. This means that for purposes of your own calendar, you should be taking the necessary action a couple of months before each of these dates.

Chapter I:

ZERO MONTHS

Time zero is when you file your regular U.S. application. This will set your "priority date" for PCT purposes if your U.S. application does not itself rely on any previously filed application for priority purposes. All of the PCT time periods that are hereinafter mentioned are keyed off of your priority date.

TWELVE MONTHS

File Your PCT Application

No later than twelve months from your previously U.S. filed application above, you must file your PCT Application. Your PCT application should contain the following parts.

- ***cover letter.*** It is a good idea to include a cover letter in which you let the PTO know what you are sending for any of your communications with the PTO. You can use the cover letter that is in Appendix E or type your own similar letter.

- ***transmittal.*** Instructions on obtaining a transmittal from the PTO website are in Appendix E on page 294.

  In Part I be sure to fill out and sign the express mailing label section.

  In Part II, check the box for a "new international application" and be sure to list your earliest previously filled application for which you are claiming priority (this is usually the date that you filed your prior U.S. application). You should also check Box C and fill in your relevant information for your priority application. If your application is identical to the one that you previously filed with the PTO, you should check the appropriate Box in item D.

Author's Note

Note that dates are written a little bit different when you are dealing with anything abroad. When writing dates in your PCT application or any associated correspondence you should first indicate the day, then the name of the month followed by the year. You should then ideally repeat in parenthesis this order using just numbers. For example, June 10, 1986 would be written as follows: 10 June 1986 (10.06.86).

In Part III, Check Box E to indicate that you are submitting a fee calculation sheet (form PCT/RO/101 annex).

- ***request (Form PCT/RO/101).*** A blank copy of this form can be found on the PTO website, and is listed in Appendix E. Instructions for the form can also be accessed at the WIPO's website (**www.wipo.int/pct/en/index.html**) under "Notes to the Request Form (PCT/RO/101)."

Make your designation of states where you want to pursue foreign filings in Box V of your request. The most important countries that I would recommend checking are EA (this will enable you to obtain a patent in Europe), AT (for Austria), and JP (for Japan). You do not need to check the box for the U.S. since your previously filed U.S. application will still be active.

Author's Note

One circumstance where you would want to designate the U.S. is if you desired to file a continuation or CIP of your previously filed U.S. application. By designating the U.S. now, you could then use your PCT application to file your continuation or CIP later. By designating the U.S. you are saying that you do want to enter the national stage in this country later and file a new application there.

Another circumstance where you might want to designate the U.S. is where you file your PCT application before you file your U.S. In such a case, you may want to designate the U.S. so that you can file in the U.S. later when you enter the national stage in the U.S. under the PCT.

You will note at the bottom of Box V that there is a *precautionary designation statement*. This statement allows you to add any additional countries that you do not specifically designate now, so long as you confirm in writing the addition of these states within fifteen months from your priority date. This serves as a type of safety net if you want to add any countries a little later on.

In Box VI, make sure that you list each of your previously filed applications for your invention in order to obtain their priority date. In the example above you will see that the PCT application is not only claiming priority to the earlier September 1, 2000 U.S. application, but even to a later regional application filed in the EP on March 9, 2001.

Author's Note

You will need to make a declaration of the claim of priority at the time of filing your international application and either file a certified copy of the priority document with the international application, or submit a certified copy of the priority document to the International Bureau within a specified time (Rule 17 of the PCT Regulations). If you have previously filed a U.S. application with the PTO as your receiving office, then you should check the appropriate boxes under Box No. VI indicating that you request the PTO to prepare and transmit to the IB a certified copy of your earlier application(s).

Box VII is where you list your choice for your ISA. The choice listed above is the U.S.

Author's Note

If you are designating the EP in your patent application, I recommend that you chose the European Patent Office (EPO) as your ISA instead of the U.S. The reasons for this are outlined in MPEP Sec. 1840 and include such reasons as:

- the EPO search fee need not be paid upon entering the EP as a designated office and,
- the European Patent Office search will provide you with the benefit of a European art search that may be different from the search already conducted by the PTO with respect to your previously filed U.S. application. (Given that one of the advantages for the PCT listed at the start of this chapter is to give you the benefit of an international search which can highlight any problems with your invention before you go to the great expense of foreign filing, this is advantageous.)

However, be forewarned that the EPO has recently curtailed the types of applications which it will agree to serve as an ISA as stated at the start of this chapter. For example, the EPO will not serve as an ISA for nationals or residents of the U.S. for applications containing claim(s) relating to biotechnology or business methods. So your only option may be to choose the PTO as your ISA.

There is also a space to indicate whether you want the results of any previously international search to be used. In this case, the applicant is requesting that the search conducted in its previously filed U.S. application be used. The PTO performs an international-type search on all U.S. national applications filed on and after 01 June 1978. This can save you money since international searching authorities like the U.S. provide for a reduced search fee where there is a corresponding prior national non-provisional application.

You finally must sign the request in Box IX.

PCT Fee Calculation Sheet (Form PCT/RO/101 Annex). A blank copy of this form is contained in Appendix E. Appendix E also contains notes on how to fill out each of the items of the fee calculation sheet.

You should check the PTO website for any changes in fees since they change regularly. (See Sec. 1730 of the MPEP for the various PCT fees.)

In item 2, be sure to indicate whether you want the U.S. or the EPO as your international searching authority. The fee is higher if you choose the EPO, but there are advantages to choosing the EPO if the EP is a designated state as mentioned previously.

Make a copy of your U.S. specification and drawings that you previously submitted to the PTO. The only difference here is that you should make sure that you use A4 paper rather than 8½ x 11. Color drawings are also not accepted.

Any required sequence listing. (See Chapter 4 for information about sequence listings.)

Author's Note

You should send your PCT application using Express Mail. To be absolutely safe, also try to send your application and any other PCT papers that you file soon enough so that you insure it arrives before your absolute cut-off date. While U.S. law gives you the date that you deposit your Express Mail papers with the post office, PCT Rule 20.1(a) provides for marking the date of actual receipt on the request. (MPEP Sec. 1805.) To obviate any possible disagreement about which law is right, see if you can get your papers in so that they arrive no later than your absolute cut-off-date.

FIFTEEN MONTHS

Confirm any Precautionary Designations

Remember that statement included on your demand that says you are making a precautionary designation in your demand as to all other states that you did not specifically designate in your demand? Well, that clause will come in handy now if there are any states that you want to add to your list of designated states. However, you will need to let the PTO know now that you want to confirm any such additional designations.

The form that you can use is called a "Notice of Confirmation of Precautionary Designations" and is listed in Appendix E. Of course, you will have to pay the appropriate additional fee for each state that you list if you do this.

Chapter II

NINETEEN MONTHS

Preliminary Examination Demand

No later than nineteen months from your priority date, you have the right to make what is called a *demand for preliminary examination* of your application. This was recently required if you wanted to delay the time for when you had to start filing national stage applications to thirty months. However, the law has recently changed and now everyone is given thirty months from the time they file a PCT application to the time a national stage application needs to be filed, regardless of whether a demand for preliminary examination has been made.

However, a *demand* for preliminary examination is still something that you will want to consider making. If you make a demand for preliminary examination, an international preliminary examination report will be issued concerning your application.

Author's Note

The term *demand* is a term that denotes that you want to start the process of Chapter II of the PCT process and should be distinguished between the term *elect* which is used to denote those states where you want to delay entry into the national stage phase. In most cases, the states that you elect to enter the national stage will match the states that you designated in your PCT Request form in Chapter I of the PCT process.

Your demand should be filed on PCT Form PCT/IPEA/401 along with a fee transmittal sheet, Form PCT/IPEA/401 (Annex). Following are instructions on how to complete these two forms. Blank copies of these forms are listed in Appendix E.

In Box I, you should put all relevant information about your PCT application.

Box V of your demand is where you "elect" states for the purposes of your preliminary examination and thereby delay entry into the national stage for those elected states. You can only elect those states that you previously "designated" in your request under Chapter I of the PCT process. (Usually you will elect all the states that you have previously designated, but there is a space to write in those designated states that you do not want to elect.)

Mail your demand and appropriate fees to the specific IPEA that you desire to prepare your International Preliminary Examination Report. The PTO will act as an IPEA for U.S. residents and nationals even if the EPO served as your ISA. To use the PTO as your IPEA, send your demand to:

Commissioner for Patents
Box PCT
Washington, DC 20231

If your international search report was prepared by the EPO you can also request the EPO as your IPEA. If you elect this choice, you should mail your demand to:

European Patent Office
Erhardstrasse 27
D-80331 Munich
Federal Republic of Germany

TWENTY-EIGHT MONTHS

Preliminary Examination Report of IPEA

By twenty-eight months from your priority date, the IPEA examiner of will issue the preliminary examination report, which presents the examiner's final position as to whether each claim of your invention is "novel," involves an "inventive step," and is "industrially applicable." This report is nonbonding on your elected states, although they are also free to adopt the positions in the report when you are in the national stage. A copy of this report will be sent to you as well as to the IB. The IB then sends a copy of the report to each of your elected offices.

At this stage in the game, you are ready for entry into the national stage of the PCT.

THIRTY MONTHS

National Stage

Before the expiration of thirty months from your priority date, you will need to hire foreign associates in each of the countries that you want to pursue foreign patent rights. These countries must be ones selected from the list of countries that you previously designated in your Demand.

Author's Note

Ideally, the best way to find a foreign associate is to get the name of one that someone else has used in the past and recommends to you to use in the future. If a recommendation is not available, go to the EPO website at **www.epo.co.at** and click onto "search engines" and then click "european patent attorneys database." Another useful website to find patent agents in the United Kingdom (UK) can be found at **www.cipa.org.uk.**

You can also contact the patent department in a U.S. law firm. Firms that have intellectual property departments will also have foreign associates that they use for foreign filings. They will more than likely be delighted to give names of such a contacts since they usually expect that any business they refer will be returned in their favor by the foreign firm.

Entering the National Stage in the U.S. under United States Code, Title 35, Section 371. There are two routes for entering the national stage in the U.S. One route is if you have not made a demand for preliminary examination and the other route is if you have made a demand for preliminary examination. Under the first route, an international application designating the U.S. will enter the national stage via the U.S. Designated Office. Under the second route where a demand electing the U.S. is filed prior to the expiration of nineteen months from the priority date, entry will be via the U.S. Elected Office.

The procedure for entry via the U.S. Designated Office is as prescribed in C.F.R., Title 37, Sec. 1.494(b). The procedure for entry via the U.S. Elected Office is as prescribed in C.F.R., Title 37, Sec. 1.495(b).

In either case, you will need to submit the following parts to the PTO in order to enter the national stage:

- transmittal letter;
- declaration;
- fees; and,
- IDS.

Transmittal Letter and necessary items specified in the transmittal (Form PTO-1382). This form is listed in Appendix E. You need to complete this special transmittal form because you need to specifically identify that you are filing a national stage application under U.S.C., Title 35, Sec. 371. If you do not do this, your application will be treated by the PTO as a regular non-provisional application. (U.S.C., Title 35, Sec. 111(a).)

Check Box 3 indicating that you request the commencement of national examination procedures.

Make sure that a copy of your international application (PCT) has been provided to the PTO. A copy should be provided to each designated office by the IB about eighteen months from your priority date. The IB then mails you confirmation (Form IB/308). You can rely on this confirmation instead of providing a copy of your international application to the PTO.

If for some reason you filed your PCT application in a language other than English, you must provide a translation (item 6).

Declaration. You should also include a declaration (item 9). If you do not submit this now, the PTO will send you a *Notice of Missing Requirements* giving you one month to submit it.

Fees. You must also include a basic national fee (item 21). This national fee is not extendable and your application will go abandoned in the U.S. if you do not pay this fee before the time has expired for you to commence the national stage (twenty or thirty months from your priority date). (C.F.R., Title 37, Sec. 1.492.)

However, be sure to check the PTO website for the most current fees. National stage fees are always subject to change. Remember you absolutely *must* include at least the amount of the basic national fee due or your application will go abandoned.

Information Disclosure Statement (IDS). You should complete and file an IDS now just as you would if you were filing your regular U.S. nonprovisional application. (see Chapter 6).

If your application is accepted for entry into the national stage, you will be mailed Form PCT/DO/EO/903 indicating acceptance of your application as a national stage filing. (U.S.C., Title 35, Sec. 371.)

Amending Your PCT Application

It is possible to amend your PCT Application even before you enter the national stage for each of your designated countries.

PCT Article 19 amendments are exclusively amendments to your claims. You have two months from the mailing date of the International Search Report by the ISA or sixteen months from your priority date—whichever occurs later—to make an amendment to the claims of your application. Your amendments must be filed with the International Bureau, whose duties are performed by the World Intellectual Property Organization (WIPO) in Geneva, Switzerland. Since the national laws of some designated offices may grant provisional protection on your invention from the date of publication of your claims, you may want to take advantage of this opportunity under Article 19 to polish your claims before such publication.

You also have the right to make amendments to your claims, description, and/or drawings during the Chapter II examination phase. (PCT Article 34(2)(b).) Such amendments sometimes are done in response to a written opinion issued during your preliminary examination proceedings under Chapter II of the PCT. Written opinions are issued by your examiner before he or she issues the final preliminary examination report for your application.

Such an opinion might tell you that your application does not comply with formal matters or point out substantive matter such as your claims are not directed to inventions that have novelty, inventive step and industrial applicability. Any amendments you make must be made by submitting a replacement sheet for every sheet of your application that differs from the sheet it replaces unless the entire sheet is cancelled. You must also include a description of how the replacement sheet differs from the replaced sheet. (MPEP Sec. 1878.02.)

NOTE: *You can always make amendments to your application at the time you enter the national stage of your designated country according to the amendment practice for that designated state.*

ADDITIONAL INFORMATION

The MPEP devotes its entire Chapter 18 to the PCT. You can also find the text of the PCT Applicant's Guide, a monthly PCT Newsletter, a weekly PCT Gazette, downloadable PCT forms, and other information about the processing of international application at the WIPO's website:

www.wipo.int/pct

The PCT Help Desk provides information and assistance on the PCT process and can be reached at 703-305-3257 between the hours of 9:00 AM and 4:30 PM (EST), Monday through Friday.

OTHER FOREIGN FILING ROUTES

The procedure in the previous section where you file a PCT application within one year of filing your regular U.S. patent application is a recommended way to file your patent application abroad. However, there are alternate routes to foreign filing.

FILE IN EACH FOREIGN COUNTRY OR REGION INDIVIDUALLY

One alternative route to the one presented earlier is to file in each of the foreign countries that you desire patent protection. This is, in effect, what you are doing in the PCT process. However, as noted above, the PCT process gives you added time to make individual foreign filings in each of the countries that you designate. Also, your individual national filings in each of your designated states are usually less burdensome and therefore less costly when you enter such states by way of the PCT. This is because many of these states will rely on things that have already occurred in your PCT application—like your international search.

If you know that you will be selling your invention in only one or two specific countries abroad, then foreign filing individually in each of those countries may be a good idea as opposed to a PCT application. Another case where individual foreign filing might be done is for non-U.S. residents who want to file in their own home state first. Such non-residents file their patent application in their own country and then file here in the U.S.

Foreign filing license. If your invention was made in the United States, a *Foreign Filing License* is necessary to apply abroad. If a foreign filing license is required, but not obtained for your invention, you can be barred from obtaining a U.S. patent on that same invention. Since the U.S. is by far the largest market place for your invention, this is something that you never want to happen.

When you apply for a U.S. patent, you will usually be granted a foreign filing license by the PTO when you receive your filing receipt several months later. If you look on your filing receipt, you will see the phrase "Foreign Filing License Granted" and the date printed on it. Even if the PTO did not grant you a foreign filing license on your receipt, you would automatically be entitled to the license six months from your filing date. However, if you foreign file before you apply for a U.S. patent application, you will have no filing receipt from the PTO granting you a foreign filing license. In such a case, you will need to petition the PTO for a foreign filing license before you file your foreign patent application. Consult MPEP Section 140 for how to go about submitting a petition to the PTO for a foreign filing license.

Before you file your PCT, you will have obtained a filing receipt for your U.S. granting you a foreign filing license or else six months will have elapsed. There is even a safety net with PCT applications since if for some reason you have not obtained a foreign filing license before you file your PCT application and you are found to need it, it is current practice to construe your PCT filing as petition for the license which should normally be granted. (MPEP Sec. 1832.)

If for some reason you do not obtain a foreign filing license before you foreign file, there is a procedure to petition for a retroactive foreign filing license (so long as your error occurred without deceptive intent). However, you do not want to be placed in such a circumstance.

Claiming priority to the earlier foreign application. If you file a foreign patent application first and later file your regular U.S. non-provisional application, you have one year (twelve months from the date of your foreign filing) to claim priority to your previously filed foreign application. (U.S.C., Title 35, Sec. 119 and MPEP Sec. 201.13.) You cannot obtain the earlier effective filing date of applications filed in every foreign country, but for most foreign countries you can. (You can find a list of recognized foreign countries in MPEP Sec. 201.13.)

NOTE: *If you file a design patent application abroad, you only have six months to make your claim of priority.*

In computing your twelve (or six month time period in the case of design patent applications) to claim priority, the first day is not counted.

Example: You file an application in Canada on January 3, 1983. You may file your U.S. nonprovisional application on January 3, 1984, and still claim priority to the earlier filing date of your Canadian application.

This twelve month period (or six month period in the case of designs) is from the date of the earliest foreign filing and not from any subsequent foreign filings (unless the first filing has been withdrawn or abandoned for some reason.)

Example: You file an application in France on January 4, 1982, and an identical application in the United Kingdom on March 3, 1982. You then file in the U.S. on February 2, 1983. You are not entitled to a right of priority at all. You are not entitled to the date of the French application because this application was filed more than twelve months before your U.S. application. You are not entitled to the benefit of the date of the United Kingdom application since this application is not the first one filed.

If the last day of the twelve months is a Saturday, Sunday, or Federal holiday within the District of Columbia, then you may still make your claim of priority even if you file your U.S. nonprovisional application on the next succeeding business day.

Example: You file a foreign application on September 4, 1981. Your U.S. nonprovisional application is still timely if filed on September 7, 1982, since September 4, 1982 was a Saturday and September 5, 1982, was a Sunday and September 6, 1982, was a Federal holiday.

If you use Express Mail to submit your non-provisional application, your date filed will be considered the date that you deposit your application with the post office. So, if you deposited your express mail on Saturday, September 4, 1982, you would not even have to rely upon this special rule about Saturdays, Sundays, and holidays.

In order to make a claim of priority to your previously filed foreign application, there must be an identity of inventors between your U.S. application and your previously filed foreign application. (See MPEP Sec. 201.13 for the exact requirements that must be fulfilled in order to make a proper claim of priority.) This is a little different from a domestic claim of priority (a claim of priority from one U.S. application to a previously filed U.S. application where only one inventor needs to be the same).

Just as with earlier filed domestic application, the disclosure of a foreign application may be insufficient (e.g., lacks enablement, written description, etc.) to support a priority claim for a later filed application in this country. Thus your foreign application must be written just like your U.S. application (e.g., must be enabling, pass the written description requirement, etc.).

You make your foreign priority claim just as you would with a domestic priority claim as explained in the last chapter by including a specific reference to the foreign application. You can make this reference in your Specification, your application transmittal letter, your application data sheet or even in your declaration. You must identify the foreign application by specifying its application number, the foreign country and the day, month, and year of its filing. The various application numbers should be presented in proper form. (Consult MPEP Sec. 201.14(d) for how to properly cite the application numbers of various foreign countries.)

You must also file a certified copy of your foreign application with the PTO. (U.S.C., Title 35, Sec. 119(b).) This means that you must submit a copy of your foreign application (the Specification and drawings) as filed in that country. The copy must include a certification by the patent office of the foreign country in which it was filed.

The foreign application does not need to be translated at the time you file your later domestic application. Your examiner will only request translations if the filing date of your foreign application comes into issue as where it must be relied upon to overcome a rejection. (MPEP Sec. 201.15.) If you are later required to provide a translation, the translation must be filed with a statement that the translation of the certified copy is accurate.

If the benefit of a foreign filing date based on a foreign application is claimed in a later filed application (i.e., continuation, continuation-in-part, division), and a certified copy of the foreign application as filed has already been filed in a parent application, it is not necessary to file an additional certified copy in the later application. (MPEP Sec. 201.14(b).)

File Your Foreign PCT Application

It is perfectly acceptable practice to file your PCT application *before* you file your domestic U.S. application. If you decide to file your PCT application before your domestic U.S. application, there are two ways that you can later file your U.S. application. The easiest way is to simply designate the U.S. as one of your designated states in your PCT Request. Then either twenty or thirty months from your priority date (depending on whether you have submitted a demand) you will need to enter the national stage in the U.S. (U.S.C., Title 35, Sec. 371.)

The second way that you can later file your U.S. application is to file a regular U.S. domestic application under U.S.C., Title 35, Sec. 111(a) during the pendency (prior to abandonment) of your PCT application.

The main differences between filing a national stage application under U.S.C., Title 35, Sec. 371 under the first method and a national application under U.S.C., Title 35, Sec. 111(a) under the second method are as follows:

- If you choose the first option of entering the national stage, your filing date is the filing date of your PCT application. If you choose instead to file a regular U.S. national application, your filing date is the date that you file that U.S. application (with the necessary specification, claim, and any necessary drawing).

- The filing fees are different. For a national stage application you should consult C.F.R., Title 37, Sec. 1.492 for your filing fee whereas for a national application under U.S.C., Title 35, Sec. 111(a) you should consult C.F.R., Title 37, Sec. 1.16 for your filing fee.
- You will not ordinarily need to submit a certified copy of any application for which you are claiming priority if you choose to enter the national stage under U.S.C., Title 35, Sec. 371 so long as you have previously submitted such certified copy in your PCT application. However, you will need to submit a certified copy of your priority document (including the PCT application) if you file a regular U.S. application under U.S.C., Title 35, Sec. 111(a).
- The rules for claiming priority are slightly different. When you enter the U.S. via the national stage route (option 1), you do not need to claim priority to the PCT application that you filed leading up to your national stage application. However, you will need to make a claim of priority either in your application data sheet or first sentence of your specification to any other applications that your PCT application itself relies on for priority (This must be done within the later of four months from the date on which the national stage commenced or sixteen months from the filing date of the prior application).

  The reason that you need not make a claim of priority to your PCT application is because your national stage U.S. application takes on the same filing date as your PCT application. However, if you file a regular United States U.S.C., Title 35, Sec. 111(a) application (option 2), you will need to make a specific claim of priority to your filing date of your PCT application that you previously filed. In order to make a proper claim of priority, you need to comply with the general rules for claiming foreign priority as well as the specific rules below.

Author's Note

If your application filed on or after November 29, 2000, claims benefit to an international application, the first sentence of your specification must also be amended to indicate whether the international application was published under PCT Article 21(2) in English, regardless of whether benefit for such application is claimed in the application data sheet. (C.F.R., Title 37, Sec. 1.78(a)(2) and MPEP Secs.. 201.11 and 202.01.) Make sure that you claim priority to your earlier filed PCT application in your specification.

Example: Joe files a PCT application on January 4, 1990. Before abandonment of the PCT application, Joe files a 35 U.S.C. 111(a) U.S. non-provisional application. Joe should write the following as the first sentence of his specification: "This application claims priority to International Application PCT/EP90/00000, with an international filing date of January 4, 1990, published in English under PCT Article 21(2)."

The filing date of your international stage application (your PCT application) will also be the filing date for your national stage U.S. application. Your application will be examined in the same manner as for a regular domestic U.S. application. You will learn more about examination of U.S. applications in the following chapters.

FILE A PROVISIONAL APPLICATION, *THEN* FILE A PCT APPLICATION

If a provisional application was your first application, do not be concerned. You can file your PCT Application within twelve months from the filing date of your provisional. You can then enter the national stage in the U.S. through your PCT application or you can alternatively file a U.S.C., Title 35, Sec. 111(a) U.S. non-provisional application that claims priority to your PCT application.

I recommend that you enter the U.S. by designating the U.S. In either case, you should claim priority to your previously filed U.S. provisional application at the time that you enter the national stage or file your U.S.C., Title 35, Sec. 111(a) application in the U.S., either in an application data sheet (C.F.R., Title 37, Sec. 1.76) or in the first sentence of your specification.

Under this same scenario, you could also conceivably file your provisional application, then a regular U.S. non-provisional application within twelve months, and then file your PCT application within twelve months. The effect of this would be to give you even more time before you need to enter the national stage in any of the foreign states that you designate in your PCT application.

Section 3:

After You File Your Application

9 After You File Your Patent Application

After you have submitted your patent application, it is received by the Mail Room and stamped with a provisional serial number and the current date. This will become the official filing date of the application. The application is then forwarded to the *Office of Initial Patent Examination* (OIPE) of the PTO to confirm that it contains all the necessary parts.

Your application is then sent to the Licensing and Review Branch that determines whether it is a candidate for a secrecy order or whether it is drafted to certain subject matter, such as nuclear materials. Your application is then assigned to a *group art unit*. A filing receipt identifying the inventors, the title of the invention, the serial number and the filing date is issued to you by the Applications branch.

NOTE: *Issuing the filing receipt ordinarily occurs three or four months from the date of filing of the application. Your application is then assigned to an examiner who has expertise in the area of technology related to your invention. Your application is examined for compliance with all legal requirements and makes a search through both U.S. and foreign patent documents, as well as literature to make sure that your invention is novel, non-obvious, and meets all the necessary disclosure requirements. The examiner will then notify you in writing of his or her decision in a document that is referred to as an office action.*

Relatively few applications are allowed by the examiner as filed. In most cases, one or even all of the claims will be rejected on some legal ground. If you have received an action from the examiner that rejects some or all of your claims, you must either change or cancel some of your rejected claims or persuade the examiner why he or she is wrong.

Author's Note

A *rejection* is a term that the PTO uses when your claims are not allowed because your subject matter as claimed is considered unpatentable by the PTO. An *objection* is a term that the PTO uses when the form of your claims is considered improper. Rejections are about substance, while objections are about forms.

The practical difference between a rejection and an objections is that a rejection, involving the merits of the claim, is subject to review by the Board of Patent Appeals and Interferences. On the other hand, an objection may be reviewed only by way of petition to the Commissioner if you disagree with the reasoning of your examiner. (MPEP Sec. 706.01.)

Length of Time to Approve Application

The time it takes from the date you file your application up to the date that you are granted a patent will really depend on a host of factors, such as the complexity of your invention, the scope of your claims, and how diligent you are in prosecuting your application. Some generalities can be made, however, based on past data.

In 1995, the average patent pending period was around nineteen months. In 1996, it climbed to twenty months and then to twenty-two months in 1997 and twenty-four months in 1998. In 1999 the average time shot up to twenty-five months! The average time has hovered around twenty-four months in 2000. In general, you can expect it to take at least two years before you have a patent in hand.

Petitions to Make Special

Speeding Up Approval

There are a host of reasons why you may want to try to speed up examination (and therefore issuance) of your patent application. Some of the major reasons are as follows:

- If you plan to license your patented invention, your ability to attract potential licensees may be stronger with either a patent in hand or notice from the PTO that your patent application has been allowed. The same rationale applies equally with attracting potential investors in any company you may be forming. Patents simply look good to investors.
- Because your patent term will be measured twenty years from your application filing date and not the date that your patent actually issues, it is to your advantage to try and keep examination of your patent application as short as possible and have your patent issue as soon as possible. The time you spend in the examination phase is using up the term of any patent which you may obtain.
- Patents can not be enforced again potential infringers until they issue. Therefore, it is to your advantage to get that patent as soon as possible so that you can quickly go after potential infringers.

It is possible to speed up the examination of your application by filing what is known as a *petition to make special*. This can sometimes save you several months in the examination process. There are a host of reasons on which you can file this petition. Some of these reasons are deemed so important by the PTO that you do not even need to file a fee with your petition. Other grounds, while important, still require you to file a fee.

Petition to Make Special—No Fee

The following grounds can be used in a petition to make special and do not require a special fee:

- you are over the age of 65;
- your health is such that you might not be able to assist in the prosecution of the application if it were to be examined in its normal course;

- your invention would materially enhance the quality of the environment;
- your invention would contribute to the development of energy resources or to the more efficient utilization of energy resources. Examples include developments in fossil fuels, nuclear energy, solar energy and inventions relating to the reduction of energy consumption in combustion systems, industrial equipment and household appliances; or,
- your invention relates to superconductivity.

Petition to Make Special—Fee

The following grounds can serve as the basis for a petition to make special, but require you to pay a fee. (C.F.R., Title 37, Sec. 1.17(h).)

- a prospective manufacturer will not manufacture or increase present manufacture of your invention unless certain a patent for the invention is granted (see MPEP Sec. 708.02 for what you must specifically allege in your petition);
- there exists an infringing device or product actually on the market or a method in use (see MPEP Sec. 708.02 for what you must specifically allege);
- your invention relates to HIV/AIDS and cancer;
- your invention can be used to counter terrorism;
- your invention relates to safety of research in the field of recombinant DNA;
- your application is a new application in which a preexamination search has been made. Your petition to make special must be filed prior to the examiner's first action. The petition must be accompanied by a search report based on a search conducted by an attorney, a professional searcher, the inventor, or a foreign patent office. One copy of each reference considered most closely related to the subject matter of the claims should also be submitted. In addition, there must be a detailed discussion of the references, pointing out how the claimed subject matter is distinguished from them. Finally, the the field of the search must be listed in the petition; and,

- biotechnology applications for small entities. You must state that the subject of your patent application is a major asset of your small entity and that development of the technology will be significantly impaired if examination of your patent application is delayed, including an explanation of the basis for making the statement.

First Office Action

After you file your patent application, your application will be examined and you will receive back your first office action. Past data shows that the PTO needed an average of 13.5 months in 1999 to take its first office action on 81 percent of applications (see the New York Times, December 31, 2001, page C4 for this data).

The first office action that you receive will either allow your claims or, more typically, reject some or all of your claims.

Your Response or Reply

After an office action, you as the applicant or patent owner must request reconsideration by your examiner with or without an amendment if your action is adverse in any respect. In most cases you will present your reply in the form of an amendment. (The specifics of drafting an amendment appear later in this chapter.)

Whether you submit arguments or an amendment as your reply, you must distinctly and specifically point out the supposed errors in your examiner's action. You must respond to every ground of objection and rejection in the action.

You must also point out the specific distinctions you believe renders your claims patentable over any references that your examiner is applying against you. For example, if the issue surrounding your rejected claims is novelty, then you must point out the patentable novelty of your amended claims in the "Remarks" section of your amendment. A general allegation that your claims are patentable without *specifically* pointing out why is not a sufficient reply. (MPEP Sec. 714.02.)

You should also point out the justification behind any amendments that you have made to your specification. In other words, you should point out that any changes you have made are supported by your original disclosure as filed (i.e., do not constitute new matter).

Length of Time to Respond

By statute, you are given up to six months to respond to any action that the PTO sends you. This is an absolute cut-off period and cannot be altered by the PTO. This means that even if you can buy another extension of time, you will not be able to use such extension to avoid abandonment of your application if it means that your response is after six months from the mailing date of your office action.

The PTO typically sets a three-month period to respond to your office action, unless the action relates to a preliminary matter. If this is the case, the PTO typically gives you only one month to respond. This three-month time period to respond is often called a *shortened statutory period*. It is called shortened because as stated above, a statute sets a longer six-month absolute cut-off period to respond to actions from the PTO. However, this same statute gives the PTO the right to set shorter time periods that the PTO has done. Your action will tell you the shortened statutory period that the PTO has set for response to your action. Just keep in mind, however, that even though you may be able to buy more months, you can never respond later than six months.

The actual time it takes you to reply to your office action is calculated from the date stamped or printed on your office action to the PTO's date of receipt (or, if you use Express Mail, the date of deposit with the post office).

When the PTO says that you have three months to respond to an action, this time period is calculated by months. The PTO does not take into account fractions of a day, unless it has given you one month to respond. Then you are given at least thirty days to send in your response.

When the last day that you have to respond to an action falls on a Saturday, Sunday, or Federal holiday, the time period that you can file your response is can file your response is extended to the next business day that the PTO is open for business. This rule does not, however, apply when you are using an extension of time.

This is a lot to remember, but if you file your responses at least several days before the due date, you will not have to worry about whether you are filing your response on the absolute cut-off date.

FAILING TO RESPOND ON TIME

If you fail to reply to an office action or fail to file a complete and proper reply within the fixed statutory period, then your application becomes abandoned. An *abandoned application* dies and it can no longer issue into a patent unless you are able to win a petition to revive your application. (See Chapter 13 on how to file a *petition to revive.*)

If you cannot revive your application, your only alternative is to pay a new filing fee and file a new patent application for your invention. This can be a fatal course of action because your priority date will now be the date that you file your subsequent patent application. Any prior art that exists before this date could prevent you from obtaining a patent on your invention.

Your examiner is authorized to accept a timely reply by you to a non-final office action that is made in good faith and is substantially complete except for an inadvertent omission. (C.F.R., Title 37, Sec. 1.135(c).) Such inadvertent omissions include unsigned amendments or amendments that present additional claims but do not include the fees necessary for such claims. In such circumstances, your examiner may consider your reply adequate to avoid abandonment and give you a shortened statutory time period of one month to correct your omission.

Supplemental Replies

Sometimes you make a reply only to realize later that you forgot to add something to your reply or you wish to update your reply with new information. It is possible to submit such information in a *supplemental reply*. However, your examiner has the right to refuse it if it "unduly interferes" with the preparation of the office action that your examiner may be working on in respect to your original reply.

An extension of time under C.F.R., Title 37, Sec. 1.136 is not necessary when submitting a supplemental reply to an office action if you have already completed a timely first reply. (MPEP Sec. 710.02(e).)

Consider an Interview with Your Examiner

An interview is the personal, telephone, or video conference appearence by you, your agent, or attorney with your examiner. Interviews are not allowed until you have received a first office action by the PTO—except in the case of continuing or substitute applications.

An interview after final rejection (see the next section) may be granted by your examiner, although you have no automatic right to one at that stage in your application. Thus the usual time that you will be asking for an interview is after you receive your first office action. You can request in your Action reply that your examiner defer taking any further action on the case until you have had a chance to confer with your examiner in Washington.

You should arrange for an interview in advance either by letter, fax, or telephone. You must usually arrange to go directly to the PTO in Washington D.C. to conduct a face-to-face interview with your examiner. However, there are certain cites outside of Washington D.C. where a video conference can be held.

Interviews are a very useful way for you to present arguments to your examiner. However, you need to prepare for your interview. It is advisable for you to indicate in advance to your examiner what you desire to discuss at the interview by submitting, in writing, a proposed reply to your office action in the form of an amendment (discussed in the next chapter). The PTO does not allow interviews merely for "feeling out" an examiner as to the patentability of your application.

The substance of any interview must be recorded in your application. (MPEP Sec. 713.04.) At the conclusion of your interview, your examiner will give you a copy of the *Examiner Interview Summary Form* (Form PTOL-413). In the case of telephone or video interviews, this copy will be mailed to you. Unless the examiner has checked the box at the bottom of this form indicating that you do not need to submit a record of the substance of what occurred at your interview, you are required to submit such a written record. A complete and proper recording of the substance of any interview must include at least the following items:

- a brief description of the nature of any exhibit shown or any demonstration conduction;
- identification of specific prior art discussed;
- identification of the principal proposed amendments of a substantive nature discussed;
- the general thrust of arguments made by you and your examiner;
- a general indication of any other pertinent matters discussed; and,
- the general results or outcome of the interview.

FINAL REJECTION

After your examiner gives you a proper *final rejection*, you no longer have any automatic right to further prosecution of your application. The things that you can do after final rejection are quite limited.

In general, you are restricted to making only those amendments to your claims that will bring your application into condition for allowance or in better form for an appeal of your examiner's decision if you have filed a *Notice of Appeal*.

Changes that you can make after final rejection usually includes things like canceling some of your rejected claims or adopting suggestions by your examiner.

If you are submitting a reply to your final rejection in the form of an amendment, you do so under C.F.R., Title 37, Sec. 1.116. If you want to make only arguments and no amendment, then your reply is filed under C.F.R., Title 37, Sec. 1.113. (You can still use the amendment form provided in the next chapter to do this, just change the heading to "REPLY UNDER C.F.R., Title 37, Sec. 1.113" and make your arguments in the "Remarks" section.)

You may have to obtain more than one extension of time in order to keep your application from being abandoned after a Final Rejection.

Example: You are mailed a Final Rejection on October 20, 1998. setting a three month statutory shortened period to respond. Your response filed on February 20, 1998, together with an automatic one month extension of time is timely. If your response does not result in allowance of your application by the PTO, you could file a second response on March 20, 1998, together with a two month extension of time. While you must pay for the full two month extension, you will receive a credit for the one month extension that you have already paid. You can keep obtaining extensions of time up until the statutory six month cut-off date of April 20, 1998, in this case.

Your reply after final action does not place your application in condition for allowance, so the period set for your reply will simply continue to run until you file a reply that does. Of course, if you do not do this by the six month deadline, your application will go abandoned.

Request for Continued Examination (RCE)

If you have run up against a dead-end with respect to your examiner in getting your application allowed, and the six month statutory deadline is approaching, you will need to consider some other options in order to keep your application alive. One possible option is for you to file a continuing application such as a *Request for Continued Examination* (RCE) under C.F.R., Title 37, Sec. 1.114. (As explained in Chapter 7, you will need to accompany your RCE by a *submission*. This will usually mean that you will need to submit a proper reply to your outstanding office action as well as the requisite fee.)

Notice of Appeal

Another option that you have after a final rejection is to appeal your examiner's decision. To do this, you will need to file a *Notice of Appeal* and the requisite appeal fee. Appeals will require that you obtain the assistance of an experienced patent attorney or agent in this field as explained later. However, you can and should file a Notice of Appeal to preserve your right to appeal if you want to pursue this option. By filing a Notice of Appeal, you will stop the statutory period for abandonment of your application. Instead, new time periods begin with respect to what you must do concerning your Notice of Appeal.

NOTE: *If you have submitted an amendment at or near the end of the statutory period, you should always accompany your amendment with a Notice of Appeal. If you do not do this, your application may go abandoned even before your examiner has considered your amendment after final action.*

When an Office Action is Improper

Under the current practice at the PTO, any subsequent action that you receive from your examiner on the merits will be made final. There is one exception to this rule, however. If your examiner introduces a new ground for his or her rejection that was neither necessitated by your amendment of your claims, nor based on information that you filed in an information disclosure statement during the allotted time period, then a final rejection is improper. (C.F.R., Title 37, Sec. 1.97(c).)

Example 1: An important claim in Joe's patent application is rejected in a first office action on the basis of obviousness over prior art. In his response, Joe argues that his claims are not obvious in respect to the references cited.

In a second rejection, the examiner continues the rejection and adds a further rejection based on 102(a) citing a prior publication that teaches each of Joe's limitations in his claim. This final rejection is improper because the newly added rejection made by the examiner was not necessitated by anything that Joe had done in his response.

Example 2: Joe's claim is rejected in a first official action for the same reasons as above. In his response, Joe amends his claims to add a new limitation, and argues that this new limitation makes his invention nonobvious.

The examiner issues a final rejection that is based now on a 102(e) publication that was found in a new search. Since Joe's amendment of adding a new limitation forced the examiner to conduct a new search that revealed the publication, this second action is a proper final rejection.

Some special rules as to when a final rejection can be made apply to continuing application. If you file a continuation, the first action that you receive in that application can be made final where all the claims of the new application are drawn to the same invention claimed in the earlier application and would have been properly finally rejected the office action in that earlier application. Making a first office action final in a continuing or substitute application, however, is never proper where such application contains material that was presented in the earlier application after final rejection, but was denied entry either because new issues or matter were raised that required further consideration.

If you believe that your examiner has incorrectly made a final rejection in your application, you should raise the issue with your examiner. If your examiner still disagrees and you think you are right, your only option is to file a petition for review of your examiners decision. (C.F.R., Title 37, Sec. 1.181.)

Length of Time to Respond to Final Rejection

You will be given a three-month *shortened statutory period* for responding to the final rejection. However, it is to your advantage to submit a first reply prior to the expiration of two months from the mailing date of your final office action. If you do this, your shortened statutory period will expire at the later end of three months or on the date that the PTO mails you an *advisory action*. Thus a variable reply period is established if you get your first reply to the PTO within two months from the date of your final office action. (MPEP Sec. 706.02(f).)

Example: A final rejection is mailed to Joe on June 30, 1998, setting a three-month shortened statutory period to respond. Joe responds to the final rejection by submitting an amendment along with arguments as to why his changes overcome the examiner's rejection within two months from June 30.

Joe's examiner mails out an advisory action that states Joe's response does not place his application in condition for allowance and reaffirms the final rejection. If that advisory action was mailed out after three months from June 30, then the shortened statutory time period will be considered to expire on the date the advisory action was mailed.

If Joe now makes a second reply, any extension of time that Joe needs to pay for will be calculated from the mailing date of the advisory action and not from the time period originally set forth in Joe's final rejection.

Your examiner will consider any reply that you submit after final rejection quickly, usually within ten calendar days from the time you submit your reply. You can expect a response from your examiner usually within thirty days from your amendment.

Advisory Action

An *advisory action* (Form PTOL-303) is sent to you by your examiner to acknowledge receipt of your reply to your final office action where your reply is prior to your filing an appeal brief and does not place your application in condition for allowance. This form is used by your examiner to advise you of the disposition of your proposed amendments to your claims and of the effect of any argument or affidavit that you submitted that did not place your application in condition for allowance.

Appeal of Your Examiner's Decision

If any of your claims have been rejected twice by the PTO or you have been given a final rejection in your patent application, you have the right to appeal the decision to the *Board of Patent Appeals and Interferences*. You must, however, make your appeal within the time allowed for your response, given any extensions of time that you can obtain. You must also pay an appeal fee. The PTO will still charge an appeal fee even if your amendment ends up not being entered by your examiner.

Only questions affecting the merits of the claims, i.e., priority and patentability—prior art and sufficiency of disclosure issues—are appropriate for decision by the Board. Formal objections or purely procedural matters will not be ruled upon in a Board decision. Such matters should be undertaken by petition to the Commissioner prior to the appeal process.

Appeals to the Board of Patent Appeals and Inteferences is a subject that is beyond the scope of this book. You will want to consider obtaining the assistance of a patent attorney or agent who has experience in making such appeals. However, I will briefly review the appeal process here so that you have an understanding of some of the critical dates and can at least preserve your right to appeal.

Deciding to Appeal

Your decision whether to appeal a rejection of your claims will depend on whether further prosecution is either undesirable or not possible and you believe there is some likelihood of success in reversing the rejection of at least one important claim. If your application contains some allowed claims, a better course of action may be to respond to the final office action by cancelling the rejected claims in favor of their presentation, with or without amendment, in a continuation application. This will place your pending application (with your allowed claims) in condition for allowance. Prosecution can now proceed on your non-allowed claims in the continuation application.

Time Line of Events for Appeal

Notice of Appeal. You must file a *Notice of Appeal* in writing within the period for response to your pending final office action, and this period may be appropriately extended if necessary. The Notice of Appeal stops the time clock with respect to abandonment of your application.

Example: You receive a final rejection dated May 8, 1997, setting a three month period to respond. You respond to the rejection on September 8, 1997, after the three-month due date has passed together with a one-month automatic extension of time. You receive an advisory action by the PTO on October 1, 1997, continuing your rejection. On October 8, 1997, you file a Notice of Appeal together with a two-month extension of time. This Notice of Appeal stops the clock in respect to the six-month deadline that you have to respond to actions.

You now can concentrate on the appeal process and filing your appeal brief without having to worry about November 8, 1997—the date that your application would have become abandoned under the six month rule. In fact, if you decide to file a continuation of your pending application on November 30, 1997, you do not have to even obtain any further extensions of time since by filing your Notice of Appeal your application is not up against any due date with respect to your final rejection.

A form provided by the PTO that you can use as your Notice of Appeal is reproduced in Appendix E. Your Notice of Appeal must identify the rejected claim(s) that you want to appeal and must be signed by you. You must also include the appropriate fee.

File An Appeal Brief. You must file an appeal brief in triplicate within two months from the date that your Notice of Appeal is received by the PTO, or within the time allowed for reply to the action from which the appeal was taken, if such time is later. If you fail to file your appeal brief in a timely fashion, your application will go abandoned as of the date that your brief is due if you have no allowed claims in your appeal. If you have claims that were previously allowed by your examiner, your application will be returned to your examiner as to those allowed claims.

The time for filing your appeal brief can be extended automatically. This time period is also not a shortened statutory period so you can even take extensions up to five months under C.F.R., Title 37, Sec. 1.193(a), which give you beyond a six-month period to reply. (MPEP Sec. 710.02(e).)

Examiners Answer: After you have filed your appeal brief, your examiner has the right to file an *examiner's answer.* This is a written statement in answer to your brief. The examiner may not set forth new grounds of rejection in the answer unless your examiner reopens prosecution on such new grounds.

Reply Brief. You may file a reply brief within two months of the date of the examiner's answer. (C.F.R., Title 37, Sec. 1.193.)

Oral Hearing. If you believe that a hearing is necessary or desirable for a proper presentation of your appeal, you have the right to request an oral hearing accompanied by the appropriate fee within two months from the date of your examiner's answer. You will be notified as to the time and place of your hearing.

Board's Decision. After the Board of Patent Appeals and Interferences has considered the record, including your appeal brief and the examiner's answer, it will write its decision either affirming your examiner in whole or in part or reversing your examiner's decision. The Board also has the right to set forth a new ground of rejection. A copy of the Board's decision will be mailed to you and the original will be placed in your application file.

REQUEST FOR RECONSIDERATION

You have the right to request reconsideration by the Board of its decision within one month from the date of the decision. In the event that the Board makes a new rejection of one or more of your appealed claims, you have the right to either ask that the Board reconsider the new rejection or you can have the new rejection considered by your examiner just as if you were prosecuting a new application. If your rejected claim(s) are not allowed by your examiner, then you have the right to make a brand new appeal before the Board with respect to such rejection. If you do not appeal, the Board will make its original decision final.

Judicial Review. If you are dissatisfied with a final decision of the Board of Patent Appeals and Interferences, you may appeal the decision either to the U.S. Court of Appeals for the Federal Circuit or to the U.S. District Court for the District of Columbia. You have two months from the date of the Board's decision to do this.

To start an appeal before the Court of Appeals you must file a written notice of appeal in the PTO and also file a copy of this notice alone with the necessary fee in the Court of Appeals. To commence an appeal with the District Court, you must file a complaint in that court, as well as file copies of this complaint on certain designated officials. In an appeal to the District Court, you have the right to present evidence not previously submitted to the PTO.

The hearing at the district court is a *de novo* (or fresh) hearing, whereas an appeal to the Federal Circuit is based on the PTO prosecution history. A *de novo* appeal to the district court requires much more work than an appeal to the Federal Circuit, but is advantageous if the prosecution history is inadequate to support your case. If based on a strong record, an appeal to the Federal Circuit can be advantageous, as Federal Circuit judges are more experienced in patent issues.

Notice of Allowance or Allowability

If after examination of your application your examiner concludes that you are entitled to a patent, you will be mailed a *Notice of Allowance,* also called a *Notice of Allowability* (Form PTOL-37). If your examiner believes that the record as a whole does not make clear the reasons for allowing your claim(s), the examiner may also attach a separate written *statement of Reasons for Allowance*. You have the right, but are under no obligation, to file a statement commenting on such reasons for allowance.

When the notice of allowance is mailed, the examiner relinquishes jurisdiction of the application, which is forwarded to the issuance branch of the PTO for final processing and printing. Any papers you submit to the PTO following issuance of the Notice of Allowance should be accompanied by the *batch number* printed on the Notice of Allowance.

In situations where informalities such as drawing corrections are noted on your Notice of Allowance, you must make such corrections within three months from the mailing date of your Notice. No extensions of time are permitted to do this. (MPEP Sec. 710.02(e).)

Patent Term Adjustments

Extended Patent Term

Under some circumstances the PTO will add more time to the twenty year (for plant and utility patents) and fourteen year (for design patents) patent term. Examples of each of these circumstances are more particularly noted as follows:

- If the PTO fails to initially act on your application within fourteen months of its filing date (or that date on which your application fulfills the requirements for entering the national stage if you have filed a PCT application), then the PTO will need to extend your patent term. The term of a patent may be adjusted one day for each day by that the PTO misses this deadline.

  Not all communications you receive from the PTO are considered actions that stop the fourteen month time clock. For example, preliminary examination communications such as a *Notice of Incomplete Nonprovisional Application* (PTO-1123), a *Notice of Omitted Items(s) in a Nonprovisional Application* (PTO-1669), a *Notice to File Missing Parts of Application* (PTO-1533), a *Notice of Informal Application* (PTO-152), a *Notice to File Corrected Application Papers Filing Date Granted* (PTO-1660), or a *Notice to Comply with Requirements for Patent Applications Containing Nucleotide Sequence and/or Amino Acid Sequence Disclosures* (PTO-1661) are not considered actions by the PTO that will stop this fourteen-month clock. (These types of actions are discussed further in Chapter 11.)

- The PTO fails to issue a patent within three years of the actual filing date of your application. Note that for utility patents that have a twenty-year term, this rule effectively guarantees you a term for your patent of seventeen years so long as you are diligent in the prosecution of your application. Consult C.F.R., Title 37, Sec. 1.702(b) for more information on this three-year rule.

- Delays caused if an interference is declared between your application and the patent application or patent of another. This can occur where there is controversy about whether you or someone else was actually the first to invent what you are claiming to be your invention. You can consult C.F.R., Title 37, Sec. 1.703(c) for more information about this circumstance.

- If your application becomes subject to a secrecy order, the PTO will need to add time to your patent term for the period during which your application is under the secrecy order. (C.F.R., Title 37, Sec. 1.703(d).)

- You have filed a Notice of Appeal to the Board of Patent Appeals and Interferences and the Board or federal court has rendered a decision in your favor. (C.F.R., Title 37, Sec. 1.703(e).)

- The PTO fails to issue your patent more than four months after the date that you have paid your issue fee, having complied with all of the requirements necessary for issuance of your patent.

Patent Terms Reduced

In calculating any *patent term adjustment* (PTA), any overlaps in time caused by the above circumstances are counted only once.

Any term adjustment that you are entitled to receive due to the previously listed failures of the PTO are reduced by your own failures. The PTO calls this a failure to engage in "reasonable efforts to conclude prosecution" and reduces any term adjustment according to the days that you lack such efforts.

The PTO lists a host of examples where you have failed to engage in reasonable efforts. (C.F.R., Title 37, Sec. 1.704(c).) You have failed to engage in reasonable efforts if:

- you take longer than three months to respond to a notice from the Office making any rejection, objection, argument or other request. This three month period is measured from the date the notice was given or mailed to you by the PTO. From this time forward until the date that you make your response (considered to be on the day that the PTO receives your response if you mail or fax it or the date you deposit it in the mail if you use Express Mailing procedures), any term adjustment will be reduced on a day-by-day basis;

- you submit a reply that omits something (i.e., fails to respond to a pending issue);

- you pay your issue fee late;
- you fail to file a petition to withdraw a holding of abandonment or to revive an application within two months from the mailing date of a notice of abandonment;
- you submit a preliminary amendment less than one month before the mailing of an office action or notice of allowance that requires the mailing of a supplemental office action or notice of allowance; or,
- you file a continuing application, in which case the period of adjustment shall not include any period that is prior to the actual filing date of the application that resulted in the patent.

You will be notified by the PTO of any adjustment to the term of your patent if your patent application is approved at the time the PTO sends you a *Notice of Allowance and Issue Fee Due* (Form PTOL-85).

Contesting Calculation of Term Adjustment

If you believe the PTO has figured out your term adjustment incorrectly, you can file an application for patent term adjustment. However, you must file any such request before you pay the issue fee on your patent

As you might have guessed, your application for patent term adjustment also requires a fee. At the time this book was published, the current fee was $200. (C.F.R., Title 37, Sec. 1.18(e).) In addition to the fee, your application must contain a statement of the facts involved specifying the correct patent term adjustment and the grounds for such adjustment under C.F.R., Title 37, Sec. 1.702. There are a host of other things that your application must include. You should look at C.F.R., Title 37, Sec. 1.705 for everything that your application should contain if you intend to file an application for patent term adjustment.

If the PTO has reduced your patent term for failing to reply to a rejection, objection, argument, or other request within three months of the date of mailing of the office communication and that despite all due care you were unable to reply to such a communication, your application for patent term adjustment must be submitted in the form of a request for reinstatement of all or part of the period of adjustment under C.F.R., Title 37, Sec. 1.705(c). The fee for such a request was $400 at the time this book was published. (C.F.R., Title 37, Sec. 1.18(f).) The things that must be included in such a request for reinstatement are specified in C.F.R., Title 37, Sec. 1.705(c).

Payment of Issue and Publication Fee

Within three months from the date of your Notice of Allowance you must pay an *issue fee* in the amount shown on your Notice of Allowance (small entities get one-half off). No extensions of time are allowed to do this.

You should use the special fee transmittal form provided with your Notice of Allowance with your payment. If you fail to pay the issue fee on time, your application will go abandoned.

Pay your fee as soon as possible, rather than waiting until the end of the three months. The only time that I would recommend that you pay your issue fee towards the end of the three months is when you need that additional time to prepare a continuing application. In such a situation you need to file your continuing application while your current application is still pending. Delay of payment will insure that your current application is still co-pending with your continuing application.

In addition to an issue fee, your Notice of Allowance may also require that you pay a publication fee if your application was published. This fee must also be paid within three months from the date of mailing of your Notice of Allowance. As with your issue fee, you cannot extend the date for paying your publication fee.

10 Amending or Modifying Your Application

If you want to correct, modify, or augment information that you previously provided in your application data sheet, you should submit a supplemental application data sheet. This requires that you simply submit another application data sheet with all of the information that you provided in your prior application data sheet along with any additions underlined and any eliminations striked through.

A form that you can use to submit your required information is contained in Appendix E. It is the same form that you used when submitting your initial application data sheet except for two minor changes. First, the heading now reads "Supplemental Application Data Sheet." Second, the footer has been modified to read "supplemental" in place of "initial," and you should type in your application number followed by the filing date of your application and the date that you have prepared your supplemental application data sheet (this can correspond to the date that you Express Mail your supplemental data sheet to the PTO).

Author's Note

As stated earlier, you should be careful about amending your claims because you will lose any range of equivalents as to element(s) that you have amended. In a perfect world it would be nice to say that you will not need to make amendments to your claims. However, this is not a perfect world and often you will have no other option but to amend claims in order to get your claims allowed.

Due to the fact that you will lose any range of equivalents for those elements that you make amendments, you may want to now more seriously consider opposing your examiner's push for you to make amendments. This, however, is not an easy thing to do and will entail that you make arguments in your remarks section to try and convince your examiner that your claims are patentable as you have written them.

The other thing that you can do is to file an appeal of your examiner's rejection. This was already touched upon in the last chapter. The actual process of making an appeal, however, is outside the scope of this book and will require you to obtain the assistance of a patent attorney or agent with experience in making such appeals. The cost, however, could be worth it for the broader coverage of your invention that you could obtain if you win.

AMENDING YOUR SPECIFICATION

When you make amendments prior to any official action by the PTO, your amendments are referred to as *preliminary amendments*. Sometimes you may need to do this if you have forgotten to add something to your specification when you filed your application.

NOTE: *Preliminary amendments do not enjoy the status as part of your original disclosure unless they are referred to in the first oath or declaration that you file.*

This is an important point to keep in mind if you run into written description problems in any office action later on. In order to negate any written description rejection, you will need to rely upon your disclosure as originally filed. The written description requirement and responding to office actions are discussed more throughly in Chapter 13.

Although preliminary amendments are those amendments submitted prior to the date you received your first office action, you should submit any preliminary amendments as soon as possible after you file your application. This is because once your examiner has started to prepare his or her first office action, entry of a preliminary amendment submitted by you may be disapproved if it unduly interferes with the preparation of your examiner's office action. However, your preliminary amendment will be approved if it is filed no later than three months from the filing date of your application. (MPEP Sec. 714.03(a).)

You can also make amendments to your application after you receive a first action from the PTO and usually such amendments are necessary in order to overcome some rejection in your action. (C.F.R., Title 37, Sec. 1.111.)

After you receive a final rejection of your application, your rights to amend your application are restricted. (C.F.R., Title 37, Sec. 1.116.) The PTO is of the opinion that after a final rejection is made, prosecution of your application should ordinarily be concluded and thus you should not have the unrestricted right to make amendments, as it will create a lot of new work for the PTO.

After a final rejection, you are permitted to submit an amendment that cancels all your rejected claims or otherwise places your application, in condition for allowance. (C.F.R., Title 37, Sec. 1.116.)

You do not have an automatic right to amend your application after the PTO mails you a Notice of Allowance. However, the PTO will generally consider such amendments after a Notice of Allowance if they are needed for proper disclosure or protection of your invention and require no substantial amount of additional work on the part of the PTO. (C.F.R., Title 37, Sec. 1.312.)

One type of amendment that you may want to make after Notice of Allowance is one in which you consolidate all your previous versions of pending claims from a series of separate amendment papers into a single clean version. This can be useful for patent printing purposes. You will learn how to do this in the next section. No amendments should be filed after the date you pay your issue fee.

FORMAT OF YOUR AMMENDMENT

Your amendment should be divided into the following three separate parts. Each part should begin on a separate page.

1. Your first part should include a clean version of any paragraphs in your specification or claims that you want to amend.

2. The second part of your amendment papers is a *remarks* section. This is where you should restate any objections/rejections that your examiner has made in your *office action* and where you specifically deal with each and every one of those objections/rejections. This part of your amendment contains your arguments for allowance of your application. You will learn about arguments that you can make with respect to objections and rejections in the coming chapters.

   Your remarks must address all issues raised by the examiner, pointing out errors in the examiner's position and supporting patentability of your claims as they will appear following entry of your amendment.

   The remarks should also summarize the changes that you have made and confirm that no new matter is added to your specification. If you are adding new claims or amending any of your claims, you should specifically point out where those claims are supported in your original application as you filed it. (See Chapter 13 and the written description requirement for more about the importance of showing that new or amended claims are supported by your original disclosure.)

   NOTE: *The less superfluous material that you say in your remarks section, the better. Be brief and to the point. Anything that you say in your amendment can be held against you later on as an admission.*

Author's Note

You can never make amendments to your patent application that are not supported by your original application's disclosure.

Example: In July 1995, Harry filed a patent application for his invention of a floating pool stool. On August 20, 1997, Harry discovered that the foot rests, as shown in his drawings, were not included in his description or set forth in the claims, however, Harry still wanted to claim the stool with foot rests.

Harry could amend his claims to include the foot rests only if he also made an amendment to include the foot rest in the detailed description of his invention. If Harry did not also make an amendment to include the foot rests in the description, then the claimed foot rest would not be supported by the written description.

3. The third part of your amendment papers is a separate page entitled "Version with marking to show changes made." Underneath this section you must show any amendments made to your specification outside your claims as well as any changes made to your claims. The way you do this will be explained in the next two sections.

Amending Your Specifications Outside Your Claims

To amend your specification outside your claims you must do two things. First, you must unambiguously identify the location where you want to delete one or more paragraphs of the specification, replace a deleted paragraph with one or more replacement paragraphs, or add one or more paragraphs (see the sample amendment below for the proper format that is described).

Example: You want to add the word "melted" in a paragraph of your specification. You know that you should number your paragraphs when drafting your specification. You can now easily refer to any specific paragraph in your specification by number in order to amend it. Suppose that the paragraph number you want to replace is [0071]. You can now create a section heading in your amendment and state your changes.

<u>In the Specification:</u>

Please replace paragraph [0071], with the following rewritten paragraph:

In this construction the electric heating elements are positioned directly beneath the iron grid bars and melted fat is carried off in grooves formed in the upper surfaces of the bars.

Be sure that when you replace a paragraph, your amended paragraph takes on the same number as the paragraph you are replacing. If you want to replace your paragraph with more than one paragraph, then your added paragraphs should be numbered using the number of your original paragraph for the first replacement paragraph, followed by increasing decimal numbers for the second and subsequent added paragraphs. For example, your original paragraph [0071] might be replaced with paragraphs [0071], [0071.1], and [0071.2].

The second thing that you must do is provide a version of any of your replacement paragraph(s) on one or more pages after your remarks section, marked-up to show all the changes relative to the old version. You do not, however, have to provide a marked up version for an added paragraph or a deleted paragraph as it is sufficient to simply state that a particular paragraph has been added or deleted.

Example: Using the earlier example on p. 200, you must show the changes that you have made on a separate page. After your remarks section, create a separate page entitled as follows:

<u>VERSION WITH MARKINGS TO SHOW CHANGES MADE"</u>

Underneath this heading creating a subheading entitled as follows:

<u>In the specification:</u>

Underneath this subheading you could state the following:

> Paragraph [0071] has been amended as follows: In this construction the electric heating elements are positioned directly beneath the iron grid bars and melted fat is carried off in grooves formed in the upper surfaces of the bars.

Note that you are also allowed to amend entire sections. You do this in the same manner as above for amending paragraphs (i.e., you need to provide a clean form or your sections that your amending without any marking as well as a separate marked-up version showing the changes in the section relative to the previous version).

If you want to submit an entirely amended specification (outside your claims), you are also allowed to submit an instruction to replace your old specification with a substitute specification. You should provide a clean version of your substitute specification as well as another version of the substitute specification, separate from the substitute specification, marked-up to show all changes relative to the previous version of the specification. The changes may be shown by brackets (for deleted matter), underlining (for added matter), or by any equivalent marking system. Sometimes your examiner will require that you submit a substitute specification if the number of amendments to your application makes it difficult to examine or print your patent.

Ammending Your Claims

Your claims may be amended in any of the following ways:

- by canceling particular claims;
- by presenting new claims; or,
- by rewriting particular claims.

The format of making changes to your claims is very similar to the format discussed earlier for making changes to your specification. In both instances you must provide a clean form of your amended claim as well as a marked-up version separate from your amendment to indicate changes that have been made (See the sample amendment following for the proper format). However, a marked-up version does not have to be supplied where all you are doing to your application is adding or canceling claims. You only need to provide the marked-up version if you are making changes to the claims which currently exist in your application. If you do provide a marked-up version to show changes made to any amended claims, however, you should identify (in the marked-up version) any added or canceled claims with a statement, such as, "Claim 6 has been canceled."

One difference between amending paragraphs in your specification and amending claims is that you must write the number of the claim that you are amending followed by either the word "amended," "twice amended," or "three times amended" in parentheses depending on how many times you have amended your claims since its original presentation.

The first thing you must do (as with amending in your specification outside your claims) is to provide a clean form of any rewritten or newly added claims. You do this before your remarks section of your claims.

Example: You want to cancel Claim 6 and amend Claim 7. In your amendment before the remarks section, you should create the following entitled section:

In the claims:

You would could then state the following:

Please cancel Claim 6.

Please amend Claim 7 as follows:

7. (Amended) A griller as claimed in Claim 1 wherein the power consumption of the heater element is 1250 watts and the weight of the grill member is about 3.5 kg.

The second thing you must then do is provide a version of any amended claim on a separate page showing any changes made by either brackets (for deleted matter), or underlining (for added matter), or by any equivalent marking system. As stated, a marked-up version does not have to be supplied if all you are doing is presenting an added claim or canceled claim as it is sufficient to state that a particular claim has been added, or canceled. However, if you do provide a marked-up version to show changes made to any amended claims, you should identify (in the marked-up version) any added or canceled claims.

Example: A separate page of your amendment after your remarks section should be entitled as following:

`VERSION WITH MARKINGS TO SHOW CHANGES MADE`

You would then create the following heading:

`In the claims`

You can then state something like the following:

`Claim 6 has been canceled.`

`Claim 7 has been amended as follows:`

`7. (Amended) A griller as claimed in claim 1 wherein the power consumption of the heater element is 1250 [1600] watts and the weight of the grill is about 3.5 kg."`

You may also amend your claims by canceling claim(s) that you no longer want and replacing them with new claims that you do want. The number of the new claims that you want to add must begin with the next highest number in your claim numbering.

Example: You wish to cancel Claims 1 and 2 and replace them by a new single Claim 3. To do this you can state in your amendment the following:

```
Please cancel claims 1-2 and add the follow-
ing Claim 3.
```

You would then write out your new claim 3.

If you have made a lot of amendments during the prosecution of your application, you may submit a clean version (with no marking) of all of your pending claims into one amendment paper. (MPEP Sec. 714.) This can be beneficial for clarity and printing purposes.

When rewriting a claim in the clean set, the parenthetical expression (i.e., "Amending," "Twice Amending") should *not* appear. The only time a parenthetical expression should appear in the clean set is when the claim is actually being amended. The submission of a clean version of all your pending claims will be construed as directing the cancellation of all your previous claim versions. You do not need to submit a marked-up version of your consolidation if you are not making any current amendments to your claims.

SAMPLE AMENDMENT

On the next page is a sample amendment that incorporates the examples just discussed. The sample includes changes made to both a specification and the claims section in the same amendment. A blank copy of this form can also be found in Appendix E.

Applicant(s):	Joe Genius
Serial No.	09/106,043
Filed:	April 1, 2000
Title:	Griller
Group Art unit:	1744
Examiner:	John Doe
Docket N:	12345/JAS/R758

Certificate of Mailing by Express Mail
"Express Mail" Mailing
Label No. EK_______________US
Date of Deposit: ____________, 200__
I hereby certify that this paper is being deposited with the United States Postal Service as "Express Mail Post Office to Addressee" service under 37 C.F.R. §1.10 on the date indicated above in an envelope addressed to Box PCT Commissioner for Patents, Washington, D.C.. 20231

(type or print name of person making deposit)

____
Signature of person making deposit

FILED BY EXPRESS MAIL
Honorable Commissioner for Patents
Washington, D.C. 20231

AMENDMENT

Dear Examiners:

In response to the Office action of October 10, 2000, please amend the above-identified application as follows:

In The Specification:

Please replace paragraph [0071], with the following rewritten paragraph:

— In this construction the electric heating elements are positioned directly beneath the iron grid bars and melted fat is carried off in grooves formed in the upper surfaces of the bars —

In The Claims:

Please cancel Claim 6.

Please amend Claim 7 as follows:

7. (Amended) A griller as claimed in claim 1 wherein the power consumption of the heater element is 1250 watts and the weight of the grill member is about 3.5 kg."

REMARKS

Claims 1-5 and 7-10 remain in this application. Claim 6 has been canceled. Claim 7 has been amended.

The examiner has acknowledged that claims 1-5 and 7-10 are directed to allowable subject matter. Claim 6 has been canceled as being drawn to an embodiment no longer of interest to applicant. Claim 7 has now been amended to correct editorial errors and clear up any matters of form.

Claim 7 has been amended for the following reasons:

[Inserted reasons].

Attached hereto is a marked-up version of the changes made to the specification and claims by the current amendment. The attached page is captioned **"Version with markings to show changes made."**

Applicant respectfully requests that a timely Notice of Allowance be issued in this case.

Respectfully submitted,

BY______________________

Applicant

VERSION WITH MARKING TO SHOW CHANGES MADE

In the specification:

Paragraph [0071] has been amended as follows:

In this construction the electric heating elements are positioned directly beneath the iron grid bars and melted fat is carried off in grooves formed in the upper surfaces of the bars.

In the claims:

Claim 6 has been canceled.

Claim 7 has been amended as follows:

7. (Amended) A griller as claimed in claim 1 wherein the power consumption of the heater element is 1250 [1600] watts and the weight of the grill is about 3.5 kg.

AMENDING YOUR DRAWINGS

When you get a *Notice of Draftsperson's Drawing Review,* it is normally attached to the first office action that you receive from the PTO. If the *Notice* requires you to correct your drawings, you can simply make such corrections and resubmit the corrected drawings either with your response or even after you have received a Notice of Allowance. If you want to wait until after your receive your Notice of Allowance, you should state in your response the following:

"The objection to the drawings is noted. Formal drawings will be filed after allowance."

If you wait to file your corrected drawings after you receive your Notice of Allowance, you will have three months from its mailing date to file such corrected drawings. This date is non-extendable. You should try to submit your corrected drawings as soon as possible after you receive your Notice of Allowance because if the drawings are again rejected, you will have to file another set of corrected drawings within the three month time limit.

You can use the form contained in Appendix E to submit your corrected drawings for informalities to your drawings. You should file this form with your corrected drawings and then send them as a separate mailing to the official draftsperson, whose address should appear on your Notice of Draftsperson's Drawing Review.

If you want to make changes to your drawings other than changes in response to the Notice of Draftsperson's Drawing Review, you must obtain the permission to do so from your examiner. To do this, submit a copy of the sheet of your drawing that you want to change marked-up in red to show the changes that you want to make. Then attach this with a *Request for Approval of Proposed Drawing Amendment*. A copy of this form that you can use is contained in Appendix E. You then send this form and marked-up copy to the PTO just as you would if you were sending a response. If such changes are approved by your examiner, you must then file corrected drawings just as you would in response to a Notice of Informalities above.

Examiner Amendments

Small mistakes to your application such as misspelled words, grammatical errors, or other informalities may be corrected by your examiner in what is called an *examiner's amendment*. In an examiner's amendment, you do not need to submit a formal amendment to your application since your examiner makes the amendment. But if the examiner's amendment will occur after any resonse due date has passed, you must still obtain and pay for the necessary extension of time so that the examiner's amendment can be made.

Example: You receive a final rejection on March 1, 1988, setting a three-month shortened statutory period. On June 1, 1988, you file a response by Express Mail. The PTO sends you an Advisory Action on July 23, July 23, 1988, indicating that your claims will be allowed with a few minor amendments that can be made by the examiner. In order to obtain these amendments and push your application into allowance, you must obtain a two-month extension of time.

You cannot amend an oath or declaration. If your oath or declaration is defective, you must instead execute a new one. Such a new oath is called a *substitute oath*. A substitute oath must identify the application that it goes along with, preferably by giving the serial number and the filing date of the application.

If at any later time after filing your oath or declaration, you add claims to your application, you should also file a new oath or declaration, called a supplemental oath or declaration to cover such claims. (MPEP Sec. 608.01 and Rule 1.52(c).)

Correction of inventorship is not common. If you need to make a correction to the inventors that you named as inventors of your application, you should consult C.F.R., Title 37, Sec. 1.48 and the MPEP at Sec. 201.03. Here are some of the situations where you may need to correct inventorship in your application:

If your inventorship was improperly set forth in your oath or declaration that you file with your patent application you need to correct inventorship in your application. In such a case you can correct your inventorship by filing an amendment as discussed earlier, so long as you include the following in your amendment:

- a request to correct the inventorship and the desired change you want to make;
- a statement from each person that you are adding and from each person being deleted as an inventor that the error in inventorship occurred without deceptive intention on his or her part;
- a new oath/declaration by the actual inventors;
- the appropriate fee (C.F.R., Title 37, Sec. 1.17(i)); and,
- if any assignment was made by any of the original named inventors, the written consent of such assignee(s).

AMENDING OATH DECLARATIONS

You may need to correct inventorship if your oath/declaration is set for the correct inventorship, but during prosecution of your application through claim cancellation or other amendment fewer than all of the currently named inventors are the actual inventors of your remaining claims. In such a case you can submit an amendment that identifies the inventor(s) you want to delete. It must indicate that the inventor's contribution is no longer being claimed in your application. You must also submit the required fee. (C.F.R., Title 37, Sec. 1.17(i).)

If your application correctly set forth the inventorship in the oath/declaration, but you subsequently add claims to your application that requires you to add an inventor(s) who you did not previously name, you will be required to supply the following (C.F.R., Title 37, Sec. 1.48(c)):

- a request to correct the inventorship that sets forth the desired inventorship change;

- a statement from each inventor being added that that the addition is necessitated by the amendment to your claims and that the inventorship error occurred without deceptive intent on his or her part;
- an oath or declaration signed by all the inventors;
- the appropriate fee (C.F.R., Title 37, Sec. 1.17(i)); and,
- if an assignment was granted by any of the originally named inventors, the written consent of the assignee.

Correction of inventorship in your regular *non-provisional application* can also be done by filing a *continuing application*, (C.F.R., Title 37, Sec. 1.53) so long as there will be at least one common inventor between the continuation and the application that you filed (yet another purpose for a continuation application). It is also possible to correct inventorship in a *provisional application*, but you should consult C.F.R., Title 37, Sec. 1.48(d) and (e) for those situations.

11 Dealing With Preliminary Examination Communications

You will recall that in Chapter 9 you read that the PTO will usually give you a shortened statutory period of three months to respond to an office action before you need to pay for extensions of time. I also qualified that rule by saying in some cases the PTO will give you an even shorter time to respond. These cases are usually preliminary matters that will be covered here in this chapter.

Notices That Relate to an Incomplete Application

Notice of Incomplete Application

If you submitted your patent application without a description (or one that cannot be construed as a written description), any required drawing, or at least one claim, you will receive a *Notice of Incomplete Application* (PTO-1123). You will not be granted a filing date for your application until you submit the necessary parts of your application. You have the following options to deal with this notice.

- ***Assert that you submitted the required parts of your application.*** To do this, you will need to file a petition under C.F.R., Title 37, 1.53(e) along with the appropriate fee under C.F.R., Title 37, 1.17(h) asserting that

- your missing specification was submitted or,
- that your papers contained an adequate written description.

You must also present evidence such as a date stamped return postcard from the PTO that shows that you did submit the required parts of your specification.

- ***Submit your specification again.*** Submit the specification with the missing parts, including a new oath or declaration that refers to your specification being submitted. If you do this, you are basically agreeing with the PTO that you forgot to add the missing part of your specification. The filing date of your application will be the date that you provide your missing parts.

The filing date of your application will be the date that these required parts of your application are filed. (MPEP Sec. 506.)

NOTE: *Remember that you do not need to submit claims for a provisional application. Thus a provisional application will only be incomplete if you neglect to file a description or any required drawings.*

NOTICE OF OMITTED ITEMS

You receive a *Notice of Omitted Items* when you have filed everything that you need to in order to get a filing date (i.e., a written description, a claim and any necessary drawing), but you have mistakenly left out one of the pages of your specification. (MPEP Sec.601.01(d).) Your notice will state that your submitted application papers will be afforded a filing date, but are lacking some page(s) of the specification.

You have the following three options in dealing with a notice of omitted items:

File a petition. If you believe that you did, in fact, send the alleged missing pages to the PTO, you can file a petition along with the appropriate fee, proving that you did send the missing pages. (C.F.R., Title 37, secs. 1.53(e) and 1.17(h).) You can prove this through the self-addressed postcard that you should have received back from the PTO identifying receipt of all the pages of your specification. You have two months from the date of your notice of omitted items to pursue this option. If the PTO determines that you are correct, the PTO should return your petition fee.

Submit omitted pages. You can submit the omitted page(s) in your nonprovisional application within two months from the mailing date of your notice of omitted items. Extensions of time are *not* permitted. If you elect this option, you must accept as the filing date the date for your application the date that you submit such omitted pages. Thus this is really the equivalent to simply filing a new application (which, of course, you are also allowed to do). You must submit a petition along with an appropriate fee requesting the later filing date. (C.F.R., Title 37, Sec. 1.17(h) and 1.182.)

Do nothing. You can simply do nothing in response to your notice of omitted items. This will be treated as an acceptance of your application as filed with the PTO. You must then amend your specification to clean up your application so that your omission makes no difference. The problem with this last item is that if you try to add back your omissions in an amendment, this will likely be considered as adding new matter to your application. As stated earlier, the PTO will never allow the addition of new matter to a patent application.

NOTICE TO FILE MISSING PARTS

`An application number and Filing Date have been assigned to this application. However, the items indicated below are missing. The required time and fees identified below must be timely submitted ALONG WITH THE PAYMENT OF A SURCHARGE.`

You get the above notice when you have submitted all the necessary parts of your application to obtain a filing date (claim(s), specification and required drawings), but have left out other parts such as the oath/declaration or the filing fee.

You are given two months from the filing date or one month from the date of this notice to submit the missing parts in order to avoid abandonment of your application. Upon timely submission of the missing parts, your application will receive as a filing date the date your incomplete application.

You can take extensions of time up to five months under to file your missing parts., even if this will take you pass the statutory deadline of six months to respond to office actions. (C.F.R., Title 37, Sec. 1.136(a).) This is because a *Notice to File Missing Parts* is not identified on the *Notice* as a statutory period subject to U.S.C., Title 35, Sec. 133 (MPEP Sec. 710.02(d).)

Notice of Incomplete Reply

```
The reply filed on [date] is not fully responsive to the prior Office action because of the following omission(s) or matter(s) [ ]. See 37 CFR Sec. 1.111. Since the above mentioned reply appears to be bona fide, applicant is given a TIME PERIOD of ONE (1) MONTH or THRITY (30) DAYS from the mailing of this notice, which ever is longer, within which to supply the omission or correction in order to avoid abandonment. EXTENSIONS OF TIME MAY BE GRANTED UNDER 37 CFR Sec. 1.136(a).
```

You get this notice from the PTO when you have made a response to an action from the PTO, but your reply is incomplete for some reason. This could happen if you fail to respond to each and every rejection or objection in your action. (MPEP Sec. 714.03.) The PTO will usually give you a period of one month from the date of the notice to submit a proper reply. You are also allowed to obtained automatic extensions if you need even more time to correct your response.

Restriction Requirement

The PTO will not allow you to claim two or more independent or distinct inventions in a single patent application. If you try to do this, the PTO will send you a restriction requirement, which requires you to "elect" the invention that you want to pursue in your application.

For a restriction requirement to be proper, not only must the inventions be distinct, but examination of the inventions in one application must create an undue burden on the examiner. (MPEP Sec. 803.) Thus one strategy to argue against a restriction requirement is to convince the examiner that the application will not be unreasonably burdensome to examine.

NOTE: *The issue of whether a search and examination can be made without serious burden to an examiner is **not** applicable to design applications when determining whether a restriction requirement should be made.*

Dealing with a Restriction Requirement

You have a few options in dealing with a restriction requirement made by the PTO. The harder option you have is to argue that the restriction requirement is wrong and request a reconsideration of your examiner's decision. Arguing that your examiner is wrong is referred to as *traversing* the restriction requirement. Even if you traverse your examiner's restriction requirement, you must still elect which invention you want to pursue in your application.

If you are unable to overcome the restriction requirement, your examiner will make the next action final and withdraw the claims that you have not elected to pursue.

Your second, easier option in dealing with a restriction requirement, is to elect the invention you want to pursue without traversing. You can still prosecute your nonelected inventions in divisional applications. (See Chapter 7 for more information on this.) Filing a divisional application can be deferred no later than the issue date of your parent application.

Accepting a restriction requirement without traversal may be your best course of action. By traversing your restriction requirement and arguing that your claims are not distinct, there is a good chance you are going to lose the battle. Not only may you lose the battle over the restriction requirement, but by asserting that your claims are distinct you may be admitting yourself that your claims are not patentable over each other later on if you ever face litigation in court. Prior art might then be presumed to invalidate your *other* claims that you previously argued were not distinct.

An example of wording that you can use in the *remarks* section of your amendment/reply to a restriction requirement if you pursue the easier second option is the following:

> I. Response to Restriction Requirement
>
> The Examiner has imposed a restriction requirement on the application. By way of this amendment Applicants elect the Group II Claims 6, 7, 15, 26, 27, 36, 40, 41, 44-54, and 75. The non-elected claims have been cancelled without prejudice for later prosecution in a divisional or other related application. The dependencies of other claims have been modified.
>
> The Examiner has noted that upon canceling claims, the inventorship of the application must be amended if one or more inventors is no longer an inventor of the remaining subject matter. Applicants have made a good faith review of the remaining claims and believe that the named inventors each contributed to the conception of the subject matter or at least one of the remaining claims.

For more information about restriction practice, see Chapter 800 of the MPEP.

12 Overcoming Prior Art Obviousness Rejections

By far the most frequent ground of rejection is on the ground of unpatentability in view of the prior art. In other words, your claimed subject matter is either not novel or it is obvious based on prior art references. (U.S.C., Title 35, Secs. 102 and 103.)

In a proper prior art rejection, your examiner must identify and communicate to you a reason, based in law, why your claimed subject matter fails to satisfy the novelty and non-obviousness requirements. If the PTO succeeds, the burden shifts to you to rebut, or knock down, the examiner's case. You cannot achieve allowance for your rejected claims without coming forward with evidence to rebut his or her case. The only exception to this rule is where you can point to sufficient evidence of patentability in the existing prosecution record.

Your first question to ask in dealing with prior art rejections is whether each cited reference in the office action constitutes prior art against your claims under examination. The criteria for determining whether patents and publications are prior art were previously discussed in Chapter 2. Following is a more detailed examination of each of these prior art sections in order to tackle the specific rejections raised by your examiner.

As you go through the references that your examiner is using against you, make sure that such reference(s) meet the criteria under one of the prior art sections. Your examiner will state in the rejection which one of the prior art sections he or she is relying on. Go right to the relevant prior art section and make sure that the reference your examiner is using meets the necessary criteria.

Sometimes examiners can make mistakes. For example, if your examiner cites a U.S. patent filed after your filing date, you should simply (and respectfully) respond by explaining, based on the reference and filing dates, why the reference is not prior art. In such a case you would not need to submit any additional evidence because you have all of the evidence that you need correct in the record.

You should also be on the look-out for references that have insufficient disclosures. Your examiner cannot use references as prior art if such references have insufficient disclosures. A patent or printed publication is an insufficient disclosure if it is not enabling (*In re Donohue*, 766 F.2d 531 (Fed. Cir. 1985).)

A disclosure is non-enabling if it fails to place the subject matter of the claims within the possession of the public, meaning that someone with general skill in your field could have used the reference's description of your invention with their own knowledge to make your claimed invention themselves. (*In re Wilder*, 429 F.2d 447 (C.C.P.A. 1970).)

Usually it will be necessary to introduce evidence rebutting enablement of a prior art reference in the form of a 132 Affidavit, which is discussed in the following section. The affidavit must specifically identify the alleged deficiencies of the reference, and must explain why those deficiencies preclude a person of ordinary skill in the art from possessing the subject matter allegedly disclosed. (*In re Lamberti*, 545 F.2d 747(C.C.P.A. 1976).)

THE PRIOR ART SECTION

United States Code Title 35, Section 102(a)

A person shall be entitled to a patent unless (a) the invention was known or used by others in this country, or patented or described in a printed publication in this or a foreign country, before the invention thereof by the applicant for a patent.

You will see the above statement if the PTO is rejecting one or more of your claims on the basis of U.S.C., Title 35, Sec. 102(a). The third and fourth categories, (3) a patent obtained or (4) a printed publication describing all of the aspects of your claimed invention, can occur anywhere in the world.

OVERCOMING SEC. 102(A) PRIOR ART REJECTIONS

You have the following options to choose from in overcoming a Sec. 102(a) rejection.

- Argue that your claims are distinguishable from the reference(s) being used by the PTO to reject your claim(s). This is true because even if an act or document constitutes prior art under Sec.102, it will not bar patentability of your claim(s) unless it *anticipates* your claim(s). As we have previously discussed, anticipation only occurs if the prior art reference teaching each and every element of your claim(s). If you are successful in arguing that the reference does not anticipate your claims (because it is distinguishable), you will have removed that reference as a 102(a) prior art bar to the patentability of your invention.
- Amend your claims (as discussed in Chapter 10) so that they are distinguished from the prior art reference(s). This is really the same means to overcoming a Sec. 102(a) prior art rejection as just discussed, except that here you actually make changes to your claims so as to negate anticipation. Again, this can be used with any of the prior art rejections you will encounter.

- File an affidavit or declaration that shows that your invention was made prior to the effective date of the reference being applied against you by the examiner. (C.F.R., Title 37, Sec. 1.131.)

Rule 131 Affidavits/ Declarations

A Rule 131 Affidavit is sometimes referred to as swearing back of a reference which your examiner is using against you. In other words, a Rule 131 Affidavit/Declaration supports the proposition that your claimed invention was made before the date on which your cited reference became prior art under one of the categories discussed above. (A Rule 131 form that you can use is located in Appendix E.

There are three ways that you can use to establish that your invention was made prior to the effective date of your prior art reference.

- First, you can show that your invention was put to actual practice (*"reduction to practice")* prior to the effective date of your reference.
- Second, you are also allowed to show that you conceived your invention prior to the effective date (even without actual reduction to practice of your invention prior to the effective date of your cited reference). As long as you also show that you took steps with due diligence to reduce your invention to practice prior to the effective date of the cited prior art reference, it is not absolutely essential that you show you have reduced to practice your invention before the effective date of the prior art reference.
- Third, you can show *conception* of your invention before the effective date of the reference coupled with due diligence from before to the reference date up to the filing of your application (constructive reduction to practice). This is the same way as discussed in the second option above, except here you are considered to have constructively reduced to practice your invention when you file your application.

Reduction to practice may be either actual or constructive. *Actual reduction* requires that the invention is reduced to a physical or tangible form. Actual reduction for a process requires successful performance of the process. For a machine, actual reduction requires that the machine be assembled, adjusted, and used. For a manufacture, the article must be completely manufactured. For a composition, the matter must be completely composed. *Constructive reduction* is the filing of a patent application.

Example: Sally conceived of an invention on June 8, 1998, but did not start to take any actions in reducing her invention to practice (no reasonable diligence) until June 7, 1999. Just after this day on June 8, 1999, Molly claimed to invent the same invention and reduced it to practice on September 1, 1999. Even if Sally reduces the invention to practice on October 1, 1999, she is awarded priority since she took reasonable diligence to reduce the invention to practice prior to Molly's conception. However, if Sally had not taken this reasonable diligence prior to Molly's conception, the results would be the reverse.

The essential thing is that you show priority of your invention. This may be done by any satisfactory evidence of the facts. Facts, not conclusions, must be alleged in your declaration. A general allegation that your invention was completed prior to the date of your cited reference is *not* sufficient. You need factual evidence.

The allegations of fact might be supported by submitting as evidence one or more of the following:

- attached sketches;
- attached blueprints;
- attached photographs;
- attached reproductions of notebook entries;

- an accompanying model (you must comply with rule C.F.R., Title 37, Section 1.91, however, if you want to enter a model into your application file); and/or,
- attached supporting statements by witnesses, where verbal disclosures are the evidence relied upon.

Finally, you and any other co-inventor(s) must sign your declaration.

Another thing to note is that in establishing the date of your invention, you cannot only rely on inventive acts in the U.S., but also acts in a NAFTA country (Mexico or Canada) on or after December 8, 1993, and in a WTO country on or after January 1, 1996.

File an affidavit or declaration under C.F.R., Title 37, Section 1.132 showing that the prior art reference is by you and not by another person. Even when published within the year preceding the filing date of your application, inventor authored publications may constitute prior art against your claims if the authors of the publication and the inventors of your application overlap but do not completely correspond. In such a case the publication is considered the work of "another," and therefore is available as a Sec. 102(a) prior art against your claims.

You can use a 1.132 affidavit/declaration to remove such co-authored publications and co-inventored patents that your examiner seeks to use against you. Where you are one of the co-authors of a publication cited against your application, you may also remove the publication as a reference by filing a 1.132 affidavit signed by any of your co-authors which disclaims any inventive contribution to your claimed subject matter.

Perfect any priority claims to any earlier applications that you may have filed on your invention. You would do this by amending your specification to a contain a specific reference to the prior application or by filing a new application data sheet that contains a specific reference to the prior application. If you are claiming priority to an earlier filed foreign application you will need to provide a certified copy of that priority document as well as an English language translation if the document is not in English.

Conception is when the inventor forms, in his or her mind, a definite and permanent idea of the complete and operative invention as it will be applied in practice. (*Coleman v. Dines*, 754 F.2d 353, (Fed. Cir. 1985).) Conception is more than a vague idea of how to solve a problem. The requisite means themselves and their interaction must also be comprehended. Conception must include every feature or limitation of your claimed invention. (*Davis v. Reddy*. 620 F.2d 885 (C.C.P.A. 1980).) Conception is made when the invention is made sufficiently clear to enable one skilled in the art to reduce your invention to practice without the exercise of extensive experimentation.

While conception is the mental part of your inventive act, it must be capable of proof, such as by demonstrative evidence or by a complete disclosure to another person. The sufficiency of corroborative evidence is determined by the *Rule of Reason*. Accordingly, a court must make a reasonable analysis of all of the pertinent evidence to determine whether an inventor's testimony is credible.

United States Code Title 35, Section 102(b)

A person shall be entitled to a patent unless (b) the invention was patented or described in a printed publication in this or a foreign country or in public use or on sale in this country, more than one year prior to the date of application for patent in the United States.

If you have language like this in your office action then your claim(s) have been rejected. (U.S.C., Title 35, Sec. 102(b).)

The *on sale* category of Sec. 102(b) means the sale of your invention and not the sale of the rights to your invention as in an assignment. Two conditions trigger the on-sale bar. First, there must be an offer for sale. Second, the invention must be "ready for patenting." (*Pfaff v. Wells Electronics, Inc.*, 525 U.S. 55, (1998).)

An invention is "ready for patenting" if it is reduced to practice or if the inventor prepares drawings or other descriptions of the invention that are sufficient to enable one skilled in the art to practice the invention. If someone only conceives an invention,there is effectively no invention that could be placed on sale. Therefore the offer for sale would not be a bar to patentability. (*Micro Chemical, Inc. v. Great Plains Chemical Co.*, 103 F.3d 1538 (Fed. Cir. 1997).)

The main differences between a rejection under Sec.. 102(b) and Sec. 102(a) is that whereas a Sec.102(a) category act or publication must be made by "another," a Sec. 102(b) act or publication can be made by another or yourself. For example, if you disclose your own work in a publication more than one year prior to filing a patent application for that work, then you will be barred from obtaining a patent for the invention under Sec. 102(b), but not so under Sec. 102(a).

The rationale for barring you under Sec. 102(b) is that once you have decided to lift the *veil of secrecy* from your work, you must choose between the protection of a federal patent or the dedication of the idea to the public at large. Thus there are indeed penalties for revealing your invention without obtaining a patent.

The second difference between Sec. 102(a) and Sec. 102(b) is that Sec. 102(a) is keyed off of one of its categories occurring *prior to the date of your invention*, while Sec. 102(b) is keyed off of one of its categories being before *the date of your patent application*. Thus the date of invention referred to in Sec. 102(a) is sometimes termed "soft" and open for debate on a case-by-case basis, whereas the Sec. 102(b) filing date of an application is certain. Prior art that arises under Sec. 102(b) is unforgiving, and hence a bar to patentability. Sec. 102(b) is sometimes termed an *absolute statutory bar*.

Overcoming Your 102(b) Rejection

There are three possible ways that a Sec. 102(b) rejection can be overcome.

- The first way is your option of arguing that your claims are distinguishable from the prior art reference(s) being used by the PTO to reject your claims. As with Sec. 102(a), you argue that your claims are not anticipated by the references in your response.

- The second thing you can do is to amend your claims so as to distinguish your claim(s) from the prior art.
- The third way that you can overcome this rejection is if you have previously filed another U.S. application for the same invention, but you have forgotten to perfect priority to that application. In such a case, you should file a new application data sheet which contains a specific reference to the prior application so that you can obtain the earlier priority date.

Claiming foreign priority does not help you in overcoming prior art based on a Sec. 102(b) rejection. This is because the one-year bar of U.S.C., Title 35, Sec. 102(b) dates from the *U.S.* filing date and has nothing to do with any *foreign* filing date. When the statute says "prior to the date of application for patent in the U.S.", that is really what is meant. You cannot use a prior foreign application date for your invention to overcome this.

As stated earlier, your options are more limited under U.S.C., Title 35, Sec. 102(b) as compared with U.S.C., Title 35, Sec. 102(a). You cannot use a C.F.R., Title 37, Sec. 1.131 affidavit as your could in Section 102(a) because Section 102(b) is keyed off of the date of your U.S. application. On the other hand, Section 102(a) is keyed off of the date of your invention, which the PTO assumes to be the date you file your patent application but can be otherwise shown by presenting a C.F.R., Title 37, Sec. 1.131 affidavit.

You also cannot present a C.F.R., Title 37 Sec. 1.132 declaration or affidavit showing that the prior art reference is of your own work because Sec. 102(b) applies to acts or documents by *you,* unlike Sec. 102(a).

United States Code, Title 35, Section 102(c)

A person shall be entitled to a patent unless (c) he has abandoned the invention.

In order to have a rejection under this part of the prior art statute you must have abandoned your invention. The PTO must show that you have intended to abandon your invention as shown by your actions. Abandonment of an invention occurs when an inventor either does not intend to further pursue an invention, or intends to suppress or conceal it. Delay in filing a patent application is not sufficient to infer the necessary intent to abandon your invention. (MPEP Sec. 2134.)

United States Code, Title 35, Section 102(d)

A person shall be entitled to a patent unless (d) the invention was first patented or caused to be published, or was the subject of an inventor's certificate, by the applicant or his legal representatives or assignees in a foreign country prior to the date of the application for patent in this country on an application for patent or inventor's certificate filed more than twelve months before the filing of the application in the United States.

Four conditions must apply for a proper rejection under Sec. 102(d).

- There must be a foreign application filed more than twelve months before the effective filing date of your U.S. application;

  NOTE: *A U.S. design patent application must be filed within a shorter six months of the foreign filing.*

- The foreign application must have been filed by the same applicant(s) as in the U.S. or by his or her legal representatives and assigns;

- The foreign patent must have been granted prior to the U.S. filing date. Normally, an inventor's foreign patent will not issue before a U.S. filing date, making Sec. 102(d) prior art rejections rare; a patent may not issue in Japan for over a decade. However, issuance could occur in other countries, such as Belgium, where a patent may be granted in just a month after its filing; and,

- The same invention in both the foreign filing and U.S. filing must be involved. So long as the foreign patent contains the same claims as the U.S. application, there is no question as to the same invention. However, the inventions are considered the same even where the foreign application supports the subject matter of the U.S. claims.

United States Code, Title 35, Section 102(e)

A person shall be entitled to a patent unless (e) the invention was described in (1) an application for patent published under U.S.C., Title 35, Sec. 122(b) by another filed in the United States before the invention by the applicant for patent, except that an international application filed under the treaty defined in Sec. 351(a) shall have the effect under this subsection of a national application published under Sec. 122(b) only if the international application designating the United States was published under Article 21(2)(a) of treaty in the English language; or (2) a patent granted on an application for patent by another filed in the United States before the invention by the applicant for patent, except that a patent shall not be deemed filed in the United States for the purposes of this subsection based on the filing of an international application filed under the treaty defined in Sec. 351(a).

AMERICAN IVESTORS' PROTECTION ACT (AIPA)

The *American Inventors' Protection Act* (AIPA) amended U.S.C., Title 35, Sec. 102(e). This Act provides that U.S. patents, U.S. application publications, and certain international application publications can be used as prior art based on their earliest effective filing date against applications filed on or after November 29, 2000, and applications filed prior to November 29, 2000, that have been voluntarily published. Applications that were filed prior to November 29, 2000, and that were not voluntarily published, are subject to the older version of the statute.

U.S.C., Title 35, Sec. 102(e) was a complex piece of legislation even before the new revisions. With the new changes, this statute has become even more complex. Even patent attorneys and agents have great difficulty in understanding this one, and it is easy to understand why. However, if you break down the types of references that can be used against you as Sec. 102(e) prior art, then the statute can be understood.

For U.S.C., Title 35, Sec. 102(e) to apply, the reference must be a U.S. patent, a U.S. patent application publication, or an international application publication with a filing date earlier than the effective filing date of your application being examined.

There are really two important dates at play in the statute. First, there is the effective filing date of the Sec. 102(e) prior art reference which your examiner is trying to use against you. Your examiner would like this effective filing date to precede your date of invention.

The second big date is the date that you *conceive* and *reduce to practice* your invention. In other words, the second big date is your date of invention. Since your examiner does not know the actual date of your invention, your examiner will take this date to be the effective filing date of your own patent application.

Therefore, Sec. 102(e) rejections for examiners really involves comparing the effective filing date of the Sec. 102(e) reference with the effective filing date of your own application to see which one came first. For Sec. 102(e) to apply, the inventive entity of your application must be different from the reference. However, all that needs to be true for Sec. 102(e) to apply is for there to be one inventor who is different even if there are some common inventors between your application and the applied reference.

With this in mind, let's see how U.S.C., Title 35, Sec. 102(e) can apply to the various references which your examiner may use against you.

PUBLISHED U.S. PATENT APPLICATIONS

You will notice above that Sec. 102(e)(1) starts off by saying that you are not entitled to a patent if the invention was disclosed in a published application "filed in the United States before the invention by the applicant for patent."

Under this portion of the statute, as soon as a U.S. patent application is published, that patent application becomes eligible as Sec. 102(e) prior art. Its effective filing date for Sec. 102(e) prior art purposes is the U.S. filing date of that application. If this date is prior to your own application's effective filing date, your examiner has made a proper Sec. 102(e) rejection. Your only course of action in such a case will be to submit a 1.131 affidavit proving that your date of invention was earlier than your effective filing date and that it occurred before the effective filing date of the Sec. 102(e) reference.

As I said before, to determine if a reference is prior art under Sec. 102(e), you will need to know not only your date of invention but also the effective filing date of the reference. Lets look at some examples on how to determine the effective filing date of a Sec. 102(e) reference which your examiner seeks to use (I will assume that you know the invention date for your own invention).

Example 1: Competitor A files a 111(a) patent application (a U.S. regular application) on January 1, 2001, which is published under U.S.C., Title 35, Sec. 122(b) on July 1, 2002, eighteen months after its filing date. Under Sec. 102(e)(1), the published application is now a prior art reference. The effective filing date for prior art purposes is the earliest effective U.S. filing date, which is January 1, 2001. If the effective filing date for your own patent application is after January 1, 2001, the examiner has made a proper rejection.

Example 2: Competitor A files a Sec. 111(b) application (a U.S. provisional application) on January 1, 2000, and then a Sec. 111(a) application on January 1, 2001, claiming priority from the provisional application under Sec. 119(d). The 111(a) application is published on July 1, 2001. The effective filing date in this case is January 1, 2000.

PUBLISHED U.S. NATIONAL STAGE APPLICATIONS

A U.S. published application that claims priority back to a PCT application will have a Sec. 102(e) prior art date as of the date the PCT application was filed so long as the PCT application designates the U.S. and is published in English.

Example: Competitor A files an application on January 1, 1999, in a foreign country and then files a Sec. 111(a) application in the U.S. on December 31, 1999, claiming priority from the foreign application. Competitor A then files a second Sec. 111(a) application with a priority claim to the first U.S. application and published. The effective 102(e)(1) date of the publication is December 31, 1999, and not January 1,

> 1999. However, if the foreign application was a PCT application that designates the U.S and is published in English, then the effective filing date would indeed be January 1, 1999.

The publication of a U.S. national stage application will have a U.S.C., Title 35, Sec. 102(e) date for prior art purposes as of its international filing date provided that the application was published under PCT Article 21(2)(a) in the English language.

A U.S. application publication resulting from a U.S.C., Title 35, Sec. 371 application entitled to the benefit of the filing date of the provisional application will have a reference date as of the filing date of the provisional application under U.S.C., Title 35, Sec. 119(e) only if the international application was published in English pursuant to PCT Article 21(2)(a).

INTERNATIONAL APPLICATION (PCT) PUBLICATIONS

An international application is prior art under U.S.C., Title 35, Sec. 102(e) only if:

- the international application designated the United States;
- the international application was published under PCT Article 21(2)(a) in English;
- the international application was filed on or after November 29, 2000; and,
- the international application entered the national stage as to the United States. (MPEP Sec. 1857.01, 706.02(a), 2136.03.)

  NOTE: *For an application to enter the national stage, all the requirements for national stage entry such as a copy of the international application with any necessary translation, national fee and oath or declaration must be filed.*

An international application publication entitled to the filing date of a provisional application will have a reference date as of the filing date of the provisional application, but only if

- the international application designated the United States;
- the international application was published under PCT Article 21(2)(a) in English; and,
- the international application was filed on or after November 29, 2000, and the international application entered the national stage as to the U.S. (MPEP Sec. 706.02(a)).

U.S. PATENTS

102(e)(2) starts off by stating that you will not be entitled to a patent if there is another "patent granted on an application for patent by another filed in the United States before the invention by the applicant for patent." In other words, a U.S. patent has a Sec. 102(e) effective filing date for prior art purposes on the date that the patent was filed.

Since applications are usually published before they are patented, few references will qualify under this portion of the statute that do not also qualify under the portions already discussed. The only real time that your examiner may need to reach this portion of the statute to apply a Sec. 102(e) reference is where you have elected not to publish your application.

Sec. 102(e)(2) goes on to state "that a patent shall not be deemed filed in the United States for the purposes of this subsection based on the filing of an international application." Under this portion of the statute, a U.S. patent issuing from a national stage application will have no Sec. 102(e) prior art date at all. It would only be able to be used as a U.S.C., Title 35, Sec. 102 (a) or (b) reference where appropriate (MPEP Sec. 1893, 1896.)

OVERCOMING SEC. 102(E) REJECTIONS

Rejections based on Sec. 102(e) may be overcome by the following means:

- Argue that your rejected claim(s) are distinguishable from the prior art reference(s) or amend your rejected claim(s) to distinguish them from the prior art.

- File an affidavit or declaration under C.F.R., Title 37, 1.Sec. 132 showing that the referenced prior art invention is your own work and not "by another," just as you did under Sec. 102 (a).
- You can also file a Rule 130 declaration just as you would for a 102(a) rejection. Your oath or declaration under C.F.R., Title 37, Sec. 1.130 should state that your application and reference are currently owned by the same party. It should also state that the inventor named in the application is the prior inventor under U.S.C., Title 35, Sec. 104, together with a terminal disclaimer in accordance with C.F.R., Title 37, Sec. 1.321(c).
- File a Rule 1.131 affidavit/declaration showing that your invention date precedes the U.S. filing date of the PTO reference. To do this you must submit an oath or declaration alleging acts that establish a completion of the invention in this country before the effective date of the prior art. (C.F.R., Title 37, Sec. 1.131(a).)

Example: You conceive of a new invention in California on November 10, 1992, and work diligently to reduce your invention to practice on July 27, 1993. You file a patent application in the U.S. on July 12, 1994. The examiner rejects both of your claims on January 18, 1995. Your first claim is rejected as being anticipated under U.S.C., Title 35, Sec. 102(b) by a German patent filed on December 20, 1991, and issued on June 15, 1993.

Your second claim is rejected as anticipated under U.S.C., Title 35, Sec. 102(e) by a U.S patent filed on June 10, 1993, and issued October 4, 1994. Since the German patent issued on June 15, 1993, which is more than one year prior to your U.S. filling date of July 12, 1994, you cannot overcome the Sec. 102(b) rejection.

However, the Sec. 102(e) rejection *can* be overcome because your conception date, November 10, 1992, is before the U.S. patent filing date of June 10, 1993. In your response you should file an amendment canceling claim 1 and file an *ante-dating affidavit* proving that you conceived and diligently reduced it to practice prior to the U.S. filing date.

You should note that where the claims of the reference and your application are directed to the same invention, an affidavit or declaration under C.F.R., Title 37, Sec. 1.131 is not an acceptable method of overcoming your rejection. Under these circumstances, your examiner must determine whether a double patenting rejection or interference is appropriate. If there is a common assignee or inventor between your application and a patent, a double patenting rejection must be made. If there is no common assignee or inventor and the rejection under U.S.C., Title 35, Sec. 102(e) is the only possible rejection, your examiner must determine whether an interference should be declared. (MPEP Sec. 706.02(b).)

- Make any proper claim of priority back to an earlier filed application such as a foreign or provisional application which support the claims of your application. This will require you to either amend your specification, to contain a specific reference to your prior application, or file a new Application Data Sheet that contains a specific reference to your prior application. In the case of a priority claim back to an earlier foreign application, you would need to file a certified copy of the prior foreign application and if such application is not in English provide a translation.

  You are given a little bit of an advantage here. While you can reach back to a foreign priority application in order to antedate a Sec. 102(e) reference filing date, your examiner cannot use a foreign priority date in order to antedate your own effective filing date.

PROVISIONAL 35 USC 1029E) REJECTION

Claim [ ] provisionally rejected under U.S.C., Title 35, Sec. 102(e) as being anticipated by copending application no. [ ] which has a common [assignee or inventor] with the instant application. Based upon the earlier effective U.S. filing date of the co-pending application, it would constitute prior art under U.S.C., Title 25, Sec. 102(e) if published under U.S.C., Title 35, Sec. 122(b) or patented. This provisional rejection under U.S.C., Title 35, Sec. 102(e) is based upon a presumption of future publication or patenting of the co-pending application. This provisional rejection under U.S.C, Title 35, Sec.102(e) might be overcome either by a showing under C.F.R., Title 37, Sec. 1.132 that any invention disclosed but not claimed in the copending application was derived from the inventor of this application and is thus not the invention "by another," or by an appropriate showing under C.F.R., Title 37, Sec. 1.131. This rejection may not be overcome by the filing of a terminal disclaimer.

Note that it is possible for your examiner to make what is called a "provisional Sec. 102(e) rejection" even though the reference has not been published or issued as a patent. The examiner can do this only in the case of co-pending U.S. applications that have at least one common inventor or where the applications are commonly assigned.

This rejection is termed "provisional" because the reference that the examiner is using has not actually been published or patented so as to constitute 102(e) prior art under the statute. However, the examiner can still make a provisional rejection based upon a presumption of future publication or patenting of the co-pending application.

Author's Note

You may ask why can't the examiner also make a provisional rejection for co-pending applications that do not have a common inventor or assignee? The reason has to do with the confidential status of applications which you file with the PTO. If there are no common inventors or assignees, the PTO would not be able to divulge to you that there is another co-pending U.S. patent application that discloses subject matter that would anticipate your claims. The PTO would have to wait until such prior application becomes public knowledge as by publishing.

Overcoming Provisional Rejections

A provisional rejection can be overcome in any of the ways discussed above. A provisional rejection can also be overcome by abandoning the two applications and filing a new application containing the subject matter of both applications.

United States Code, Title 35, Section 102(f)

A person shall be entitled to a patent unless (f) he did not himself invent the subject matter sought to be patented.

Where it can be shown that you derived an invention from another person, then a rejection is made under Sec. 102(f). Derivation requires that someone *else* completely conceived the invention and communicated it to you before any date on which it can be shown that you had knowledge of the invention. The main focus of derivation is on the originality of the invention.

United States Code, Title 35, Section 102(g)

A person shall be entitled to a patent unless (g) before the applicant's invention therefor the invention was made in this country by another who had not abandoned, suppressed, or concealed it. In determining priority of invention there shall be considered not only the respective dates of conception and reduction to practice of the invention, but also the reasonable diligence of one who was first to conceive and last to reduce to practice, from a time prior to conception by the other.

U.S.C., Title 35, Sec. 102(g) bars the issuance of a patent where another person made your invention in the U.S. before you and that other person has not abandoned, suppressed, or concealed the invention. Sec. 102(g) is the basis of *interference practice*. Interference practice is a lengthy expensive proceeding that is beyond the scope of this book. If your patent application becomes involved in an interference, you will need to retain the assistance of a patent attorney who has experience in interference practice.

Sec. 102(g) has three main requirements;

1. The first requirement is that the prior art must be an invention that is made in the U.S.;

2. Second, the prior art invention must be made by someone other than you who has not abandoned, suppressed or concealed the invention. There are two types of suppression and concealment:

   - cases in which the inventor deliberately suppresses or conceals his invention and,
   - cases in which it is inferred that there is suppression or concealment because there was "too long" a delay in filing a patent application.

   Intentional suppression requires more than the passage of time. It requires evidence that the inventor intentionally delayed filing in order to prolong the period during which the invention is maintained in secret. There are no minimum or maximum periods necessary to establish an inference of suppression or concealment. The time elapsed is not the controlling factor, but rather the total conduct of the first inventor is considered.

3. The third requirement of Sec. 102(g) is that the prior art invention must be made at a time prior to your invention, considering the date of conception, and also the date of reduction to practice and the inventor's diligence in doing this.

You might be wondering whether you can overcome a U.S.C., Title 35, Sec. 102(g) rejection using a C.F.R., Title 37 Sec. 1.131 as you can when faced with rejections under Sec. 102(a) and 102(e) as above. The answer is *No*. The reason for this is that subject matter that is available under U.S.C., Title 35, Sec. 102(g) by definition must have been made before you made your invention. By contrast, references under U.S.C., Title 35, Sec. 102(a) and (e) merely establish a *presumption* that their subject matter was made before your invention date. It is this presumption that may be rebutted by evidence submitted under C.F.R., Title 37, Sec. 1.131.

Obviousness (35 U.S.C. Sec. 103(a))

A patent may not be obtained though the invention is not identically disclosed or described as set forth in section 102 of this title, if the difference between the subject matter sought to be patented and the prior art are such that the subject matter as a whole would have been obvious at the time the invention was made to a person having ordinary sill in the art to which the subject matter pertains. Patentability shall not be negatived by the manner in which the invention was made.

You will get the above rejection if your invention is thought to be an obvious one in light of the prior art. The PTO can take any reference that qualifies as prior art under any one of the 102 sections that we have looked at so far, combine it with any other 102 prior art reference(s), and then reject your claim(s) on the basis that such claim(s) are obvious with respect to the prior art references. This is stated in Section 103.

The following basic criteria must be met. (MPEP Sec. 706.02(J).)

- To support the conclusion that your claimed invention is directed to obvious subject matter, either the references must expressly or impliedly suggest your claimed invention or your examiner must present a convincing line of reasoning as to why the artisan would have found your claimed invention to have been obvious in light of the teachings of the references. (*Ex part Clapp*, 227 U.S.P.Q. 972 (Bd. Pat. App. & Inter. 1985).)

  If the proposed modification would render the prior art invention unsatisfactory for its intended purpose, then there is no suggestion or motivation to make the proposed modification, nad therefore it is not an *obvious* modification. (*In re Gordon*, 733 F.2d 900,(Fed. Cir. 1984).)

  Example: Joe claimed a new blood filter assembly device for use during medical procedures. In the device, the inlet and outlet for the blood were located at the bottom end of the filter assembly and a gas vent was present at the top of the assembly.

The examiner rejected Joe's claims based on a prior art reference which taught a liquid strainer for removing dirt and water from gasoline wherein the inlet and outlet were at the top of the device. The examiner thought it was obvious.

The court reversed, however, reasoning that if the prior art device was turned upside down it would be inoperable for its intended purpose because the gasoline to be filtered would be trapped at the top and water sought to be separated would flow out of the outlet instead of the purified gasoline. Therefore it was not an obvious invention.

- In order for it to be obvious, there must also be a reasonable expectation, at the time of the invention, that the modification or combination of the prior art references will be successful. (*Ex part Erlich*, 3 USPQ2d 1011 (Bd. Pat. App. & Inter. 1996).)
- The prior art reference (or combination of references if more than one is being used) must teach or suggest all your claim limitations.

NOTE: *If the product in a product-by-process claim is the same as or obvious from a product of the prior art, the claim is unpatentable even though the prior product was made by a different process.(In re* Thorpe, 777 F.2d 695 (Fed. Cir. 1985).)

One common scenario where obviousness exists (in the absence of new of unexpected results) is where an inventor merely changes the order of performing process steps. Differences in concentration or temperature will generally be obvious unless there is evidence indicating such concentration or temperature is critical.

OVERCOMING A REJECTION BASED ON OBVIOUSNES

Use any or all of the following lines of attack in order to overcome your Obviousness rejection.

- Argue that any one of the applied reference(s) do not qualify as prior art under any one of the 102 sections above that we have looked at. If such reference(s) do not constitute prior art under one of those sections, then your examiner is wrong to use it as a reference in an obviousness rejection against you.

In determining whether a particular reference constitutes prior art under one of the sections previously discussed, you should make sure that the cited references meet all of the criteria necessary to constitute prior art under the particular relevant section.

- If the prior art that your examiner is using against you is prior art under Sec. 102(e), 102(f) or 102(g), then you should note the following rule:

  If your invention and the referenced inventions were, at the time you made your invention, owned by the same person or subject to an obligation of assignment to the same person, then the references can not be considered as prior art under Sec. 102(e), 102(f) or 102(g) for 103 obvious use purposes (see U.S.C., Title 35, Sec. 103(c) and MPEP 706.01l).)

  Common ownership requires that the person(s) or organization(s) own 100 percent of the subject matter and 100 percent of the claimed invention at the time the claimed invention was made. (MPEP Sec. 706.02(l)(2).)

  The requirement for common ownership *at the time your claimed invention* was made is intended to preclude you from obtaining ownership of subject matter *after* the invention was made in order to disqualify that subject matter as prior art against your claimed invention.

  NOTE: *In situations where you file an application with joint inventors, your examiner will presume that the subject matter of your various claims was commonly owned at the time any inventions covered by such claims were made absent any evidence to the contrary. You have the duty to inform your examiner if this is not the case.*

- As with any U.S.C., Title 35, Sec. 102 rejection, you can point out or amend your claims to include an element not shown in any of the cited reference(s). This element may be a separate structural element, chemical component or step, or a novel relationship among other elements or steps of the claim.

To the extent that a rejected claim includes elements not found in the combination, your response should highlight the specific claim language that distinguishes the combination, and show why the undisclosed features, in combination with the rest of the claimed features, are significant in achieving the benefits of the invention.

You can make a special heading in your amendment/response entitled something like the following:

<u>The References Do Not fully Teach The Claimed Combination</u>

Under this section heading, you can then state something like the following:

even if the references were within the proper field of endeavor, an assertion which is strenuously traversed, the combined teaching of the cited references still fail to fully teach the invention recited herein.

You should then continue to argue why this is so.

- State that the references your examiner wants to apply against you do not come from analogous art, and therefore are not within the "scope and content of the prior art" as required by U.S.C., Title 35, Sec. 103(a).

  A reference is considered *analogous*, and, therefore, available for use in an obviousness rejection, if it is either

  - within the field of the inventor's endeavor or,
  - reasonably pertinent to the particular problem with which the inventor was involved. (*In re Deminski*, 796 F.2d 436 (Fed. Cir. 1986).)

  Example: In your remarks section your create the following title:

The Combination Draws Upon Non-Analogous Art References

You then state the following:

It is well settled that in order to combine references properly, each of the references must be relevant to the field of endeavor recited in the claimed invention or problem addressed by the invention. Such is clearly not the case with the cited references.

You then continue to explain why.

While PTO classification of your references and cross-references are some evidence of *nonanalogy* or *analogy*, the important factors to consider are the similarities and differences in structure and function of the inventions. (*In re Ellis*, 476 F.2d 1370, (C.C.P.A. 1978).)

- It may also be possible to attack a rejection based on a combination of references on the ground that nothing in the references themselves would suggest the combination. If the references are not each directed toward solving the same problem to which the invention is also directed, then the rejection should be withdrawn. The examiner must specifically explain where motivation to combine references comes from. This requires more than an allegation that the level of skill in the art is high. (*In re Rouffet*, 149 F.3d 1350 (Fed. Cir. 1998).)

  You could create a heading in your remarks section, entitled something like the following:

  The References Lack Suggestion to Combine

  You can then go on to state something like the following:

```
Of course, even if the references were from the
proper field of endeavor, and fully taught the
invention herein, there still must be some
affirmative teaching in the references to make
the cited combination. Such suggestion is
asserted to be lacking in the references cited
against the present claims.
```

You should then continue to explain why this is so.

Use any prior art disclosure that teaches away from, or discourages the making of your claimed invention. A reference *teaches away* when a person of ordinary skill, upon reading the reference, would be discouraged from following the path set out in the reference, or would be led in a direction divergent from the path that was taken by the applicant. (*In re Gurley*, 27 F.3d 551 (Fed. Cir. 1994).)

If you are lucky, you may find that one of the applied references has an explicit teaching against the combination proposed by the examiner. A contrary teaching may be explicit or implicit in the structure or purpose of one of the references. The proposed combination, for example, might disrupt the operation of the structure of one of the references or obstruct its intended result.

- Submit evidence of *secondary considerations*. Evidence of factors called "secondary considerations" indicates that your invention is not obvious. You can submit evidence of secondary consideration in a Sec. 1.132 affidavit/declaration.

  As was already discussed under 102(a), your declaration should consist of facts and not conclusions. Although you are allowed to make the affidavit yourself, an affidavit/declaration as to the advantages of your claimed invention will be more persuasive if it is made by a person with no vested interest in your invention. A form for a Sec. 1.132 declaration is contained in Appendix E.

(You will of course need to adapt this skeleton form to your own unique situation.)

The following are all secondary considerations that you should consider submitting evidence to show that any one of them is present in your case:

- *Unexpected results.* For example, if your claimed invention shows an additive result whereas a diminished result would have been expected based on a combination of the prior art, this is persuasive evidence that your invention is nonobvious

  Sometimes unexpected results can be shown through evidence of unobvious or unexpected advantageous properties of your claimed invention, or by showing that your claimed invention lacks a property that would have been expected to possess based on the teachings of the prior art.

- *Commercial success of your invention.* If your invention is highly sought after, then most likely it is something new and should be considered nonobvious.

  In considering evidence of commercial success, be careful to develop a link between the commercial success and your invention and not other extraneous factors such as heavy promotion or advertising. In other words, you must show that your claimed features were responsible for the commercial success of your invention. Merely showing that there was commercial success of an article that embodies your invention is not sufficient. This can be especially difficult in design cases. Evidence of commercial success must be clearly attributable to the design and not to brand name recognition or some other factor.

- *Skepticism by experts in your field that an invention like yours would work.*

- *Licensing of your invention.*

- *Copying of your invention by others.* More than the mere fact of copying is necessary to establish this factor because copying may be attributable to other factors such as someone's unconscientious or resentful attitude about patent protection. Evidence of copying is persuasive, however, where you can show an alleged infringer tried for a substantial length of time to design a product or process similar to your claimed invention, but failed and then copied your invention instead.
- *Long-felt need and failure of others.* Establishing this factor requires objective evidence that your art recognized that a problem existed in your art for a long period of time without solution. You must show three things;
  - First, you must show a need was a persistent one that was recognized by those of ordinary skill in your art.
  - Second, you must establish that the long-felt need was not satisfied by another before your invention.
  - Third, your invention must in fact satisfy the long-felt need.

13 How to Overcome Other Types of Rejections

In this chapter, we will look at some other common substantive rejections that are encountered in the prosecution of patent applications.

Rejections under United States Code, Title 35, Section 112, Second Paragraph

This statute contains two separate and distinct requirements:

- the claim(s) set forth the subject matter that you regard as your invention, and
- your claim(s) particularly point out and distinctly claim your invention.

Each of these requirements are discussed in the next two sections.

Failure to Claim Your Invention

Claim [ ] rejected under 35 U.S.C. sec. 112, second paragraph, as failing to set forth the subject matter which applicant(s) regard as their invention. Evidence that claim [ ] fail(s) to correspond in scope with that which applicant(s) regard as the invention can be found in Paper No. [ ] filed [ ]. In that paper, applicant has stated [ ], and this statement indicates that the invention is different from what is defined in the claim(s) because [ ].

You will receive this rejection if you have stated somewhere other than in your application as filed, that your invention is something different from what is defined in your claim(s). This is not a common rejection. So do not make it any more common by stating that your invention is something other than what you have claimed.

INDEFINITE CLAIMS. *Claim(s) (your claim #s that are being rejected) rejected under 35 U.S.C. sec. 112, second paragraph, as being indefinite for failing to particularly point out and distinctly claim the subject matter which applicant regards as the invention.*

You will get this rejection if you have claims in your application that are not definite. Following the above language, the examiner will state why he or she regards your claim as indefinite. The primary purpose of the definiteness requirement is to ensure that the scope of your claims are clear so the public is informed of the boundaries of what constitutes infringement later on.

The following are common reasons why your claims could be considered indefinite:

- You may have used a term in your claim that is contrary to the usual meaning of that term. Due to potential confusion, you are not allowed to use a meaning of a term that *is different* from the usual meaning of that term.
- You have included a process claim, but have not set forth any steps involved in the process. (You need to set forth positive "ing" steps for your process claim.)
- You use indefinite claim language. One such phrase is "such as." This is considered indefinite because it is unclear whether the limitations following the phrase are merely exemplary of your claim or a required feature of your claim. The same is true for phrase like "for example."

- You use a trademark to identify or describe a particular material or produce. (A trademark is used to identify a source of goods, and can not be used to identify the goods themselves.)

You should review Chapter 5 on drafting your claims if you have questions as to how to write definite claims. Fortunately, these types of rejections should not be a problem for you to overcome. All you need to do is to submit an amendment in which your claims are rewritten using more definite language.

New Matter Rejections under United States Code, Title 35, Section 132

The amendment filed is objected to under U.S.C., Title 35, sec. 132 because it introduces new matter into the disclosure. U.S.C., Title 35, sec. 132 states no amendment shall introduce new matter into the disclosure of the invention. The added material that is not supported by the original disclosure is as follows [identification where the new matter is in your specification].

This type of objection can arise when you amend your application and add something that was not present in your original specification. Once you submit your oath or declaration identifying the papers that you have reviewed and understand, the original disclosure of your application is said to be "defined," and you can not thereafter alter it.

The addition of new matter is defined very inclusively by the PTO. For example, if in your original written description you state a range 10–20%, you can not latter change your description by stating "15%" since your have altered your description by changing the broad range to a specific range. Even the latter deletion of a step in a method will be considered by the PTO as new matter.

There are really two ways that the PTO objects to the addition of new matter. If the new matter does not concern your claims, then the issue is treated using the new matter objection above. On the other hand, if the new matter involves your claims, the PTO rejects your claims based on the written description requirement that is covered in the next section.

If the new matter affects both your claims and other parts of your specification, then both an objection above and rejection of your claims is made.

The following circumstances should not be considered new matter.

- *Rephrasing.* Rewording of a passage in your specification where the same meaning remains intact is permissible.
- *Correction of obvious errors.* An amendment to correct an obvious error in your specification does not constitute new matter where one skilled in the art would not only recognize the existence of the error in the specification, but also the appropriate correction.

Overcoming New Matter Rejections

The easiest way to overcome an objection or rejection based on new matter is to make an amendment deleting what the PTO considers as new matter.

The harder way to deal with the objection is to argue that you have not added new matter. To argue against the PTO you must show how your additions already existed in some part of your application as filed.

A rejection of your claims is reviewable by the *Board of Patent Appeals and Interference.* However, an objection and requirement to delete new matter from other parts of your specification is subject to supervisory review by petition under C.F.R., Title 37, Sec. 1.181. If both an objection and rejection are made, the issue is appealable and should not be decided by petition. (MPEP Secs. 608.04 and 706.03(o).)

Rejections under United States Code, Title 35, Section 112, First Paragraph

Written Description

Claim [ ] rejected under U.S.C., Title 35, Sec. 112, first paragraph, as the specification does not contain a written description of the claimed invention, in that the disclosure does not reasonably convey to one skilled in the relevant art that the inventor(s) had possession of the claimed invention at the time the application was filed.

The *written description requirement* is the first of three requirements under the first paragraph of U.S.C., Title 35, Sec. 112. The second and third requirements, "enablement" and "best mode" will be discussed in the next two sections.

The written description requirement prevents you from claiming subject matter that was not described in your application as filed. In fact, it prevents you from doing anything to your claims that are not supported by your written description in your application.

The essential goal of the written description requirement is to clearly convey the subject matter that an applicant has invented. The requirement for an adequate disclosure ensures that the public receives something in return for the exclusionary rights that are granted to you by a patent.

To satisfy the written description requirement, a patent specification must describe the claimed invention in sufficient detail that one skilled in the art can reasonably conclude that the applicant had possession of the claimed invention. An applicant shows possession of the claimed invention by describing the invention with all of its limitations using such descriptive means as words, structures, figures, diagrams, and formulas that fully set forth the invention.

Possession can be shown by describing an actual reduction to practice of your invention. A specification may describe an actual reduction to practice by showing that the inventor constructed an embodiment or performed a process that met all the limitations of the claim and determined that the invention would work for its intended purpose.

Possession can also be shown by showing that your invention was "ready for patenting" such as by the disclosure of drawings or structural chemical formulas that show your invention was complete, or by describing distinguishing identifying characteristics sufficient to show that you were in possession of your claimed invention.

Author's Note

As discussed earlier, a means-plus-function claim under U.S.C., Title 35, Sec. 112, must be interpreted to cover the corresponding struture, materials, or acts in the specification or equivalents thereof. A means-plus-function claim limitation is adequately described for written description purposes if your specification adequately links or associates adequately described particular structure, material, or acts to the function recited in your means-plus-function claim limitation. It is also adequately described if is clear, based on the facts of your application, that one skilled in your art would have known what structure, material, or acts perform the function recited in the means-plus-function limitation.

Written description rejections are most common in the more unpredictable arts like biology and chemistry. This is because where an art is more unpredictable, the PTO will require a better disclosure to show that you were in possession of your invention as claimed. For inventions in emerging and unpredictable technologies, or for inventions characterized by factors not reasonably predictable that are known to one of ordinary skill in the art, more evidence is required to show possession of the invention.

Example: A claim to a gene will usually require that you have sequenced the gene to show possession. You would not, for example, be able to claim the gene and show possession merely by stating that the gene codes for some particular protein. This is because a gene is a chemical compound and conception of a chemical compound requires that you be able to define it so as to distinguish it from other materials, and describe how to obtain it.

Problems with the written description requirement arise in the following scenarios.

- ***New or amended claims.*** This is the most common situation. You add or amend one of your claims after you file your application and the PTO rejects your new or amended claims on the basis that such claims are not supported by the description of your invention in the application that you filed. Newly added claim limitations must be supported in your specification through express, implicit, or inherent disclosure. Thus if you amend a claim to include subject matter, limitations, or terminology not present in your application as filed, involving a departure from, addition to, or deletion from your disclosure as filed, your examiner will conclude that your claimed subject matter is not described in your application.

  Sometimes an amendment to your specification can indirectly affect your claim, even though your amendment is not directly to the claim, thereby triggering a written description rejection. This could happen, for example, where you change the definition of a term in your specification, thereby affecting the old definition of the term that was used in your claim.

- ***Original claims.*** Sometimes your original claims as filed in your original application may be rejected on the basis that persons skilled in the art would not recognize in your disclosure a description of your invention as defined in your original claims. This is somewhat less common than when you file new or amended claims because the claims that you file in your original application are part of your disclosure. There is a also presumption that if a claim was in your patent application as filed, then the invention covered by that claim is within the "written description" provided in the application as filed. (*In re Anderson*, 471 F.2d 1237, (C.C.P.A. 1973).)

Author's Note

The rule that your original claims are part of your original disclosure means that if your examiner rejects any of your claim(s) on the basis that there is no support for the claim in your written description, you should always look to see whether the written support which you need can be found in any of your original claim(s) that you filed. If you can find the subject matter that you need in your original claims, you should be able to amend your application so as to include this subject matter in your written description. This is because your original claims are part of your original disclosure.

- ***Entitlement to an earlier priority date.*** Written description problems can also arise when you make a claim of priority to an earlier application that you filed. This can happen when you make a claim of priority under U.S.C., Title 35, Sec. 120 to the filing date of an earlier filed U.S. application, to the filing date of a provisional application under U.S.C., Title 35, Sec. 119(e) or to the filing date of a foreign application under U.S.C., Title 35, Sec. 119(a). To be entitled to such an earlier priority date, your claims must be supported by the description of the invention in such earlier filed application.

- ***Inteference.*** As stated before, interference practice is beyond the scope of this book. But I will just mention here that written description problems can also arise in this contest. The issue is whether your specification provides support for a claim corresponding to a count in the inteference.

The following cases are also common fact patterns where a lack of written description has been found to exist.

- An element that you described in your disclosure as essential or critical to your invention does not appear in your claim. Earlier in the book we discussed the need to be careful of emphasizing the criticality of any features of your invention unless such features were truly critical to the operation of your invention. Now you understand the rationale.

Example: Anne's written description in her originally filed application described the location of a claim element, "the control means" as the only possible location for such control means. Anne would not be able to claim her invention with the control means in a different location. (*Gentry Gallery*, 134 F.3d 1473 (Fed. Cir. 1998).)

NOTE: *A claim that omits matter disclosed to be essential to the invention as described in the specification may also be subject to a rejection under the enablement requirement discussed below.*

- You claim a genus but do not describe enough representative species of that genus.

You can think of a *genus* as a large circle and a species as a small circle within that genus. In general, a genus includes no more material elements then those that are included in the species which make up the genus.

OVERCOMING REJECTIONS BASED ON WRITTEN DESCRIPTION

Your examiner has the initial burden of presenting a preponderance of evidence why a person skilled in your art would not recognize in your disclosure a description of the invention defined by your claims.

To overcome a rejection after your examiner has met his or her initial burden, you must either point out where and how your originally filed written description supports the changes made to your claim(s) or else make an amendment to your rejected claim(s) so as to eliminate the material that the PTO finds objectionable.

ENABLEMENT

Claim [ ] rejected under U.S.C., Title 35, Sec. 112, first paragraph, as containing subject matter which was not described in the specification in such a way as to enable one skilled in the art to which its pertains, or with which it is most nearly connected, to make and/or use the invention.

Or

Claims (PTO inserts one or more of your claims) rejected under U.S.C., Title 35, Sec. 112, first paragraph, because the specification, while being enabling for (PTO inserts claimed subject matter for which your specification is enabling), does not reasonably provide enablement for (PTO inserts your claims). The specification does not enable any person skilled in the art to which it pertains, or with which it is most nearly connected, to make and use the invention commensurate in scope with these claims.

If you see either of the above paragraphs in your office action, your claims have been rejected for lack of enablement. The first paragraph above will be used by your examiner when it is your examiner's position that nothing within the scope of your claims is enabled. The second paragraph form will be used when it is your examiner's position that something within the scope of your claims is enabled, but your claims are not limited in scope to what is enabled. (See Chapter 2 for additional information on enablement.)

LACK OF ESSENTIAL FEATURES

Claim [ ] rejected under U.S.C., Title 35, Sec. 112, first paragraph, as based on a disclosure which is not enabling. [recited subject matter omitted form your claims] critical or essential to the practice of the invention, but not included in the claim(s) is not enabled by the disclosure.

Your examiner may also reject any of your claim(s) where any feature considered critical or essential to the practice of your claim invention is missing from your claim(s). Such essentiality will be determined by looking at your specification and looking to see if you have recited any feature as being critical to the practice of your claims. Again, you must be very careful about emphasizing the criticality of any feature of your invention.

Example: Where the only mode of operation of a process disclosed by Joe in the specification involved the use of a cooling zone at

> a particular location in the processing cycle, the examiner made a proper rejection of Joe's claims because they failed to specify either a cooling step or the location of the step in the process. (*In re Mayhew*, 527 F.2d 1229 (C.C.P.A. 1976).)

Depositing Biological Materials. *MPEP Sec. 2402, paragraph 1 states that "where the invention involves a biological material and words alone cannot sufficiently describe how to make and use the invention in a reproducible manner, access to the biological material may be necessary for the satisfaction of the requirement for patentability under U.S.C., Title 35, Sec.112."*

Thus, a deposit of biological material is necessary when the material is essential for the practice of the invention and

- the material is not known and readily available to the public or,
- when the material cannot be made or isolated without undue experimentation.

If an application as filed includes sequence information and references a deposit of the sequenced material made in accordance with the requirements of C.F.R., Title 37, beginning with Section 1.801, corrections of minor errors in the sequence may be possible based on the argument that one of skill in the art would have resequenced the deposited material and would have immediately recognized the minor error.

It may also be useful to deposit essential biological materials if the material is only referred to in a publication, but is not commercially available. MPEP Sec. 2404.01 states that "those applicants that rely on evidence of accessibility other than a deposit take the risk that the patent may no longer be enforceable if the biological material necessary to satisfy the requirements of U.S.C., Title 35, Sec. 112 ceases to be accessible." If at some point during the patent term the material becomes unavailable and cannot be obtained without undue experimentation, the patent would become unenforceable.

You must also make reference to your biological deposit in your specification by indicating

- the name and address of the depositary institution with which the deposit was made;
- the date of deposit of the biological material with that institution;
- the accession number given to the deposit by that institution; and,
- to the extent possible, a taxonomic description of the biological material.

Computer Programs. While no specific universally applicable rule exists for recognizing an insufficiently disclosed application involving computer programs, the failure to include either the computer program itself or a reasonably detailed flowchart that delineates the sequence of operations the program must perform are subject to challenge by your examiner.

Moreover, as the complexity of functions and the generality of the individual components of a flowchart increase, the basis for challenging the sufficiency of such a flowchart becomes more reasonable because the likelihood of more than routine experimentation being required to generate a working program from such a flowchart also increase. (MPEP Sec. 2106.02.)

Overcoming Enablement Rejections

Once your examiner has advanced a reasonable basis to question the adequacy of your disclosure, you must show that your specification would enable one of ordinary skill in the art to make and use your claimed invention without resorting to undue experimentation. This will involve making arguments as to why your specification is enabling based on what has been said about enablement above. You may also want to reference prior art patents or technical publications and explain how these materials show that your specification is enabling.

You should also consider submitting a *factual affidavit/declaration* under C.F.R., Title 37, Sec. 1.132 to show what one skilled in the art knew at the time your filed your application. (See Chapter 12 for a discussion of these affidavits.) Your Sec. 1.132 affidavit will be more convincing if it is made by someone other than yourself. It should be made by a person who has a skill level and qualifications that is routine in your art. If the level of skill is too high, your examiner may challenge the affidavit since it would not help in determining the amount of experimentation required by a routineer in the art to implement your invention.

Your affiant should submit as many facts as possible and show how these facts support the argument that your invention is enabling. Concentrate on the factors above and see what evidence you can include to argue those factors in your favor. Mere conclusions by your affiant/declarant will not be persuasive.

The state of the art existing at the filing date of your application is used to determine whether a particular disclosure is enabling as of your filing date. Therefore, publications dated after your filing date providing information publicly first disclosed after your filing date generally cannot be used to show what was known at the time you filed your application. (MPEP Sec. 2164.05(a).)

Although a later dated publication cannot supplement an insufficient disclosure in a prior dated application to make it enabling, you can offer the testimony of an expert based on the publication as evidence of the level of skill in the art at the time you filed your application. (*Gould v. Quigg*, 822 F.2d 1074 (Fed. Cir. 1987).)

Although you must demonstrate that your disclosure, as filed, would have enabled your claimed invention for one skilled in the art at the time of filing, this does not preclude you from providing a declaration after your filing date that demonstrates your claimed invention works (MPEP Sec. 2164.05(a).)

BEST MODE

Claim [ ] rejected under U.S.C., Title 35, Sec. 112, first paragraph, because the best mode contemplated by the inventor has not been disclosed. Evidence of concealment of the best mode is based upon [ ].

Rejections based on the *best mode requirement* are rare in the prosecution of your application. This is because the information that is necessary to form the basis for a rejection is rarely accessible to your examiner, but is generally uncovered during discovery procedures in litigation. One case where this rejection could arise is where the quality of your disclosure is so poor as to effectively result in concealment.

UTILITY REJECTIONS UNDER UNITED STATES CODE, TITLE 35, SEC. 101

LACK OF UTILITY

Whoever invents or discovers any new and useful process, machine, manufacture, or composition of matter or any new and useful improvement thereof, may obtain a patent therefore, subject to the conditions and requirements of this title.

The above is a quotation from U.S.C., Title 35, Sec. 101. We already touched upon the fact, back in Chapter 2, that your invention has to have some practical use or "utility" in order to be patentible. Where you have made no explicit mention in your specification of how your invention might have some practical application and none can be inferred from the nature of your invention, then a rejection based on lack of utility is likely.

OVERCOMING REJECTIONS BASED ON LACK OF UTILITY

You can overcome a rejection based on lack of utility in two main ways. First, you can argue that your invention has utility in your response. Under this option you are arguing that the PTO is just plain wrong about their assertion that your invention lacks any practical value. The best way to argue this is to point out in your specification where you have stated some practical application of your invention since you only need one such assertion to show utility. If you have made no mention of practicality, then you might argue that your invention has a well established utility.

Your second option to overcome a utility rejection is to amend your application so that you state a practical application of your invention. (For more information on amending your application, see Chapter 10.)

You can also submit an affidavit/declaration under C.F.R., Title 37, Sec. 1.132 so as to present new evidence that shows that your invention has utility. Your new evidence must be relevant to the issues raised in your rejection. For example, declarations in which conclusions are set forth without establishing a link between the conclusions and the supporting evidence, or that merely express opinions, may be of limited value in rebutting your examiner's case.

DOUBLE PATENTING REJECTIONS

Claim [your claim] rejected under U.S.C., Title 35, 101 as claiming the same invention as that of claim [relevant claim] of prior U.S. Patent No. [ ]. This is a double patenting rejection.

Double patenting was discussed back in Chapter 10 and prevents you from trying to extend patent protection on your invention by trying to file a second patent application for the same invention. An interference is a proceeding that is conducted at the PTO to determine who is the first inventor of a claimed invention.

Example: If Rob submits a patent application claiming Invention X and Bob submits a patent application claiming Invention X, the proper course of action is an interference proceeding.

SAME INVENTION TYPE REJECTIONS

Double patenting rejections seek to prevent any person from unjustly extending the patent term over a claimed invention by trying to patent the invention twice. There are two types of double patenting rejections. The first type that is the subject of this section is called a *same invention* type double patenting rejection. Same invention type double patenting is also sometimes called *statutory double patenting* because it is based on U.S.C., Title 35, 101 which states that you may only obtain a patent for any new or useful invention.

The test to determine whether a statutory basis for double patenting exists is whether the same invention is being claimed twice by either the same inventive entity or by an entity that has at least one common inventor or by an entity which has a common assignee. "Same invention" means identical subject matter.

Statutory double patenting rejections can be made in your application with respect to an issued patent or with respect to another pending patent application. In the case of double patenting rejections with two pending applications, your examiner will give provisional double patenting rejections in each of the applications.

OVERCOMING STATUTORY REJECTIONS

You can overcome a statutory type double patenting by canceling the conflicting claims in all but one of your applications or by amending your conflicting claims in one application so that they are not the same as the other application.

OBVIOUS-TYPE REJECTION

Claim [your claim] rejected under the judicially created doctrine of obviousness-type double patenting as being unpatentable over claim [relevant claim] of U.S. Patent No. [ ]. Although the conflicting claims are not identical, they are not patentibly distinct from each other because [reasons].

This is the second type of double patenting rejection that you can receive. *Obviousness-type double patenting* is a judicially created doctrine based on the rationale that the public should be able to freely use not only the invention claimed in a patent after the expiration of its term but also on modifications that would have been obvious to those of ordinary skill in the art at the time the invention was made.

The purpose of the rule against double patenting is to prevent an inventor from effectively extending the term of exclusivity by the subsequent patenting of variations that are not patentably distinct from the first-patented invention.

A rejection based on non statutory double patenting is based on a judicially created doctrine grounded in public policy so as to prevent the unjustified or improper timewise extension of the right to exclude granted by a patent. (*In re Goodman,* 11 F.3d 1046 (Fed. Cir. 1993).)

OVERCOMING OBVIOUS-TYPE REJECTION A

The easiest way to overcome a rejection based on a nonstatutory type double patenting rejection (obvious-type) is by filing what is called a *terminal disclaimer.* A terminal disclaimer is a statement in which you give up that portion of time on a patent to issue so that it will end at the same time as the patent being used as the reference for double patenting.

The terminal disclaimer must cover all of your claims in your application. A terminal disclaimer form that you can use to obviate a double patenting rejection over a prior patent is listed in Appendix E. The PTO website also has another form that you can use to obviate a provisional double patenting rejection over a pending second application.

A terminal disclaimer provision under C.F.R., Title 37, Sec. 1.321 must include the following provision:

"any patent granted on that application shall be enforceable only for and during such period that said patent is commonly owned with the application or patent which formed the basis for the rejection." (MPEP Sec. 1490.)

Author's Note

It is not appropriate for your examiner to issue a double patenting rejection against a divisional application that you later filed on an invention which your examiner required you to take out of your original filed patent application due to a restriction requirement. If you are up against such a double patenting requirement in your divisional application, you should point out to your examiner that U.S.C., Title 35, Section 121 prohibits this.

Abandonment of Your Application

The application is abandoned in view of applicant's failure to submit a response to the office action mailed on [date] within the required period for response.

Abandonment is not something that you like to see happen during the course of your prosecution. Abandonment means essentially that your application has died and the PTO has taken it out of the examination process. Abandonment is not a rejection of your application for some statutory reason. However, I have included it in this chapter under other types of rejections because as with a statutory rejection, you will need to take action to deal with a *Notice of Abandonment* if you want a patent.

There are many reasons that you may get an abandonment notice. The most common reason, of course, is that you have failed to respond to an office action within the statutory six month requirement. Recall that you are allowed to take extensions of time to respond to an office action, but that the cut-off date is six months from the mailing date of the action. After that time, your application will go abandoned, and the PTO will notify you of this in a notice of abandonment (Form PTOL-1432) with language similar to the above.

Overcoming a Notice of Abandonment

You have several options to overcome a notice of abandonment of your application. If you think the PTO is wrong in its holding of abandonment, you can file a petition under C.F.R., Title 37, 1.181(a) to withdraw the holding of abandonment. This may occur where you disagree as to the dates used by your examiner in determining that your application became abandoned. There is no fee for this petition, but you must file it within two months from the mail date of your notice of abandonment. If your petition is granted, your application is considered to never have been abandoned. (MPEP Sec. 711.03(c).)

A second option that you have at your disposal is to simply file a new patent application. Such an application is referred to as a *substitute application* because it is not filed while your prior application is still alive; thus it is not *copending* as with a continuation. The problem with filing a substitute application is that you loose the effective filing date of your earlier filed application which could cause difficulties with any prior art.

A third option, and more ordinary course of action to overcome a notice of abandonment, is to file a petition to revive your application along with the appropriate fee.

Reviving an Abandoned Application

There are two ways to revive an abandoned application. The first way is on the basis that your *delay* was *unavoidable. Unavoidable* means that something occurred beyond your control. This is a less common way to revive your abandoned application because it requires you to do more.

The second way to revive your abandoned patent application is on the basis that your *delay was unintentional*. This is the more usual way that one goes about reviving an abandoned patent application. It is easier to do than on the basis your delay was unavoidable. However, it does cost more.

Whether you choose to revive based on unavoidable or unintentional delay, you must include a petition and a petition fee. This is set forth in C.F.R., Title 37, Sec. 1.17(l) if you are claiming unavoidable delay or in C.F.R., Title 37, Sec. 1.137(b) if you are claiming unintentional delay.

If your petition for revival is based on unavoidable delay, you must submit evidence proving that your abandonment was unavoidable. Such unforeseen circumstances, like your office action never having been sent to you (due to some problem with the mail), could be used by you to show that your abandonment was unavoidable.

Delay resulting from things like lack of knowledge of the patent statute or the MPEP, however, cannot serve as a basis for unavoidable delay. (MPEP Sec. 711.03(c).) You will need to show not only that the delay that resulted in abandonment of your application was unavoidable, but also unavoidable delay from the time you were notified of abandonment to the time you file your petition to revive.

Obtaining a revival of your application based on unintentional delay is much easier than based on unavoidable delay. Filing your petition is also easier. If your petition for revival is based on unintentional delay, you need only state that your delay was unintentional. You should include the statement that "the entire delay in filing the required reply from the due date for the reply until the filing of a grantable petition pursuant to C.F.R., Title 37, Sec. 1.137(b) was unintentional." (A petition that you can use for unavoidable delay is contained in the MPEP at Sec. 711.03(c).)

The PTO does not generally question whether your delay is unintentional so long as you file your petition within three months of the date you are first notified that your application is abandoned. It also should be filed within one year of the date of abandonment of your application. So it is to your advantage to file your petition as soon as possible after your notice of abandonment.

If you file your petition to revive more than three months from the date of your notice of abandonment, you should include a showing as to how such delay was unintentional. If your petition is not filed within one year of the date of abandonment of your application, you will also need to submit information as to when you first became aware of the abandonment of your application and a showing as to how the delay in discovering the abandoned status of the application occurred despite the exercise of due care or diligence on your part.

You must also include a complete and proper reply to the outstanding office action deal that you failed to respond to resulting in the abandonment of your application. This reply is usually in the form of an amendment. However, your reply can also be satisfied by filing a continuation or *Request for Continued Examination.*

If your abandoned application is a design application or a utility or plant application filed before June 8, 1995, you will also need to file a terminal disclaimer and pay a fee as set forth in Sec. 1.321 where you give up any term of your patent that is equivalent to the period of abandonment of your application. In the event that this rule applies to you, you can find terminal disclaimer forms in the MPEP at Sec. 711.03(c).

You should use Form (PTO/SB/64) as your petition to revive your application. This form is listed in Appendix E and can also be obtained from the PTO website. You must include a cover letter entitled "Petition to Revive" with your petition.

If you are unhappy with a decision of the PTO to revive your application, you should make a request for reconsideration within twelve months from the date of the decision.

You should mail your petition to the following address:

Assistant Commissioner for Patents
Box DAC
Washington, D.C. 20231

Conclusion

If you have made it this far I congratulate you on a job well done. Patent law, as I have said, is not an easy subject, but I truly believe that inventors are in the best position to understand the technology of their own inventions. All they need is a little help understanding patent law and to this end I hope my book has helped you.

If you have found my book useful in the prosecution of your patent or have questions or comments about my book, please let me know. I can be reached at my website, **www.Ypatent.com**. This site also contains useful links to patent sites as well as other sites of interest. I hope you will check it out.

In addition to my website, I hope that you will consider taking a look at my new companion book, entitled *Protect Your Patent* by Sphinx Publishing. Due to publish in late summer of 2003, the book takes a look at how best to protect your patent after it issues, as well as how to to maximize the financial profits from your invention.

GLOSSARY

A

abandoned application. An application that is removed from the PTO docket of pending applications either (a) through formal abandonment by the applicant, attorney or agent of record, (b) through failure of applicant to take appropriate action at some state in the prosecution of the application, or (c) for failure to pay the issue fee, or (d) in the case of a provisional application, automatically after twelve months after the filing date of the provisional application.

advisory action. A form sent to you in response to your reply to a final office action from the PTO. This action will advise you of the disposition of your reply and why your application is still not in condition for allowance.

allowed application. An application which, having been examined, is passed to issue as a patent, subject to payment of the issue fee.

amendment. Opportunity to make changes to either your claims or specification outside your claims, as well as arguments, in order to try to bring your application into condition for allowance.

antecedent basis. If you fail to expressly define a term or if the term does not have an inherent meaning, you are not allowed to introduce the term in your claim by using the word "said" since your term is undefined.

anticipation. Art term used to describe a reference which teaches each and every element of your claimed invention.

application data sheet. A sheet which contains information about your patent application. One of the important parts of information which it can contain is any claims of priority that you make to previously filed domestic or foreign applications.

B

body of claim. The portion of your claim which contains the elements or limitations of your invention.

C

continuation application. A second or even later filed application covering the same invention for which you previously filed a patent application. By filing a continuation, you maintain the ability to change the scope of your claims in case a cunning competitor is successful in designing around your claims of your issued patent.

continuation-in-part application(CIP). CIPs are applications which are filed later so as to include new matter to your specification which was not included in your originally filed application.

D

declaration. A statement that warns you about willful false statements.

dependent claim. A claim that refers back and further restricts a single preceding claim.

design patent application. Type of application that protects the ornamental appearance of something. It is one of three types of patent applications, the others being utility and plant patent applications.

docket number. A number that you create to identify your application.

double-patenting. There are two types of double-patenting. The first is based on U.S.C., Title 35, Sec. 101, which says that you are entitled to only a patent. This requirement has been interpreted by courts to mean that you cannot claim the same invention twice. You are not allowed, for example, to file a patent application for invention X and then several years down the road file a new patent application for invention X.

A second type of double-patenting is a so called "judicial type," which prohibits you from not only claiming the same invention later, but also from claiming any inventions that are obvious from the one you previously claimed in a patent application.

divisional application. These types of applications are often filed after you receive a "restriction requirement" in an office communication from the PTO. You file your non-elected inventions in separate divisional applications.

E

effective filing date. This date can be critical for you to know to determine whether your invention is novel. It is also important in determining the date from when your patent term will run. The effective filing date of your application is usually the date on which you file your patent application. However, if you have filed previous applications before on your same application, your effective filing date will be the earliest U.S. filing date so long as you have made a claim of priority back to such earliest filed U.S. application.

enablement requirement. A statute requirement that demands your patent application teach one skilled in your art how to make and use your claimed invention.

extension of time. You can buy these in packages of up to five months in order to extend the time that you need to reply to an office action from the PTO.

F

filing date. This is the date you get when you file your patent application containing your specification, at least one claim, and any required drawings. You do not need all components of a completed application to obtain a "filing date." When everything is complete, you will receive a "filing receipt."

filing receipt. You obtain this from the PTO when your application is complete.

final rejection. This is a second or subsequent office action which you may receive from your examiner which basically tells you that your examiner rejects your claims and wants to close your file. Your options after a final rejection become more limited.

foreign filing license. Your filing receipt, that you get back from the PTO after you file your patent application, will usually have the words "foreign filing license granted" on the form. A foreign filing license is a prerequisite before you file a foreign application for your invention, if your invention was made here in the U.S. If you fail to obtain this license before your foreign file, the consequence can be loss of patent rights here in the U.S.

I

incomplete application. An application lacking some of the essential parts and not accepted for filing by the PTO.

incorporation-by-reference. Instead of reciting all the information contained in a reference that you want to include in your specification, you are allowed to incorporate various types of references into your specification. The material which you incorporate-by-reference becomes as much a part of your specification as if you had written the material directly into your specification.

information disclosure statement (IDS). You fulfill your duty to let the PTO know about anything material to the patentability of your invention by completing an IDS. If you neglect to fulfill this duty, your any patent which you later obtain may be held unenforceable.

infringement. Term relates to litigation concerning your patenting invention rather than to prosecution.

interview. An appearance before your examiner for purposes of advancing your application towards allowance.

inventor. The person who has made any contribution to the conception of your claimed invention.

issue fee. A fee which you must pay after your application is allowed in order for you to be issued a patent. This fee is due three months from the date of your notice of allowance.

M

means-plus-function claim. A style of claim format which uses the word "means" followed by a specified function. Look to the specification to determine what types of "means" carries out the specified function.

multiple-dependent claim. A claim which depends on more than one claim. As with a dependent claim, a multiple-dependent claim must further restrict the claims on which it depends.

N

new matter. When you file your patent application you have set the disclosure for your invention. If you try to add any new material to your patent application later on that new material will probably be considered new matter. You are not allowed to add new matter to your application.

notice of allowability. This form means that your examiner has allowed all of your claims and that your patent application is ready to be issued.

notice of appeal. If you disagree with the reasoning of your examiner, you have the option of filing this form to the Board of Patent Appeals and Interferences.

O

oath. A notarized statement.

obviousness. A patent term of art used to describe the combination of prior art references to anticipate your invention even though no one of the prior art references alone anticipates your invention.

office action. A written communication which you receive from the PTO concerning your patent application.

ordinary skill in the art. This refers to the level of skill which would be possessed by a person employed in the technology of the invention.

P

Patent Cooperation Treaty (PCT). The PCT allows you to file one international application in which you designate all those countries which you want to seek patent protection.

patent term adjustment. There are many situations where the PTO will add extra days, months or even years to your patent term. The PTO does this by making an adjustment to your patent term.

patent and trademark office (PTO). The administrative agency charged with handling your application for a patent.

petition to make special. A petition which you can submit to the PTO in order to speed up examination of your patent application. You or your invention must fall into one of the categories of persons which serves as the basis for such a petition.

preamble. The introductory portion of your claim. A preamble typically starts with the article "A" or "An."

preliminary amendment. An amendment that is received by the PTO on or before the mail date of your first office action. (MPEP sec. 714.01(c).)

prior art. An art term used to describe reference(s) which meet the criteria set forth in any one of the prior art sections of U.S.C., Title 35, sec. 102. If a reference constitutes prior art and it anticipates your invention, your claimed invention will be rejected.

priority date. This date is usually when you file your patent application. However, if you have filed previous applications for your same invention (either domestic or foreign), then this date can become the date that any one of those earlier applications was filed so long as you make a proper claim of priority to those earlier applications. This date can be absolutely critical with respect to negating a novelty or other prior art type rejection that you receive from the PTO.

process claims. These claims define methods of making or doing something and are characterized by their "ing" active elements steps.

product claims. These types of claims define discrete physical structures or materials.

product-by-process claim. A particular type of claim format where you recite the product, and then also recite a process of making that product.

prosecution. A term of art used to describe everything that goes on between you and the PTO after you file your patent application.

provisional application. This type of patent application is easier to complete and less expensive than a regular application. However, they only last for a year. Before the end of that year, you will need to file a regular application in order to capture the priority date of the provisional application.

R

request for continued examination (RCE). An RCE is a later patent application which you file in order to keep alive the prosecution of your previously filed patent application. You usually file an RCE when you are up against a final rejection from your examiner and want a second chance to advance your arguments before your application goes abandoned.

response or reply. After you receive an office action from the PTO, you will need to make a response/reply to the action within the specified time period or else your application will go abandoned.

restriction requirement. If you claim more than one separate invention in your patent application, your examiner will issue this. In this case, you will need to elect the invention that you want to pursue in your current application and cancel all claims to the invention(s) which you do not elect. You have the option of filing divisional applications for any of the non-elected inventions so those inventions do not become lost as a result of this requirement.

S

small entity status. Qualifying for small entity status basically gives you a 50% reduction in all fees.

shortened-statutory period. The time period which the PTO sets for your response/reply to an office action or other communication. The period is usually three months although it can be shorter. It is called "shortened" because there is a statute which provides an absolute six month time limit for responding to all Actions from the PTO.

specification. This is basically everything that makes up your patent application, minus your drawings.

supplemental application data sheet. An application data sheet which you submit to correct any errors in the previous application data sheet which you submitted to the PTO.

supplemental reply. A subsequent response/reply that you make after having previously responded/replied to an office action from the PTO. You are allowed to make as many supplemental replies as you want, so long as they do not unduly interfere with your examiner's action on your prior response(s)/replie(s).

T

terminal disclaimer. Form in which you agree that any patent issuing from your application must expire on the same date as another patent which you also own.

transition phrase. An introductory clause in your claim between the preamble and the body of the claim.

transmittal form. Form that must often be included with submissions that you make to the PTO. The form gives the PTO information about what you are submitting.

U

utility patent. One of three types of patents which are granted. This is a general patent and will probably be the type of patent which you will want to seek.

utility requirement. This is based on a statute and requires that your invention as described in your patent application has a specific, substantial, and credible use.

W

written description requirement. A statute requirement that your patent application be detailed enough to show that you were in possession of your invention.

Appendix A
Important Addresses and Telephone Numbers

Addresses, telephone numbers and email addresses can be found at the PTO website (**www.uspto.gov**) by going to the "index" and clicking on "addresses & contacts." I have reproduced some of this important contact information below.

IMPORTANT TELEPHONE NUMBERS:

For general questions regarding patents you can call 800-786-9199 or 703-308-4357

TTY: 703-305-7785. You can also email the PTO at:

usptoinfor@uspto.gov

PCT Help Desk (703) 305-3257

IMPORTANT FAX NUMBERS:

The PTO website also has a useful chart containing the fax numbers for each of the technology centers. Your application will be assigned to a particular technology center (TC) according to the type of invention. You can refer to the listings below to find fax numbers for that center. In light of the September 11th related terrorism, the PTO has actually been encouraging the use of fax for correspondence.

By using the correct number, the PTO will automatically generate a return receipt that will include the number of pages received as well as the date and time the facsimile was received. Additionally, the return receipt will include an image of the received cover page. Be careful though. You should use the certificate of facsimile transmission procedures when submitting a reply to a non-final or final office action by facsimile. You also need to retain the return receipt in the event that the office has no record of the facsimile submission, whether the facsimile submission is a reply to an office action, or a continued prosecution application under C.F.R., Title 37, Sec. 1.53(d).

TC1600: Biotechnology and Organic Chemistry

Before Final:	703-872-9306
After Final:	703-872-9307
Customer Service:	703-872-9305

TC2800: Semiconductors, Electrical, and Optical Systems and Components

Before Final:	703-872-9318
After Final:	703-872-9319
Customer Service:	703-872-9317

TC1700: Chemical and Materials Engineering

Before Final:	703-872-9310
After Final:	703-872-9311
Customer Service:	703-872-9309

TC2900: Designs for Articles of Manufacture

Before Final:	703-872-9322
After Final:	703-872-9323
Customer Service:	703-872-9321

TC2100: Computer Architecture, Software, and Information Security

Before Final:	703-746-7239
After Final:	703-746-7238
Customer Service:	703-746-7240

TC3600: Transportation, Construction, E-Commerce, Agriculture, National Security, and License and Review

Before Final:	703-872-9326
After Final:	703-872-9327
Customer Service:	703-872-9325

TC2600: Communications

Before Final:	703-872-9314
After Final:	703-872-9315
Customer Service:	703-872-9313

TC3700: Mechanical Engineering, Manufacturing, and Products

Before Final:	703-872-9302
After Final:	703-872-9303
Customer Service:	703-872-9301

IMPORTANT ADDRESSES:

It is important to place the correct Box Number on your addressee label for correspondence relating to particular documents you may have to file during the course of prosecution. The correct way to address your correspondence is as follows:

Box (insert the correct box #)
Commissioner for Patents
Washington, D.C. 20231

For example, if you are submitting a new patent application, the correct way to address your label would be as follows:

Box PATENT APPLICATION
Commissioner for Patents
Washington, D.C. 20231

The information on proper boxes can be found at the PTO website. I have listed some of the more important Box designations on the following pages. On the right side is a description of the type of correspondence you are interested in submitting and on the left side is the corresponding Box number you should place on your address labels.

Box Designations	Explanation
Box REISSUE	All new and continuing reissue application filings.
Box 313(b)	Petitions under C.F.R., Title 37, Sec. 1.313(c) to withdraw a patent application from issue after payment of the issue fee and any papers associated with the petition, including papers necessary for a continuing application or a request for continued examination (RCE).
Box AF	Expedited procedure for processing amendments and other responses after final rejection.
Box CPA	Requests for Continued Prosecution Applications (CPA's) under C.F.R., Title 37, Sec. 1.53(d).
Box DAC	Petitions decided by the Office of Petitions including petitions to revive and petitions to accept late payment of issue fees or maintenance fees.
Box Design	The filing of all design patent applications which do not request expedited examination under C.F.R., Title 37, Sec. 1.55.
Box Expedited Design	Only to be used for the initial filing of design application accompanied by a request for expedited examination under C.F.R., Title 37, Sec.. 1.155. (Design applicants seeking expedited examination may alternatively file a design application and corresponding request under C.F.R., Title 37, Sec. 1.155 by hand-delivering the application papers and request directly to the Design Group Director's office.)
Box Issue Fee	All communications following the receipt of a PTOL-85, "Notice of Allowance and Issue Fee Due," and prior to the issuance of a patent should be addressed to Box Issue Fee, unless advised to the contrary. Assignments are the exception. Assignments should be submitted in a separate envelope and not be sent to Box Issue Fee.

Box Designations	Explanation
Box Missing Parts	Response to the Notice to File Missing Parts of Application and associated papers and fees.
Box Non-Fee	Non-fee amendments to patent applications.
Box Patent Application	New patent applications and associated papers and fees.
Box Patent Ext.	Applications for patent term extension and any communications relating thereto.
Box PCT	Mail related to applications filed under the Patent Cooperation Treaty.
Box Provisional	The filing of all provisional patent applications Patent Application and any communications relating thereto.
Box RCE	Requests for continued examination under C.F.R., Title 37, Sec. 1.114.
Box Reconstruction	Correspondence pertaining to the reconstruction of lost patent files.
Box Reexam	Requests for Reexamination for original request papers only.
Box Sequence	Submission of diskette for biotechnical application.
Box SN	For fee and petitions under C.F.R., Title 37, Sec. 1.182 to obtain date received and/or serial number for patent applications prior to the Office's standard notification (return post card or the official "Filing Receipt," "Notice to File Missing Parts, or "Notice of Incomplete Application").

Appendix B
Additional Resources

Books on Patent Law

Biotechnology and the Law, by Iver P. Cooper

Deller's Patent Claims, by Ernest Bainbridge Lipscomb, III

General Information Concerning Patents
(This is a booklet that can be purchased from the Superintendent of Documents, U.S. Government Printing Office, Washington, D.C. 20402. The booklet is also available from the USPTO Web page at (http://www.uspto.gov)

Lipscomb's Walker on Patents, by Ernest Bainbridge Lipscomb, III

Patent Applications Handbook, by Stephen A. Becker
(West Group; 800-328-4880)

Patent Law: A Practitioner's Guide, by Ronald B. Hildreth
(Practicing Law Institute, Second Edition)

Patent Law Fundamentals, by Peter D. Rosenberg

Patent Law Basics, by Peter D. Rosenberg

Patent Law Practice Forms: Rules/Annotations/Commentary,
by Barry Kramer and Allen D. Brufsky

Patent Law Handbook, by Glenn Rhodes

Patent Application Practice, by James E. Hawes

Patent Law: Legal and Economic Principles, by John W. Schlicher

Patent Strategies for Business, by Stephen C. Glazier (Euromoney Publications, 1995)

Patents for Chemicals, Pharmaceuticals and Biotechnology, by Philip Grubb (Clarendon Press, 1999)

Patent Strategies for Researchers and Research Managers, by Jackson H. Knight (Wiley, 1996)

Resources on Starting Your Own Company and Obtaining Financing

Angel Investing, Mark Van Osnabrugge and Robert J. Robinson, 2000, Jossey-Bass Publishers.

The Entrepreneur's Guide to Business Law, Constance E. Bagley and Craig E. Dauchy, 1998, West Educational Publishing Company

The Entrepreneurial Venture, William A. Sahlman, Howard H. Stevenson, Michael J. Roberts, and Amar Bhide, Second Edition, 1999 Harvard Business School Press.

Resources on Trademark Law

Trademarks by Tom Blackett (Macmillan Business/Interbrand, 1998)

How to Register Your Own Trademark by Mark Warda. (Sourcebooks, 2000).

Resources on Copyright Law

"How to Register Your Own Copyright, " by Mark Warda (Sourcebooks, 2000)

www.loc.gov/copyright/
(United States Copyright Office homepage)

Popular Patent Law Journals/Magazines

The Journal of Patent and Trademark Office Society (a version of this can also be found at http://www.jptos.org/adds.shtml)

Intellectual Property Today (a version of this can also be found at http://www.iptoday.com/)

Web Sites with Information on Intellectual Property Law

www.aipla.org

(American Intellectual Property Law Association home page which is a top legal association for intellectual property attorneys)

www.bountyquest.com

(offers rewards to people who can dig up prior art that may invalidate a patent)www.bustpatents.com (a site devoted to helping you find prior art to invalidate software patents)

www.cipa.org.uk

(a site which you can use to locate patent agents in the UK)

www.heckle.org

(information for the individual inventor)

www.patents.ibm.com

(another website where you can search for patents)

www.inventorsdigest.com

(another site for the individual inventor)

www.inventing.com

(an online wealth of information for the inventor)

www.inventions.org

(offers assistance for the individual inventor)

www.inventionconvention.com/ncio/ncio.index.html

(another online source for the individual inventor)

www.lexis-nexis.com

(a commercial database for prior art)

www.micropatent.com

(allows you to search for patents)

www.patentminer.com

(commercial database for patents)

www.pl-x.com

(patent and licenses exchange where you can both buy and sell patent rights)

www.qpat.com

(commercial site to search for patents)

www.spi.org

(home site for the Software Patent Institute; this organization maintains a prior art database for software inventions)

http://ttdomino.Thomson-thomson.com/www/internat-vis.nsf

(International Guide to Trademarks)

www.tmcenter.com/

(company that does trademark searches and has information about trademarks)

www.tmexpress.com/

(trademark company that does searches and offers other services)

www.uspto.gov/web/offices/tac/doc/basic/

(the trademark page at the uspto.gov site)

http://dir.yahoo.com/Business_and_Economy/Companies/Law/Intellectual_Property/Trademarks/Services/

(Yahoo is a great site to go for intellectual property information and listings of web sites which cover this area of law)

www.yet2.com

(market place internet site where you can both sell and buy patent rights)

Patent Office Websites

www.European-patent-office.org
(European Patent Office)

www.jpo.go.jp
(Japanese Patent Office)

www.patent.gov.uk.
(UK Patent Office)

www.uspto.gov
(U.S. Patent Office)

www.wipo.int
(World Intellectual Property Organization)

Miscellaneous

Chernoff's Federal Circuit Patent Case Digests, by Karen Dana Fienberg Oster and Kevin L. Russell

Hidden Value: Profiting from the Intellectual Property Economy, edited by Bruce Berman.

IP Strategy: Complete Intellectual Property Planning, Access and Protection, by Howard C. Anawalt and Elizabeth Enayati Powers.

Inventor Assistance Source Directory, published by Pacific Northwest Laboratory, P.O. Box 999, Mail Stop K8-11, Richland, WA 99352 (lists inventors' organizations)

Rembrandts in the Attic: Unlocking the Hidden Value of Patents, by Kevin G. Rivette & David Kline. Harvard Business School Press.

Appendix C
Sample Patent Application

This is a complete patent application for a folding carrier that was discussed throughout this book. This application is here for you to examine in order to become more familiar with what each part of your application will look like.

Folding Carrier

Background of the Invention

[0001] Field of the Invention

[0002] The present invention relates to carriers that are configured to be attached to motor vehicles for carrying such objects as bicycles, skis, luggage and the like and, more particularly, is directed towards foldable carriers of the foregoing type in which the weight of the object is distributed on the carrier's feet.

Description of the Prior Art

[0003] In recent years, the popularity of bicycle riding for sport, recreation and transportation has increased. Bicycle carriers of various configurations have been designed which enable the bicycle owner to transport one or more bicycles from place to place by means of his automobile. Carriers of the type in which the weight of the bicycles is distributed on feet are shown in U.S. Pat. Nos. 3,710,999; 3,927,811; 4,290,540; and 4,332,337. Such carriers have been introduced with varying degrees of success. A need has arisen for an automobile carrier of the foregoing type which can be mounted and demounted easily and which can be collapsed into a flat configuration for easy shipment and storage.

Summary of the Invention

[0004] It is an object of the present invention to provide a folding carrier of the type in which the weight of the object being carried is distributed over upper and lower carrier feet. In addition, the folding carrier can be easily mounted to and demounted from a motor vehicle and folded into a relatively flat configuration for easy shipment and storage. The carrier includes a main frame to which a carrying member and a supporting member are pivotally mounted for movement between a collapsed position and an extended position. The carrying member is substantially U-shaped member having a front foot bar and a pair of extending arms and the supporting member is a substantially U-shaped member having a rear foot bar and a pair of extending legs. The carrying member is held in its extended position by a pair of braces and the supporting member is held in its extended position by bearing against the main frame. Straps are provided for holding the supporting member and for securing the carrier to the motor vehicle in its extended position. In the extended position, feet on the foot bars of the carrying and supporting members are in contact with the motor vehicle. As the supporting member is rotated from the collapsed position to the extended position, it bears against the main frame and is prevented from further rotation in that direction.

[0005] Other objects of the present invention will in part be obvious and will in part appear hereinafter.

[0006] The invention accordingly comprises the apparatuses and systems, together with their parts, elements and interrelationships that are exemplified in the following disclosure, the scope of which will be indicated in the appended claims.

Brief Description of the Drawings

[0007] A fuller understanding of the nature and objects of the present invention will become apparent upon consideration of the

following detailed description taken in connection with the accompanying drawings, wherein:

[0008] FIG. 1 is a perspective view of a foldable carrier embodying the invention in a collapsed or folded position;

[0009] FIG. 2 is a perspective view of the carrier of FIG. 1 in its extended position; and

[0010] FIG. 3 is a side view of the carrier of FIG. 2 in its extended position and mounted on an automobile trunk.

Detailed Description of the Preferred Embodiments

[0011] Referring now to the drawings, in FIG. 3 there is shown a folding carrier 12 embodying the present invention mounted on an automobile trunk lid. As hereinafter described, folding carrier 12 is movable between a flat collapsed position and an erect extended position. The flat collapsed or folded position is shown in FIG. 1 and the erect or extended position is shown in FIGS. 2 and 3.

[0012] Folding carrier 12 includes a main frame 14, a carrying member 16 and a supporting member 18. A pair of bracing members 20 are provided for holding carrying member 16 at a selected angular position with respect to main frame 14. Attaching hardware such as a rear strap 22 and front straps 24 secure carrier 12 to the automobile. Rear strap 22 is placed over both main frame 14 and supporting member 18. Front straps 24 are attached to opposite sides of carrying member 16. Main frame 14, a substantially U-shaped member, for example a hollow metal pipe, includes a first side leg 26, a cross member 28 and a second side leg 30. Protective covers 32 are provided on main frame 14. Carrying member 16 is pivotally mounted to an upper portion of side legs 26 and 30 by means of pins or fasteners 34, for example screws with lock nuts. Supporting member 18 is pivotally mounted to a lower end of side legs 26 and 30 by means of pins or fasteners 36, for example, screws with lock nuts. Carrying member 16 is mounted on the outside of side legs 26, 30 and supporting member 18 is mounted on the inside of side legs 26, 30.

[0013] Carrying member 16, a substantially U-shaped member, for example a hollow metal pipe, includes a pair of arms 40, 42 and a base member or front foot bar 44. The ends of arms 40 and 42 are bent upwardly to form stops 50 and 52. Opposite ends of braces 20, for example, bent rods, are received in holes 51 and 53 formed in carrying members 40,42 and side legs 26,30, respectively. The ends of braces 20 which are received in holes 53 are reversely bent to hold the braces therein. The other ends of the braces 20 which are received in the holes 51 are bent greater than ninety degrees to prevent the braces from inadventently coming out of the holes when a heavy load is being carried on the carrying arms. A suitable protective covering, such as a plastic tubing or the like, may cover all of or a portion of arms 40,42 and stops 50 and 52. A pair of feet 54, for example resilient feet such as molded rubber members with flat bottoms 56 and a split circular portion 58, are mounted on front foot bar.

[0014] Supporting member 18, a substantially U-shaped member, for example a hollow metal pipe, includes a pair of legs 60,62 and a base member or rear foot bar 64. The end portions 66 and 68 of legs 60 and 62, respectively, are bent so that the corner formed at the bend acts as a stop to hold the supporting member 18 in its extended position. Rear foot bar 64 is long enough so that it rests against side legs 26 and 30 when the supporting member 18 is in its collapsed position. The corners of basemember 64 and legs 60,62 are bent greater than ninety degrees to permit the end portions 66 and 68 to be fastened to the inside of the side legs 26 and 30. The corners of base member 64 and legs 60-62 are bent in the manner described so as to form a rear foot bar which is sufficiently long to prevent it from passing between the side legs when the supporting member 18 is in its collapsed position. That is, the length of the rear foot bar 64 is greater than the length of cross member 28. A pair of feet 70, for example, resilient feet such as molded rubber members with flat bottoms 62 and a split circular portion 74 are mounted on base 64.

[0015] When carrier 12 is mounted on an automobile as shown in FIG. 3, feet 54 press against the trunk lid 76 and feet 70 press against the lower body panel 78. Strap 22 is threaded about both the cross member 28 and the rear foot bar 64. Strap 22 is also threaded through a clamp 80 having a hooked end portion 82 which is secured to the rear bumper 84. A buckle 86 is provided to tighten strap 22. Each strap 25 is threaded through a buckle 88 which is secured to one fastener 34. A clamp 90 having a hooked end portion 92 is attached to each strap 24 and the hooked end is secured to the top of the trunk lid 76.

[0016] Movement of the folding carrier 12 from its extended position shown in FIG. 2 to its folded or collapsed position shown in FIG. 1 is accomplished by merely removing the ends of braces 20 from holes 51 and pivoting carrying member 16 and supporting member 18. When carrier 12 is in the extended position shown in FIGS. 1 and 3, the major part of carrying arms 40,42 and the major part of supporting legs 60,62 extend in opposite directions from opposite ends of frame 14 in a substantially parallel relationship to one another and in substantially perpendicular relationship to the frame. Carrying member 16 is held generally perpendicular to frame 14 when in its extended position by braces 20. The corner formed between the end portion 66 and leg 60, and the corner formed between the end portion 68 and leg 62 define stops which limit rotational movement of supporting member 18 and hold the supporting member in its extended position. When a bicycle is positioned on carrying arms 40,42, the weight of the bicycle is distributed over feet 54 and feet 70 which are fitted over front foot bar 44 and over rear foot bar 64, respectively. The flat bottoms of the feet 54 and feet 70 distribute the weight of the bicycle over a greater area than the weight distribution provided by feet in the form of caps on the ends of the tubular members. Side legs 60,62 and the parts of arms 40,42 below frame 14 are sufficiently long to keep the bicycle pedals from hitting the automobile.

[0017] When the carrier 12 is in its collapsed position, frame 14, carrying member 16 and supporting member 18 are substantially in side-by-side relationship to one another. Initially, carrying member 16 is rotated counterclockwise from the extended position shown in FIG. 2 to the collapsed position shown in FIG. 1. Then, the ends of braces 20 are inserted into holes 51. It is to be noted that carrying member 16 is mounted to main frame 14 in such a manner that front foot bar 44 passes over the top of side legs 26 and 30 when carrying member 16 is rotated from its collapsed position to its extended position. That is, the distance from screw 34 to front foot bar 44 is greater than the distance from screw 34 to the ends of side legs 26,30 of frame 14. When supporting member 18 is rotated from its collapsed position (FIG. 1) to its extended position (FIG. 2) by moving it in a counterclockwise direction, the corners of legs 60 and 62 engage the corners of side legs 26,30, thereby preventing further rotation of the supporting member. The carrying member 16 is held rigidly by braces 20 and the supporting member 18 is now braced against frame 14, thereby providing a rigid support for articles such as bicycles, for example, which are to be carried on carrying arms 40 and 42. Carrying member 16 moved from its extended position shown in FIG. 2 to its collapsed position shown in FIG. 1 first by pulling bracing members 20 out of holes 51 and then by rotating carrying member 18 clockwise to its collapsed position. Supporting member 18 is moved to its collapsed position by merely rotating it clockwise. When the folding carrier is mounted on the automobile, the supporting member 18 is held in its extended position by the strap 22 which passes over it and the cross member 28.

[0018] Since certain changes may be made in the foregoing disclosure without departing from the scope of the invention herein involved, it is intended that all matter contained in the above description and depicted in the accompanying drawings be construed in an illustrative and not in a limiting sense.

What is claimed is:

1. A folding carrier mountable on an automobile or the like, said carrier comprising:

   (a) a frame;

   (b) a carrying member pivotally mounted to said frame said carrying member movable about a first axis between an operative extended position and a collapsed position, said carrying member and said frame being in a substantially side-by-side relationship when said carrying member is in its collapsed position, a foot of said carrying member positioned to contact the automobile when said carrying member is in its operative extended position;

   (c) bracing means mounted to said frame and configured to engage and disengage said carrying member, said carrying member fixed in its extended position when said bracing means is in engagement with said carrying member; and

   (d) a supporting member pivotally mounted to said frame and constrained for limited rotational movement relative thereto between an extended position and a collapsed position about a second axis, said first axis being parallel to said second axis, when said supporting member is in its extended position, a portion of said supporting member is pressed against said frame and said supporting member is prevented from further movement relative to said frame, said supporting member and said frame being in a substantially perpendicular relationship to one another when said supporting member is in its extended position, said supporting member and said frame being in a substantially side-by-side relationship when said carrying member is in its collapsed position, a foot portion of said supporting member positioned to contact the automobile when said supporting member is in its operative extended position.

2. The folding carrier as claimed in claim 1 wherein said frame includes a first side leg, a second side leg and a cross member, said carrying member and supporting member pivotally mounted to said first and second side legs.

3. The folding carrier as claimed in claim 1 wherein said carrying member is mounted on the outside of said frame and said supporting member is mounted on the inside of said frame.

4. The folding carrier as claimed in claim 3 wherein said carrying member includes a pair of arms and a front foot bar, one of each said arms pivotally mounted to one of each said side legs of said frame, said front foot bar is positioned to contact the automobile when said carrying member is in its operative extended position.

5. The folding carrier as claimed in claim 4 wherein said supporting member includes a pair of legs and a rear foot bar, each said leg being bent adjacent its end to form a corner which bears against said frame when said supporting member is in its operative extended position, said rear foot bar is positioned to contact the automobile when said supporting member is in its operative extended position.

6. The folding carrier as claimed in claim 5 wherein said rear foot bar is longer than said cross member.

7. The folding carrier as claimed in claim 4 including feet mounted on said front and rear foot bars, the weight of an object carried on the folding carrier being distributed over said feet.

8. The folding carrier as claimed in claim 6 wherein said feet includes a pair of resilient feet mounted to each said front and rear foot bars, each said resilient foot having a substantially flat bottom.

9. A folding carrier mountable on an automobile or the like, said carrier comprising:

    (a) a frame;

(b) a supporting member pivotally mounted to said frame, said supporting member having stop means which constrains said supporting member against full rotational movement relative to said frame, said supporting member rotatable about a first axis between an operative extended position and a collapsed position, said supporting member rotated in a first direction from said extended position to said collapsed position and in a second direction from said collapsed position to said extended position, said first direction opposite said second direction, said supporting member and said frame being substantially perpendicular to one another when said supporting member is in its extended position, said supporting member and said frame being in a substantially side-by-side relationship when said carrying member is in its collapsed position, a foot portion of said supporting member positioned to contact the automobile when said supporting member is in its operative extended position;

(c) a carrying member pivotally mounted to said frame said carrying member movable about a second axis between an extended position and a collapsed position said first axis being parall to said second axis, said carrying member and said frame being in a substantially side-by-side relationship when said carrying member is in its collapsed position, a foot portion of said carrying means positioned to contact the automobile when said carrying member is in its operative extended postion; and

(d) bracing means mounted to said frame and configured to engage and disengage said carrying member, said carrying member and said frame being in a fixed relationship when said bracing means is in engagement with said carrying member.

10. The folding carrier as claimed in claim 9 wherein said frame includes a first side leg, a second side leg and a cross member, said frame having a substantially U-shaped profile.

11. The folding carrier as claimed in claim 10 wherein said supporting member includes a pair of legs and a rear foot bar, said legs having bent end portions, each said leg end portion pivotally mounted to one of each said side legs of said frame, said supporting member having a substantially U-shaped profile, said rear foot bar positioned to contact the automobile when said supporting member is in its operative extended position.

12. The folding carrier as claimed in claim 10 wherein said carrying member includes a pair of arms and a front foot bar, one of each said arms pivotally mounted to one of each said side legs of said frame, said carrying member having a substantially U-shaped profile, said front foot bar positioned to contact the automobile when said carrying member is in its operative extended position.

ABSTRACT

A folding carrier for carrying objects on an automobile or the like has a frame to which a carrying member and a supporting member are pivotally mounted for movement between collapsed and extended positions. The carrying member is held by a pair of braces in its extended position for carrying objects and the supporting member is held in its extended position by bearing against the frame. The carrying member is a substantially U-shaped member having a front foot bar and a pair of extending arms and the supporting member is a substantially U-shaped member having a rear foot bar and a pair of extending legs. When the carrier is in its operative extended position, the weight of an object being carried is distributed on feet mounted on the foot bars of each carrying and supporting members.

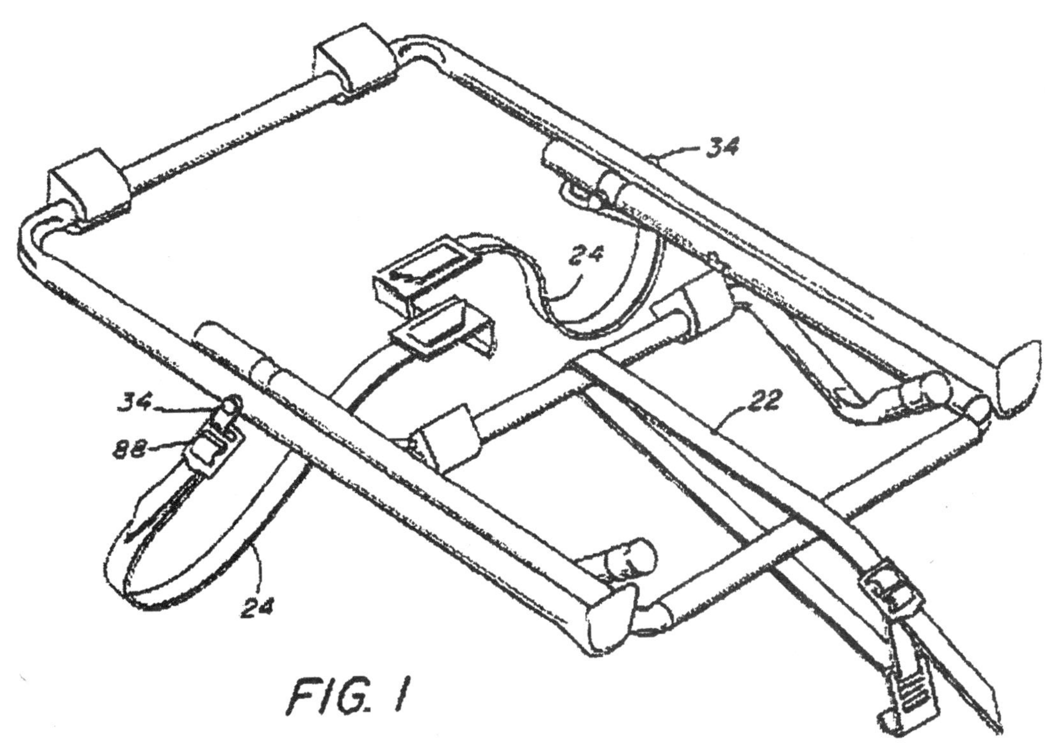

FIG. 1

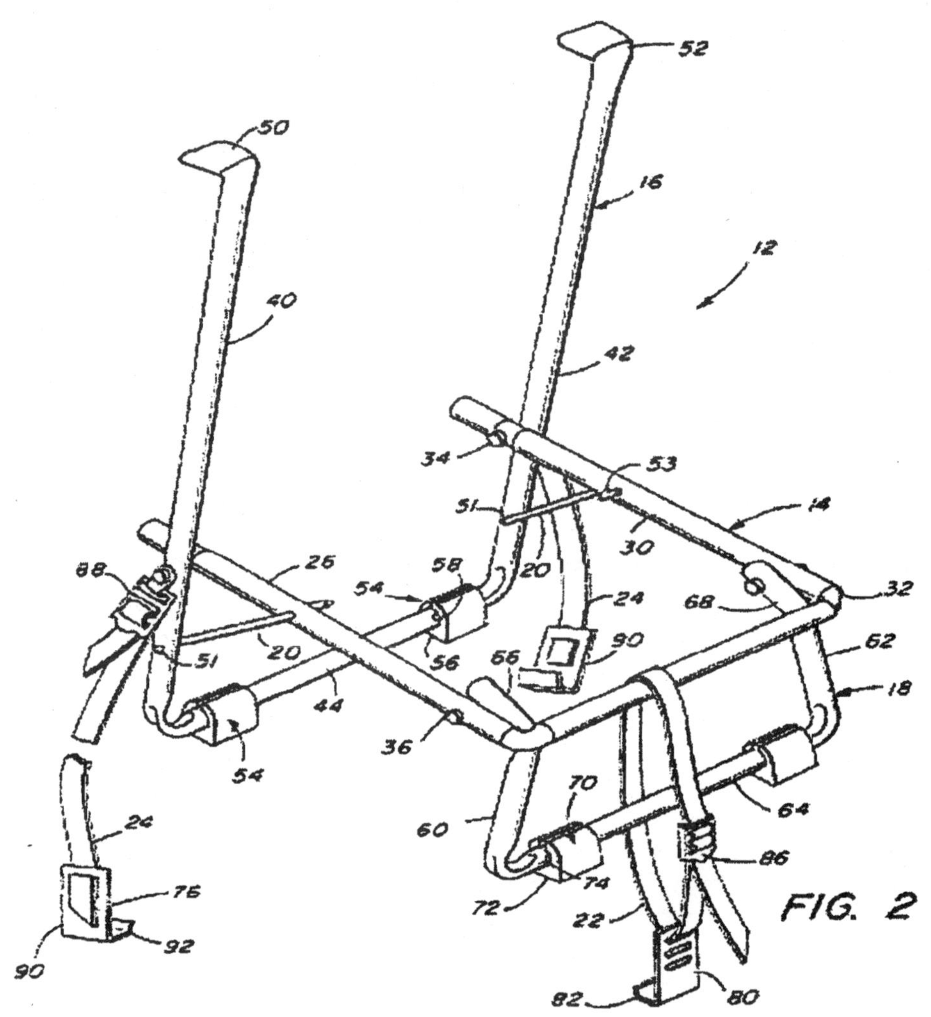
52
50
16
12
40
42
34
53
51
14
30
20
25
58
54
88
24
68
32
62
51
20
56
66
90
18
44
54
36
70
64
24
60
86
76
74
72
22
92
90
82
80
FIG. 2

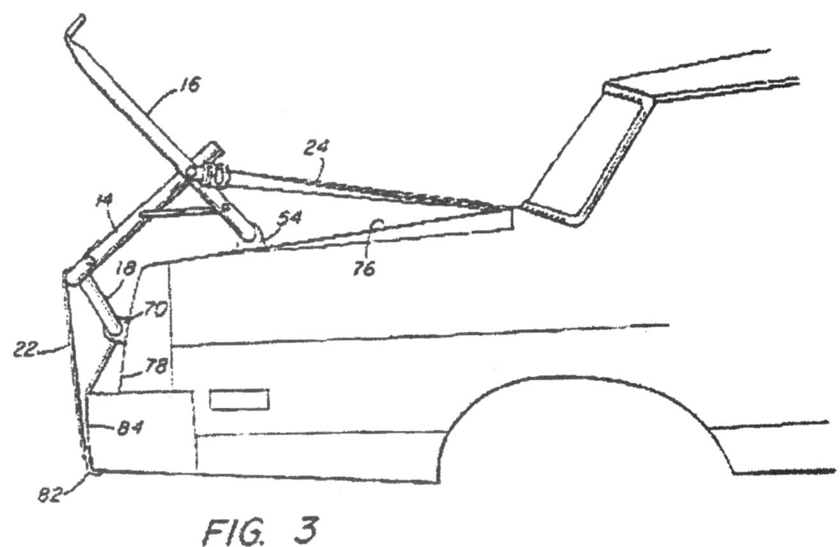

FIG. 3

Appendix D
Sample Design Patent

This is a sample design patent as discussed in Chapter 7. You may access the original by searching for and downloading patent number D296,039 on the PTO website. Reviewing this sample will help you draft your own design patent.

United States Patent [19]

Diaz

[11] Patent Number Des. 296,039

[45] Date of Patent: Jun. 7, 1988

[54] SHOE SOLE

[75] Inventors: Juan A. Diaz, Weymouth, Mass

[73] Assignee: Reebok International Ltd., Canton, Mass

[**] Term: 14 Years

[21] Appl. No: 074181

[22] Filed: July 16, 1987

[52] U.S.C. D2/320

[58] Field of search D2/264,274,314,317-321 36/103-106,114,25R,28,32R,32A,59 C,39,43,91,92

[56] References Cited

U.S. PATENT DOCUMENTS

D. 76528 10/1928 Frey D2/320
D. 257076 9/1980 Amicone et al.................. D2/320
D. 815438 12/1985 Nagano D2/320
D. 281641 12/1985 Shiki D2/320
D. 284040 6/1986 Yochitake.................... D2/320
D. 284041 6/1986 Yochitake.................... D2/320
D. 290182 6/1987 Chen D2/320
3583082 6/1971 Jordan, Jr. 36/59

U.S. PATENT DOCUMENTS

2458576 6/1976 Fed. Rep. of Germany
2520796 6/1976 Fed. Rep. of Germany

Primary Examiner—Louis S. Zarfas

Attorney Agent or Firm—Saidman, Sterne, Kessler & Goldstein

[56] CLAIM

The ornamental design for a shoe sole, as shown and described.

DESCRIPTION

FIG. 1 is a left side elevational view of a shoe sole showing my new design;
FIG. 2 is a right side elevational view thereof;
FIG. 3 is a bottom plan view thereof;
FIG. 4 is a front elevational view thereof; and
FIG. 5 is a rear elevational view thereof.
The broken line showing of a shoe upper in FIGS. 1-5 and the area within are environmental only and form no part of the claimed design.

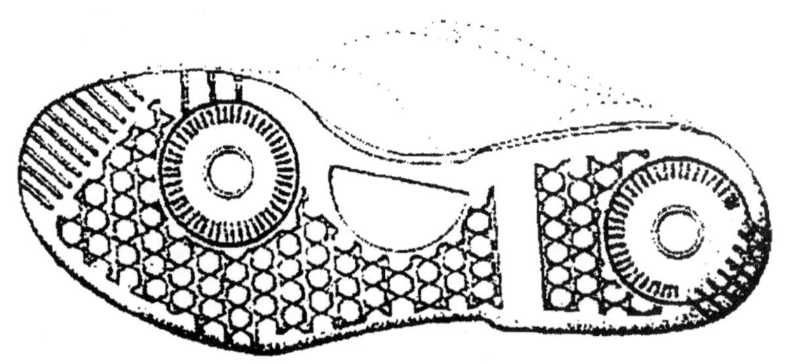

U.S. Patent Jun. 7, 1988 Sheet 1 of 2 D296,039

FIG.1

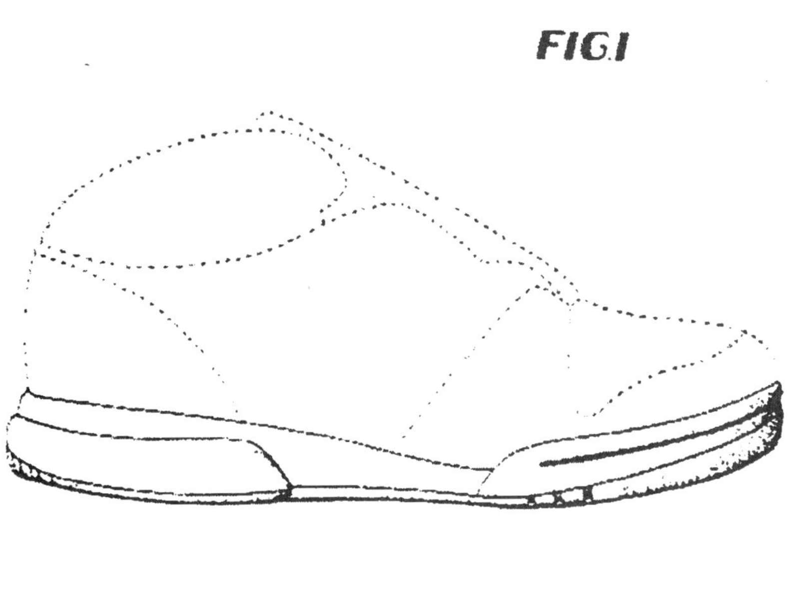

FIG.2

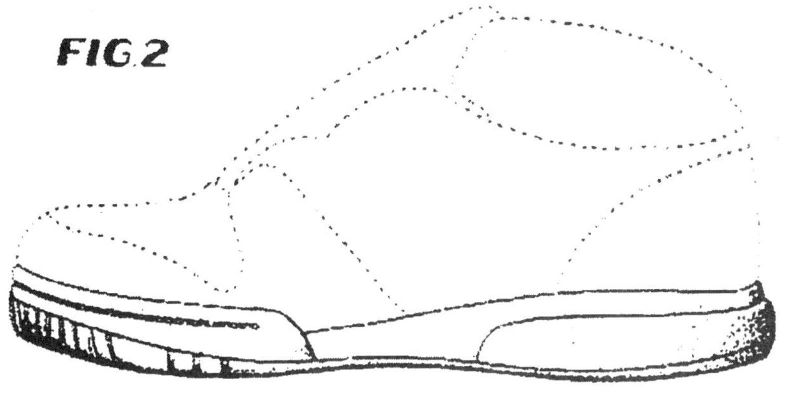

U.S. Patent Jun. 7, 1988 Sheet 2 of 2 D296,039

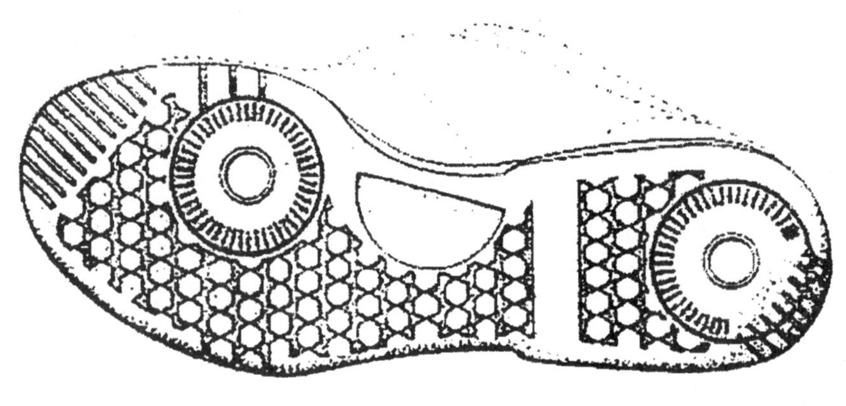

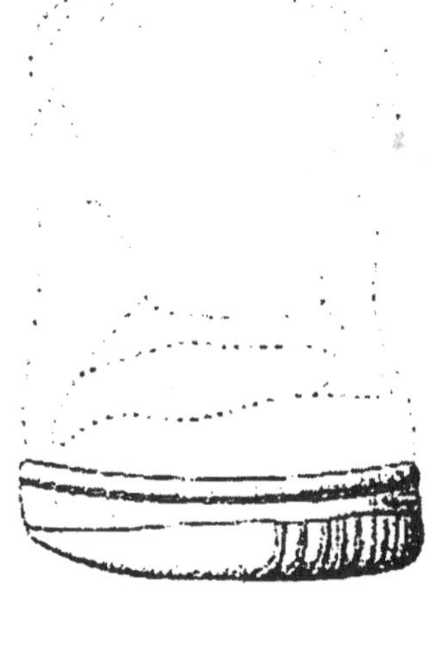

FIG 4

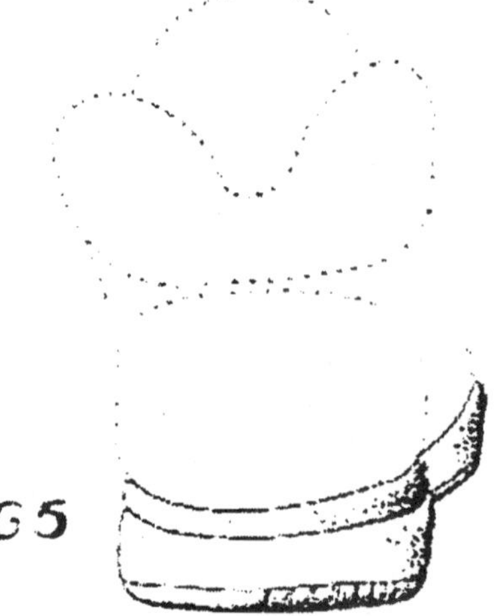

FIG 5

Appendix E
Forms

I would encourage you to use the forms that the PTO uses rather than forms you create yourself or find in patent law textbooks. Most, if not all, of the forms that you will need for patent prosecution are on the PTO website (**www.uspto.gov**). Once at the site, you should click on the "patents" icon, then click on "forms" and scroll down. The PTO forms are listed by form number and title.

Using the forms from the PTO website is in your best interest because you are more likely not to miss any updated changes or required information. A patent attorney once told me that an experienced outside lawyer which handled many of the cases for his company had been using his own declarations rather than the PTO declaration forms. The patent attorney later discovered that his experienced lawyers's forms lacked certain essential material. This created a huge problem for the company because an invalid declaration could mean an invalid patent. If the lawyer had just used the forms which existed on the PTO's website, this problem would not have occurred.

Most of the forms that you will need are contained at the PTO site. I will not reproduce those forms for you here, but rather list the form by its title, form number, and its use. In the situation where the PTO does not provide a form, I will provide you with a blank form that you can photocopy and use. I have itemized each of the forms that you will need from the PTO's website according to the chapters of the book where I have given instructions and explanations.

NOTE: *Some chapters do not have forms listed. These chapters discussed concepts, as opposed to specific forms.*

Forms for Chapter Four

form 1: Petition for Submitting Color Photographs or Drawings: Use this form if you have decided that your invention requires the submission of color photographs or drawings.

Forms for Chapter Six

form 2: Cover Letter: It is a good idea to start off the package of materials that you are sending to the PTO with a cover letter that lets the PTO know what you have included in your package.

form 3: Utility Patent Application Transmittal (PTO/SB/05): A transmittal is a form that indicates what you are sending to the PTO. You should always fill out a transmittal for any application which you send to the PTO.

form 4: Fee Transmittal (PTO/SB/17): This form is used to calculate how much money you will need to include with your application.

form 5: Patent Application Fee Determination Record (PTO/SB/06): Fill out the Part I of this record and attach this right behind your Fee Transmittal.

form 6: Multiple Dependent Claim Fee Calculation Sheet (PTO/SB/07): If you are presenting any multiple dependent claims in your application, you should fill out this form. Remember that multiple dependent claims count for the numbers of claims which are directly referenced in your multiple dependent claim.

form 7: Credit Card Payment Form (PTO-2038): If you are paying by credit card, you should fill out this form. Attach it behind your multiple fee calculation sheet or your patent application fee determination record (if you have no multiple dependent claims).

form 8: Application Data Sheet: This form should be attached directly behind your fee transmittals and fee worksheets (and credit card payment form if you use one). If a section is not applicable to you, simply leave the section blank. If pages 4 and 5 of the application data sheet do not apply to you, you can also simply not submit those pages to the PTO.

form 9: Declaration (PTO/SB/01A): Use this form for your utility patent application declaration if you have submitted an Application Data Sheet. Your declaration should be attached after your specification and drawings.

form 10: Information Disclosure Statement Cover Letter: You should submit a cover letter similar to this before the PTO IDS forms in item (1) to disclose to the PTO any prior art references which you consider material to your invention. You will see that the numbering starts with the number "1" and you can continue to number according to how many references you are going to list. There is more space to list references at the top of the second page. If you need more space to list your references beyond the pages here, simply insert an additional blank page between pages 1 and 2 of the form here.

form 11: Information Disclosure Statement (PTO/SB/08): In addition to your IDS cover letter in item (9), you must list each of your prior art references on this form. You can attach this form right beyond your IDS.

Forms for Chapter Seven

form 12: Design Patent Application Transmittal (PTO/SB/18): Whenever you submit a new patent application to the PTO, you will need to include a transmittal. Design patent applications are no exception to this rule.

form 13: Provisional Application Cover Sheet (PTO/SB/16): Start off your provisional application package materials with a cover sheet which tells the PTO exactly what you are enclosing in your envelope. A specific provisional application cover sheet from the PTO website which you can use is reproduced here.

form 14: Request for Continued Examination (RCE) (PTO/SB/30): Use this form as your transmittal for an RCE.

form 15: Supplemental Declaration (PTO/SB/04): Use this form if you have previously submitted a declaration and now you need to submit another declaration because you have made changes to you specification. A common situation where you want to execute a supplemental declaration is where you file a CIP.

Forms for Chapter Eight

form 16: Cover Letter with Express Mailing: You can use this form as your cover letter for your PCT application.

form 17: Transmittal Letter (PTO-1382): Use this form for your transmittal letter to the PTO.

form 18: PCT Request (Form PCT/RO/101): You can use this form for your Request. The Notes which accompany this form tell you how to fill out the form item by item and should not be included with the Request that you will send to the PTO.

form 19: PCT Fee Calculation Sheet (Form PCT/RO/101 (Annex)) This form must be completed to figure out how much you owe the PTO. Do not forget to include your Check payable to the Commissioner of Patents and Trademarks! If you are paying by credit card instead of check, you should fill out a credit card payment form PTO 2038 from Chapter 5. Notes on how to fill out the form are included but are not to be submitted along with the form.

form 20: Notice of Confirmation of Precautionary Designations (Form PCT/RO/144) You have no later than 15 months from your priority date to add any countries to your designation list that you filled out in your Request. By adding such countries you are telling the PTO that you would also like to enter the national stage in the countries which you have added. You can use this blank form as your notice to the PTO of the countries that you want to add.

form 21: Demand (Form PCT/IPEA/401) If you want to enter Chapter II and obtain a preliminary examination of your PCT, then you need to elect such countries in a Demand no later than 19 months from your priority date. You can use this blank form for your demand.

form 22: PCT Fee Calculation Sheet (Form PCT/IPEA/401 (Anex)) There is a fee for your Demand and this form is what you need to fill out to determine the fee that you owe.

form 23: Transmittal Letter to the United States Designated/Elected Office (DO/EO/US) Concerning a Filing Under 35 U.S.C. 371 If the U.S. is one of your designated states in your Request, then you will need to enter the national stage in the U.S. by 30 months from your priority date. To enter the national stage you need to include a transmittal letter with your papers. You can use this form for your transmittal.

Forms for Chapter Nine:

form 24: Petition to Make Special: You can use this form for your Petition to Make Special your application based on any one of the grounds listed in MPEP 708.02. This particular petition is geared towards the ground of infringement. You will need to pay the requisite fee under 37 CFR 1.17(h) and also include a declaration by you as the inventor or your attorney.

form 25: Declaration in Support of Petition to Make Special: You will need to attach this declaration behind your Petition to Make Special.

form 26: Notice of Appeal (PTO/SB/31): Use this form to file an appeal of your examiner's decision to the Board of Patent Appeals and Interferences. You will need to include the appropriate fee.

Forms for Chapter Ten

form 27: Cover Letter: You should include a cover letter and transmittal before your amendment. If you are adding more than claims that what you have previously paid for then you will also need to include the appropriate fee for such added claims.

form 28: Amendment: You can either type in the necessary information to this form as your amendment, or reproduce this form onto your word processor with your necessary information organized on the hard drive of your computer. By keeping the form on your computer, you will find that you can make changes much easier and can bring up any of your material later on if you need to.

NOTE: *This form is only a skeleton of how your amendment should look! The arguments you make and changes you make to your claims require thoughtful review of what you have read in this book.*

form 29: Supplemental Application Data Sheet: Use this form if you want to make changes to the original Application Data Sheet that you prepared from Chapter 5.

form 30: Request for Approval of Proposed Drawing Amendment: If you want to make correction to your drawings other than any corrections which are in response to a Notice from your Official Draftsperson as to informalities of your drawings, then you must obtain the prior approval of your examiner. You can use this form to seek approval of your examiner. Once you have obtained approval, you will need to submit the changes in the form of a new set of corrected drawings with your Official Draftsperson.

form 31: Submission of Corrected Drawings: Use this form to transmit corrected drawings to your Official Draftsperson. You can transmit corrected drawings even after you have received a Notice of Allowance.

Forms for Chapter Twelve

form 32: Declaration under 37 CFR Section 1.131: This is a bare bones Rule 1.131 declaration which you will need to adapt to your particular situation.

form 33: Declaration under 37 CFR Section 1.132: This is a bare bones Rule 1.131 declaration used to rebut a prima facie case of obviousness. Again, you will need to make adaptations to this form to fit your own unique situation.

Forms for Chapter Thirteen

form 34: Terminal Disclaimer to Obviate Double Patenting Rejection Over a Prior Patent (PTO/SB/26): This form can be used as your terminal disclaimer in order to obviate a double patenting rejection based on a prior patent.

form 35: Petition to Revive Unintentionally Abandoned Application (PTO/SB/64): Use this petition to revive your application which you unintentionally abandoned. You will need to include a cover letter with your petition as well as the appropriate fee under 37 CFR 1.17(m). In addition, you will need to include a reply to your last office action which you failed to respond to on time.

IN THE UNITED STATES PATENT AND TRADEMARK OFFICE

Applicant:	)	
Serial No.	)	Group Art Unit:
Filed:	)	Examiner:
Title:	)	

FILED BY EXPRESS MAIL
Honorable Commissioner
of Patents and Trademarks
Washington, D.C. 20231

PETITION FOR SUBMITTING COLOR PHOTOGRAPHS OR DRAWINGS

Dear Sirs:

Applicant respectfully petitions that the color photographs filed herewith be accepted as formal drawings. The applicable fee under 37 CFR Sec. 1.17(i) is enclosed.

These color photographs or drawings are necessary because

EXPRESS MAIL CERTIFICATE

"Express Mail" Label No.: ____________________

Deposit Date: ____________________

I hereby certify that this paper and the attachments herein are being deposited with the United States Postal Service "Express Mail Post Office to Addressee" service under 37 CFR 1.10 on the date indicated above and is addressed to the Commissioner of Patents and Trademarks, Washington DC 20231.

Respectfully submitted,

Applicant

IN THE UNITED STATES PATENT AND TRADEMARK OFFICE

Applicant(s):	)	
Serial No.	)	Group Art Unit: Unknown
Filed: Herewith	)	Ex'r: Unknown
Title:	)	

FILED BY EXPRESS MAIL

Honorable Commissioner of Patents and Trademarks
Washington, D.C. 20231

EXPRESS MAIL COVER LETTER

Dear Sirs:

Enclosed and attached hereto are the following documents:

(1) Utility Patent Application Transmittal;

(2) Fee Transmittal (in duplicate);

(3) Fee Determination Record;

EXPRESS MAIL CERTIFICATE
"Express Mail" Label No.: ______________________
Deposit Date: ______________________
I hereby certify that this paper and the attachments herein are being deposited with the United States Postal Service "Express Mail Post Office to Addressee" service under 37 CFR 1.10 on the date indicated above and is addressed to the Commissioner of Patents and Trademarks, Washington DC 20231.

(4) Credit Card Payment Form;

(5) Application Data Sheet;

(6) Specification (pages);

(7) Formal drawings (sheets);

(8) Executed Declaration;

(9) Information Disclosure Statement;

(10) Citation of references included in IDS (2 pages);

(11) Self-addressed stamped post-card.

It is respectfully requested that the attached pre-paid postcard be stamped with the date of filing of these documents and that it be returned as soon as possible.

Respectfully submitted,

____

Applicant

Docket No. ________________

Application Data Sheet

Application Information

Application Type::

Subject Matter::

Suggested Classification::

Suggested Group Art Unit::

CD-ROM or CD-R?

Title::

Attorney Docket Number::

Request for Early Publication?::

Request for Non-Publication?::

Suggested Drawing Figure::

Total Drawing Sheets::

Small Entity::

Petition included?::

Secrecy Order in Parent Appl.?::

Applicant Information

Applicant Authority Type::

Primary Citizenship Country::

Status::

Given Name::

Page # 1 Initial / /

Middle Name::

Family Name::

City of Residence::

State or Province of Residence::

Country of Residence::

Street of mailing address::

City of Mailing address::

Country of mailing address::

Postal or Zip Code of mailing address::

Applicant Authority type::

Primary Citizenship Country::

Status::

Given Name::

Middle Name::

Family Name::

City of Residence::

State or Province of Residence::

Country of Residence::

Street of mailing address::

City of mailing address::

State or Province of mailing address::

Postal or Zip Code of mailing address::

Page # 2 Initial / /

Correspondence Information

Correspondence Customer Number::

Name::

Street of mailing address::

City of mailing address::

State or Province of mailing address::

Postal or Zip Code of mailing address::

Telephone::

E-Mail address::

Domestic Priority Information

Application::	Continuity Type::	Parent Application::	Parent Filing Date::

Foreign Priority Information

Country::	Application number::	Filing Date::	Priority Claimed:

Page # 3 Initial / /

Assignee Information

Assignee name::

Street of mailing address::

City of mailing address::

State or Province of mailing address::

Country of mailing address::

Postal or Zip Code of mailing address::

Page # 4 Initial / /

IN THE UNITED STATES PATENT AND TRADEMARK OFFICE

Applicant(s):	)	
Serial No.	)	Group Art Unit: Unknown
Filed: Herewith	)	Ex'r: Unknown
Title:	)	

FILED BY EXPRESS MAIL
Honorable Commissioner of Patents and Trademarks
Washington, D.C. 20231

INFORMATION DISCLOSURE STATEMENT UNDER 37 C.F.R. §§1.56 & 1.97-1.98

Dear Sirs:

Pursuant to the provisions of 37 C.F.R. §§1.97-1.98, and in full compliance with their duty of disclosure under 37 C.F.R. §1.56, Applicant(s) are bringing the following ( ) documents to the attention of the U.S. Patent and Trademark Office and the Examiner handling their above-identified application:

1.

EXPRESS MAIL CERTIFICATE

"Express Mail" Label No.: ____________________

Deposit Date: ____________________

I hereby certify that this paper and the attachments herein are being deposited with the United States Postal Service "Express Mail Post Office to Addressee" service under 37 CFR 1.10 on the date indicated above and is addressed to the Commissioner of Patents and Trademarks, Washington DC 20231.

Copies of the above listed ( ) documents are being submitted herewith as Exhibits ( ). A completed Form PTO-1449 is also attached herewith.

By this voluntary citation of art, Applicant(s) are requesting that the documents be made of record in the instant application.

The filing of this information disclosure statement shall not be construed to be an admission that the information cited in the statement is, or is considered to be, material to patentability as defined in § 1.56(b).

Applicant(s) respectfully request that the Examiner make the above-submitted documents of record in the instant application.

This IDS is being filed in accordance with 37 C.F.R. §1.97(b)(3), that is, prior to issuance of a First Office Action on the merits. Applicant(s) believe that no fee is required.

Respectfully submitted,

____

Applicant

IN THE UNITED STATES PATENT AND TRADEMARK OFFICE

Applicant(s):

Serial No.

Filed: Herewith
Title:

EXPRESS MAIL CERTIFICATE
"Express Mail" Label No.: ____________________
Deposit Date: ____________________
I hereby certify that this paper is being deposited with the United States Postal Service as "Express Mail Post Office to Addressee" service under 37 CFR, Sec. 1.10 on the date indicated above in an envelope addressed to Box PCT Commissioner for Patents, Washington DC 20231.
(type or print name of person making deposit)
____
Signature of person making deposit

FILED BY EXPRESS MAIL
Box PCT
Commissioner for Patents
Washington, D.C. 20231

COVER LETTER WITH EXPRESS MAIL CERTIFICATE

Dear Sirs:

Enclosed and attached hereto are the following documents:
(1) Cover letter with express Mail Certificate;
(2) Transmittal Form;
(3) PCT Request;
(4) Specification (pages);
(5) Formal drawings (sheets);
(6) Executed Declaration;
(7) Check for $____________; and
(8) Self-addressed stamped post-card.

Respectfully submitted,

____

Applicant

Docket No. ____________

IN THE UNITED STATES PATENT AND TRADEMARK OFFICE

Applicant:)
Serial No.)
Filed:)
Title:)
)
Group Art Unit:)
Examiner:)
)
Docket No.)
)

FILED BY EXPRESS MAIL

Honorable Commissioner for Patents
Washington, D.C. 20231

CERTIFICATE OF MAILING BY EXPRESS MAIL
"Express Mail" Mailing
Label No. EK_______________US
Date of Deposit: ____________, 200__
I hereby certify that this paper is being deposited with the United States Postal Service as "Express Mail Post Office to Addressee" service under 37 C.F.R. §1.10 on the date indicated above in an envelope addressed to Box PCT Commissioner for Patents, Washington, D.C.. 20231
(type or print name of person making deposit)
____
Signature of person making deposit

PETITION TO MAKE SPECIAL

Pursuant to 37 C.F.R. § 1.102(d), Applicant hereby petitions the Commissioner to make the subject application special so that it may be taken out of turn for immediate action.

Attached to this Petition to Make Special is a declaration of Applicant in support of the Petition to Make Special under Rule 102(d).

Due to the fact the Applicant's claims are being infringed (see appended Declaration of Applicant's attorney) and Applicant requires a patent in order to terminate such infringement, this Petition to Make Special is being filed.

The required petition fee required under 37 C.F.R. § 1.17(h) has been calculated as $__________. A check in payment of the petition fee required under 37 C.F.R. § 1.17(h) is enclosed.

Applicant respectfully requests that this Petition be granted.

Respectfully submitted,

____________________ ____________________

Date: Applicant

IN THE UNITED STATES PATENT AND TRADEMARK OFFICE

Applicant:)
Serial No.)
Filed:)
Title:)
)
Group Art Unit:)
Examiner:)
)
Docket No.)
)

FILED BY EXPRESS MAIL

Honorable Commissioner for Patents
Washington, D.C. 20231

CERTIFICATE OF MAILING BY EXPRESS MAIL

"Express Mail" Mailing

Label No. EK________________US

Date of Deposit: ____________, 200__

I hereby certify that this paper is being deposited with the United States Postal Service as "Express Mail Post Office to Addressee" service under 37 C.F.R. §1.10 on the date indicated above in an envelope addressed to Box PCT Commissioner for Patents, Washington, D.C.. 20231

(type or print name of person making deposit)

____

Signature of person making deposit

DECLARATION IN SUPPORT OF PETITION TO MAKE SPECIAL

I, ______________________________, declare as follows:

1. I am the Applicant in the above-indicated application, which covers a ______________________.

2. On or about __________________________, it came to my attention that ____________________, of____, was distributing ______________________ under the name, "__________________________________."

3. I have compared the claims in the above-indicated application with the specimen, ________________________, distributed by "__________________________" and it is my opinion that Claims _________ of this application would be infringed by the manufacture, use or sale of said specimen.

4. I have made a careful search of the prior art and have concluded that the claims in the above-indicated application would not be anticipated or be obvious over any of the prior art references discovered.

5. One copy of each of the references which I deemed most closely related to the subject matter encompassed by the claims of the above-indicated application are attached behind this declaration. These references are the following:
____

6. As a result of reviewing this application and the prior art, I believe that all of the claims in this application are allowable.

I declare that all statements made herein of my own knowledge are true and that all statements made on information and belief are believed to be true and, further, that these statements were made with the knowledge that willful false statements and the like so made are punishable by fine or imprisonment, or both, under 18 U.S.C. § 1001 and that such false statements may jeopardize the validity of this document and the application to which it relates.

Respectfully submitted,

____________________ ____________________

Date: Applicant

IN THE UNITED STATES PATENT AND TRADEMARK OFFICE

Applicant:)
Serial No.)
Filed:)
Title:)
Group Art Unit:)
Examiner:)
Docket No.)

FILED BY EXPRESS MAIL
Box Non-Fee Amendment
Honorable Commissioner for Patents
Washington, D.C. 20231

CERTIFICATE OF MAILING BY EXPRESS MAIL
"Express Mail" Mailing
Label No. EK________________US
Date of Deposit: ____________, 200__
I hereby certify that this paper is being deposited with the United States Postal Service as "Express Mail Post Office to Addressee" service under 37 C.F.R. §1.10 on the date indicated above in an envelope addressed to Box PCT Commissioner for Patents, Washington, D.C.. 20231
(type or print name of person making deposit)
____
Signature of person making deposit

Dear Sir:

Enclosed please find the following documents for lining with the USPTO in the above-captioned matter:

(1) Transmittal Letter;

(2) Fee Transmital;

(3) Amendment;

(4) Self-addressed stamped post-card.

Respectfully submitted,

____

Applicant

IN THE UNITED STATES PATENT AND TRADEMARK OFFICE

Applicant:	)
Serial No.	)
Filed:	)
Title:	)
Group Art Unit:	)
Examiner:	)
Docket No.	)

CERTIFICATE OF MAILING BY EXPRESS MAIL

"Express Mail" Mailing

"Express Mail" Mailing

Label No. EK_______________US

Date of Deposit: ___________, 200__

I hereby certify that this paper is being deposited with the United States Postal Service as "Express Mail Post Office to Addressee" service under 37 C.F.R. §1.10 on the date indicated above in an envelope addressed to Box PCT Commissioner for Patents, Washington, D.C.. 20231

(type or print name of person making deposit)

____

Signature of person making deposit

FILED BY EXPRESS MAIL

Honorable Commissioner for Patents
Washington, D.C. 20231

AMENDMENT

Sir:

In response to the Office action of _______________, 200_), please amend the above-identified application as follows:

In The Title:

In The Specification:

In The Claims:

REMARKS

Attached hereto is a marked-up version of the changes made to the specification and claims by the current amendment. The attached page is captioned "Version with marking to show changes made."

Applicant respectfully requests that a timely Notice of Allowance be issued in this case.

Respectfully submitted,

____

Applicant

VERSION WITH MARKING TO SHOW CHANGES MADE

In the specification:

In the claims:

SUPPLEMENTAL APPLICATION DATA SHEET

Application Information

Application Type::

Subject Matter::

Suggested Classification::

Suggested Group Art Unit::

CD-ROM or CD-R?

Title::

Attorney Docket Number::

Request for Early Publication?::

Request for Non-Publication?::

Suggested Drawing Figure::

Total Drawing Sheets::

Small Entity::

Petition included?::

Secrecy Order in Parent Appl.?::

Applicant Information

Applicant Authority Type::

Primary Citizenship Country:

Status::

Given Name::

Middle Name::

Family Name::

Page # 1 Supplemental

City of Residence::

State or Province of Residence::

Country of Residence::

Street of mailing address::

City of Mailing address::

Country of mailing address::

Postal or Zip Code of mailing address::

Applicant Authority type::

Primary Citizenship Country::

Status::

Given Name::

Middle Name::

Family Name::

City of Residence::

State or Province of Residence::

Country of Residence::

Street of mailing address::

City of mailing address::

State or Province of mailing address::

Postal or Zip Code of mailing address::

Correspondence Information

Correspondence Customer Number::

Name::

Street of mailing address::

Page # 2 Supplemental

City of mailing address::

State or Province of mailing address::

Postal or Zip Code of mailing address::

Telephone::

E-Mail address::

Domestic Priority Information

Application::	Continuity Type::	Parent Application::	Parent Filing Date::

Foreign Priority Information

Country::	Application number::	Filing Date::	Priority Claimed::

Page # 3 Supplemental

Assignee Information

Assignee name::

Street of mailing address::

City of mailing address::

State or Province of mailing address::

Country of mailing address:

Postal or Zip Code of mailing address::

IN THE UNITED STATES PATENT AND TRADEMARK OFFICE

Applicant:)
Serial No.)
Filed:)
Title:)

Group Art Unit:)
Examiner:)

Docket No.)

FILED BY EXPRESS MAIL
Honorable Commissioner for Patents
Washington, D.C. 20231

CERTIFICATE OF MAILING BY EXPRESS MAIL

"Express Mail" Mailing

Label No. EK________________US

Date of Deposit: ____________, 200__

I hereby certify that this paper is being deposited with the United States Postal Service as "Express Mail Post Office to Addressee" service under 37 C.F.R. §1.10 on the date indicated above in an envelope addressed to Box PCT Commissioner for Patents, Washington, D.C.. 20231

(type or print name of person making deposit)

____

Signature of person making deposit

REQUEST FOR APPROVAL OF PROPOSED DRAWING AMENDMENT

Dear Sirs:

Applicant respectfully requests permission to amend the drawings of the above application after allowance. The proposed changes are indicated in red on the photocop(ies) of sheets ________________________ Fig.(s) ________________________.

Respectfully submitted,

____

Applicant

IN THE UNITED STATES PATENT AND TRADEMARK OFFICE

Applicant:	)
Serial No.	)
Filed:	)
Title:	)
Group Art Unit:	)
Examiner:	)
Docket No.	)

CERTIFICATE OF MAILING BY EXPRESS MAIL

"Express Mail" Mailing

Label No. EK______________US

Date of Deposit: __________, 200__

I hereby certify that this paper is being deposited with the United States Postal Service as "Express Mail Post Office to Addressee" service under 37 C.F.R. §1.10 on the date indicated above in an envelope addressed to Box PCT Commissioner for Patents, Washington, D.C.. 20231

(type or print name of person making deposit)

____

Signature of person making deposit

FILED BY EXPRESS MAIL

Honorable Commissioner for Patents
Washington, D.C. 20231
Attn: Official Draftsperson

SUBMISSION OF CORRECTED DRAWINGS

Dear Sirs:

Attached please find a copy of one set of corrected drawings (____ sheets) for the above application. Please substitute these drawings for the drawings currently on file.

Respectfully submitted,

____

Applicant

IN THE UNITED STATES PATENT AND TRADEMARK OFFICE

Applicant:)
Serial No.)
Filed:)
Title:)

Group Art Unit:)
Examiner:)

Docket No.)

FILED BY EXPRESS MAIL
Honorable Commissioner for Patents
Washington, D.C. 20231

CERTIFICATE OF MAILING BY EXPRESS MAIL

"Express Mail" Mailing

Label No. EK________________US

Date of Deposit: ____________, 200__

I hereby certify that this paper is being deposited with the United States Postal Service as "Express Mail Post Office to Addressee" service under 37 C.F.R. §1.10 on the date indicated above in an envelope addressed to Box PCT Commissioner for Patents, Washington, D.C.. 20231

(type or print name of person making deposit)

____

Signature of person making deposit

DECLARATION UNDER 37 CFR Section 1.131

Dear Sirs:

I, ____________________________, declare that I am the inventor for the above-identified patent application and that I conceived in the United States the invention claimed in the above-identified patent application prior to ______________________, the filing date of the cited U.S. Patent No. ____________________ to ____.

Attached Exhibit A is a copy of notebook records relating to this conception wherein

Pursuant to this conception, I actually reduced to practice in the United States, the invention claimed in the above-identified patent application prior to ____________________________, the filing date of the cited ____________________________ patent. Attached Exhibit B is a copy of a memorandum relating to this reduction to practice wherein

Exhibits A and B, which relate to the aforementioned conception and actual reduction to practice, correspond to the invention broadly disclosed and claimed in the above-identified patent application.

I hereby declare that all statements made herein of my own knowledge are true and that all statements made on information and belief are believed to be true; and further that these statements were made with the knowledge that willful false statements and the like so made are punishable by fine or imprisonment, or both, under Section 1001 of Title 18 of the United States Code, and that such willful false statements may jeopardize the validity of the application or any patent issued thereon.

Respectfully submitted,

____

Inventor/Applicant

IN THE UNITED STATES PATENT AND TRADEMARK OFFICE

Applicant:)
Serial No.)
Filed:)
Title:)

Group Art Unit:)
Examiner:)

Docket No.)

FILED BY EXPRESS MAIL
Honorable Commissioner for Patents
Washington, D.C. 20231

CERTIFICATE OF MAILING BY EXPRESS MAIL

"Express Mail" Mailing

Label No. EK________________US

Date of Deposit: ____________, 200__

I hereby certify that this paper is being deposited with the United States Postal Service as "Express Mail Post Office to Addressee" service under 37 C.F.R. §1.10 on the date indicated above in an envelope addressed to Box PCT Commissioner for Patents, Washington, D.C.. 20231

(type or print name of person making deposit)

____

Signature of person making deposit

DECLARATION UNDER 37 CFR Section 1.132

Dear Sirs:

I, ________________________________, declare and say:

That I am a citizen of ____ reside at ____.

That I was graduated in __________ from ___________________________ located in ______________________________ with a ______________________________ Degree in ___________________________. I was also graduated in ___________________________ from ___________________________________ located in ________________________________ with a ____________________________________ Degree in ______________________________.

That since _______________________ I have been working in the field of ____________________________. I have been employed by ______________________ since ___________________, and part of this time has been spent in this field. Since ____________________________, I have been __________________________ in the ____________________________ Department of ____________________________.

That I have been granted ____________________________ patents in the ______________ ________________________ field, and I am the author of __________________________ papers in the ____________________________ field.

That I am familiar with the above-identified patent application Serial No. _________________________ and with the following references cited by the Examiner: ____.

That a test was performed (bye me) (on behalf of applicant) described in detail hereinafter to compare ________________________ employed in the invention described and claimed in the above-identified patent application.

That in accordance with the invention, ____ ____ ____.

That the results of this test are summarized in the following table:

(Insert Table)

That the above test demonstrates clearly the (superiority of, criticality in, or synergism with) __________________ as claimed in the above-identified patent application;

That, in my opinion, the aforementioned (superiority, criticality or synergism) with respect to ______________________________ of the claimed invention is unobvious to one skilled in the art.

I hereby declare that all statements made herein of my own knowledge are true and that all statements made on information and belief are believed to be true; and further that these statements were made with the knowledge that willful false statements and the like so made are punishable by fine or imprisonment, or both, under Section 1001 of Title 18 of the United States Code, and that such willful false statements may jeopardize the validity of the application or any patent issued thereon.

Respectfully submitted,

____

Title/Name

INDEX

P

R

S

U

W

SPHINX® PUBLISHING ORDER FORM

BILL TO:		SHIP TO:	
Phone #	Terms	F.O.B. Chicago, IL	Ship Date

Charge my: ❐ VISA ❐ MasterCard ❐ American Express

❐ Money Order or Personal Check

Credit Card Number

Expiration Date

Qty	ISBN	Title	Retail	Ext.
		SPHINX PUBLISHING NATIONAL TITLES		
____	1-57248-148-X	Cómo Hacer su Propio Testamento	$16.95	____
____	1-57248-226-5	Cómo Restablecer su propio Crédito y Renegociar sus Deudas	$21.95	____
____	1-57248-147-1	Cómo Solicitar su Propio Divorcio	$24.95	____
____	1-57248-238-9	The 529 College Savings Plan	$16.95	____
____	1-57248-166-8	The Complete Book of Corporate Forms	$24.95	____
____	1-57248-229-X	The Complete Legal Guide to Senior Care	$21.95	____
____	1-57248-201-X	The Complete Patent Book	$26.95	____
____	1-57248-163-3	Crime Victim's Guide to Justice (2E)	$21.95	____
____	1-57248-251-6	The Entrepreneur's Internet Handbook	$21.95	____
____	1-57248-159-5	Essential Guide to Real Estate Contracts	$18.95	____
____	1-57248-160-9	Essential Guide to Real Estate Leases	$18.95	____
____	1-57248-139-0	Grandparents' Rights (3E)	$24.95	____
____	1-57248-188-9	Guía de Inmigración a Estados Unidos (3E)	$24.95	____
____	1-57248-187-0	Guía de Justicia para Víctimas del Crimen	$21.95	____
____	1-57248-103-X	Help Your Lawyer Win Your Case (2E)	$14.95	____
____	1-57248-164-1	How to Buy a Condominium or Townhome (2E)	$19.95	____
____	1-57248-191-9	How to File Your Own Bankruptcy (5E)	$21.95	____
____	1-57248-132-3	How to File Your Own Divorce (4E)	$24.95	____
____	1-57248-083-1	How to Form a Limited Liability Company	$22.95	____
____	1-57248-231-1	How to Form a Nonprofit Corporation (2E)	$24.95	____
____	1-57248-133-1	How to Form Your Own Corporation (3E)	$24.95	____
____	1-57248-224-9	How to Form Your Own Partnership (2E)	$24.95	____
____	1-57248-232-X	How to Make Your Own Simple Will (3E)	$18.95	____
____	1-57248-200-1	How to Register Your Own Copyright (4E)	$24.95	____
____	1-57248-104-8	How to Register Your Own Trademark (3E)	$21.95	____
____	1-57248-233-8	How to Write Your Own Living Will (3E)	$18.95	____
____	1-57248-156-0	How to Write Your Own Premarital Agreement (3E)	$24.95	____
____	1-57248-230-3	Incorporate in Delaware from Any State	$24.95	____
____	1-57248-158-7	Incorporate in Nevada from Any State	$24.95	____
____	1-57071-333-2	Jurors' Rights (2E)	$12.95	____
____	1-57248-223-0	Legal Research Made Easy (3E)	$21.95	____
____	1-57248-165-X	Living Trusts and Other Ways to Avoid Probate (3E)	$24.95	____
____	1-57248-186-2	Manual de Beneficios para el Seguro Social	$18.95	____
____	1-57248-220-6	Mastering the MBE	$16.95	____
____	1-57248-167-6	Most Valuable Bus. Legal Forms You'll Ever Need (3E)	$21.95	____
____	1-57248-130-7	Most Valuable Personal Legal Forms You'll Ever Need	$24.95	____
____	1-57248-098-X	The Nanny and Domestic Help Legal Kit	$22.95	____
____	1-57248-089-0	Neighbor v. Neighbor (2E)	$16.95	____
____	1-57248-169-2	The Power of Attorney Handbook (4E)	$19.95	____
____	1-57248-149-8	Repair Your Own Credit and Deal with Debt	$18.95	____
____	1-57248-217-6	Sexual Harassment: Your Guide to Legal Action	$18.95	____
____	1-57248-219-2	The Small Business Owner's Guide to Bankruptcy	$21.95	____
____	1-57248-168-4	The Social Security Benefits Handbook (3E)	$18.95	____
____	1-57248-216-8	Social Security Q&A	$12.95	____
____	1-57248-221-4	Teen RIghts	$22.95	____
____	1-57248-236-2	Unmarried Parents' Rights (2E)	$19.95	____
____	1-57248-161-7	U.S.A. Immigration Guide (4E)	$24.95	____
____	1-57248-192-7	The Visitation Handbook	$18.95	____
____	1-57248-225-7	Win Your Unemployment Compensation Claim (2E)	$21.95	____
____	1-57248-138-2	Winning Your Personal Injury Claim (2E)	$24.95	____
____	1-57248-162-5	Your Right to Child Custody, Visitation and Support (2E)	$24.95	____
____	1-57248-157-9	Your Rights When You Owe Too Much	$16.95	____
		CALIFORNIA TITLES		
____	1-57248-150-1	CA Power of Attorney Handbook (2E)	$18.95	____
____	1-57248-151-X	How to File for Divorce in CA (3E)	$26.95	____
____	1-57071-356-1	How to Make a CA Will	$16.95	____
____	1-57248-145-5	How to Probate and Settle an Estate in California	$26.95	____
____	1-57248-146-3	How to Start a Business in CA	$18.95	____
____	1-57248-194-3	How to Win in Small Claims Court in CA (2E)	$18.95	____
____	1-57248-196-X	The Landlord's Legal Guide in CA	$24.95	____
		FLORIDA TITLES		
____	1-57071-363-4	Florida Power of Attorney Handbook (2E)	$16.95	____
____	1-57248-176-5	How to File for Divorce in FL (7E)	$26.95	____
____	1-57248-177-3	How to Form a Corporation in FL (5E)	$24.95	____
____	1-57248-203-6	How to Form a Limited Liability Co. in FL (2E)	$24.95	____
____	1-57071-401-0	How to Form a Partnership in FL	$22.95	____

Form Continued on Following Page **SUBTOTAL**

To order, call Sourcebooks at 1-800-432-7444 or FAX (630) 961-2168 (Bookstores, libraries, wholesalers—please call for discount)

Prices are subject to change without notice.

Find more legal information at: www.SphinxLegal.com

SPHINX® PUBLISHING ORDER FORM

Qty	ISBN	Title	Retail	Ext.
	1-57248-113-7	How to Make a FL Will (6E)	$16.95	
	1-57248-088-2	How to Modify Your FL Divorce Judgment (4E)	$24.95	
	1-57248-144-7	How to Probate and Settle an Estate in FL (4E)	$26.95	
	1-57248-081-5	How to Start a Business in FL (5E)	$16.95	
	1-57248-204-4	How to Win in Small Claims Court in FL (7E)	$18.95	
	1-57248-202-8	Land Trusts in Florida (6E)	$29.95	
	1-57248-123-4	Landlords' Rights and Duties in FL (8E)	$21.95	
		GEORGIA TITLES		
	1-57248-137-4	How to File for Divorce in GA (4E)	$21.95	
	1-57248-180-3	How to Make a GA Will (4E)	$21.95	
	1-57248-140-4	How to Start a Business in Georgia (2E)	$16.95	
		ILLINOIS TITLES		
	1-57248-244-3	Child Custody, Visitation, and Support in IL	$24.95	
	1-57248-206-0	How to File for Divorce in IL (3E)	$24.95	
	1-57248-170-6	How to Make an IL Will (3E)	$16.95	
	1-57248-247-8	How to Start a Business in IL (3E)	$21.95	
	1-57248-252-4	The Landlord's Legal Guide in IL	$24.95	
		MASSACHUSETTS TITLES		
	1-57248-128-5	How to File for Divorce in MA (3E)	$24.95	
	1-57248-115-3	How to Form a Corporation in MA	$24.95	
	1-57248-108-0	How to Make a MA Will (2E)	$16.95	
	1-57248-106-4	How to Start a Business in MA (2E)	$18.95	
	1-57248-209-5	The Landlord's Legal Guide in MA	$24.95	
		MICHIGAN TITLES		
	1-57248-215-X	How to File for Divorce in MI (3E)	$24.95	
	1-57248-182-X	How to Make a MI Will (3E)	$16.95	
	1-57248-183-8	How to Start a Business in MI (3E)	$18.95	
		MINNESOTA TITLES		
	1-57248-142-0	How to File for Divorce in MN	$21.95	
	1-57248-179-X	How to Form a Corporation in MN	$24.95	
	1-57248-178-1	How to Make a MN Will (2E)	$16.95	
		NEW YORK TITLES		
	1-57248-193-5	Child Custody, Visitation and Support in NY	$26.95	
	1-57248-141-2	How to File for Divorce in NY (2E)	$26.95	
	1-57248-249-4	How to Form a Corporation in NY (2E)	$24.95	
	1-57248-095-5	How to Make a NY Will (2E)	$16.95	
	1-57248-199-4	How to Start a Business in NY (2E)	$18.95	

Qty	ISBN	Title	Retail	Ext.
	1-57248-198-6	How to Win in Small Claims Court in NY (2E)	$18.95	
	1-57248-197-8	Landlords' Legal Guide in NY	$24.95	
	1-57071-188-7	New York Power of Attorney Handbook	$19.95	
	1-57248-122-6	Tenants' Rights in NY	$21.95	
		NEW JERSEY TITLES		
	1-57248-239-7	How to File for Divorce in NJ	$24.95	
		NORTH CAROLINA TITLES		
	1-57248-185-4	How to File for Divorce in NC (3E)	$22.95	
	1-57248-129-3	How to Make a NC Will (3E)	$16.95	
	1-57248-184-6	How to Start a Business in NC (3E)	$18.95	
	1-57248-091-2	Landlords' Rights & Duties in NC	$21.95	
		OHIO TITLES		
	1-57248-190-0	How to File for Divorce in OH (2E)	$24.95	
	1-57248-174-9	How to Form a Corporation in OH	$24.95	
	1-57248-173-0	How to Make an OH Will	$16.95	
		PENNSYLVANIA TITLES		
	1-57248-242-7	Child Custody, Visitation and Support in Pennsylvania	$26.95	
	1-57248-211-7	How to File for Divorce in PA (3E)	$26.95	
	1-57248-094-7	How to Make a PA Will (2E)	$16.95	
	1-57248-112-9	How to Start a Business in PA (2E)	$18.95	
	1-57248-245-1	The Landlord's Legal Guide in PA	$24.95	
		TEXAS TITLES		
	1-57248-171-4	Child Custody, Visitation, and Support in TX	$22.95	
	1-57248-172-2	How to File for Divorce in TX (3E)	$24.95	
	1-57248-114-5	How to Form a Corporation in TX (2E)	$24.95	
	1-57248-255-9	How to Make a TX Will (3E)	$16.95	
	1-57248-214-1	How to Probate and Settle an Estate in TX (3E)	$26.95	
	1-57248-228-1	How to Start a Business in TX (3E)	$18.95	
	1-57248-111-0	How to Win in Small Claims Court in TX (2E)	$16.95	
	1-57248-110-2	Landlords' Rights and Duties in TX (2E)	$21.95	

SUBTOTAL THIS PAGE ______

SUBTOTAL PREVIOUS PAGE ______

Shipping— $5.00 for 1st book, $1.00 each additional ______

Illinois residents add 6.75% sales tax ______

Connecticut residents add 6.00% sales tax ______

TOTAL ______

To order, call Sourcebooks at 1-800-432-7444 or FAX (630) 961-2168 (Bookstores, libraries, wholesalers—please call for discount)

Prices are subject to change without notice.

Find more legal information at: **www.SphinxLegal.com**